Rebuilding the Temple

Rebuilding the Temple

Spirituality in Classic Christian Literature

ROBERT P. VANDE KAPPELLE

WIPF & STOCK · Eugene, Oregon

REBUILDING THE TEMPLE
Spirituality in Classic Christian Literature

Copyright © 2022 Robert P. Vande Kappelle. All rights reserved. Except for brief quotations in critical publications or reviews, no part of this book may be reproduced in any manner without prior written permission from the publisher. Write: Permissions, Wipf and Stock Publishers, 199 W. 8th Ave., Suite 3, Eugene, OR 97401.

Wipf & Stock
An Imprint of Wipf and Stock Publishers
199 W. 8th Ave., Suite 3
Eugene, OR 97401

www.wipfandstock.com

PAPERBACK ISBN: 978-1-6667-4201-5
HARDCOVER ISBN: 978-1-6667-4202-2
EBOOK ISBN: 978-1-6667-4203-9

APRIL 5, 2022 11:58 AM

Unless otherwise noted, Bible quotations are from the *New Revised Standard Version of the Bible*, copyright © 1989 by the Division of Christian Education of the National Council of the Churches of Christ in the United States of America. Used by permission.

Contents

Preface | vii

CHAPTER 1
Introduction | 1

CHAPTER 2
Biblical Spirituality | 9

CHAPTER 3
Augustine's *Confessions* and *Enchiridion* | 27

CHAPTER 4
Dante Alighieri's *Divine Comedy* | 45

CHAPTER 5
Martin Luther's *Freedom of a Christian* and John Calvin's *Institutes* | 65

CHAPTER 6
Teresa of Ávila's *Interior Castle*
and John of the Cross's *Dark Night of the Soul* | 85

CHAPTER 7
Blaise Pascal's *Pensées* and George Fox's *Journal* | 104

CHAPTER 8
John Milton's *Paradise Lost*
and William Blake's *The Marriage of Heaven and Hell* | 123

CHAPTER 9
Tozer's *Pursuit of God*, Drummond's *Greatest Thing in the World*,
and Murray's *Humility* | 145

CHAPTER 10
Nouwen's *Reaching Out*, Conway's *Acres of Diamonds*,
and McLaren's *Generous Orthodoxy* | 163

CHAPTER 11
Matthew Fox's *Original Blessing* and Richard Rohr's *The Naked Now* | 181

CHAPTER 12
John Shelby Spong's *Why Christianity Must Change*
and Marcus Borg's *Heart of Christianity* | 200

CHAPTER 13
Conclusion | 217

Bibliography | 233

Index | 237

Preface

LITERATURE, AS ALL ART, is a gift of divine grace, a pathway to mystery. Each literary experience is slightly beyond our horizon of understanding. What a gift literature is! When it enhances spirituality, each literary moment confounds in order to keep us going and growing.

As you read classic Christian literature, I suggest you apply to your pondering and meditating a contemplative way of reading sacred writings known as *lectio divina*. This approach applies four stages of spiritual exercise to a literary passage: reading, meditation, prayer, and contemplation. These steps make a ladder that connects us with the divine. The ladder has few rungs, yet its length is immense and wonderful, for its lower end rests upon the earth, but its top teaches heavenly secrets. The intention behind *lectio divina* is both practical and unitive, for it helps us focus on God's presence about us and within us. Ultimately, the spiritual journey has one goal—experiencing God's presence in our life. Reading scripture and other writings this way sees literature as one long love letter from God.

The first rung of the ladder asks to read scripture and all great literature as sacred, and hence, as a way of seeking God. As you read selections from classic Christian literature suggested in this study, listen for God's word in it for you. By this I mean, learn to be attentive to God's voice reverberating not only in scripture or devotional literature, but in poems, novels, artwork, and the refrains of songs, as well as through news reports, conversations with others, random thoughts in your head, and promptings in your heart.

As you stand firmly on the first rung of the ladder to God, you will become more receptive and open to God's presence and voice in your life, more receptive to the love of God and others, and more empowered to share that love with God and others.

The task before us is daunting, because to select some two dozen books to study from the vast body of Christian literature, spanning two millennia, is nigh to impossible.¹ While no two people would agree on the final list, due to such personal and subjective considerations as upbringing, theological persuasion, and educational training, the following criteria were helpful in my selective process:

1. influential quality (Augustine, Dante, Luther, and Calvin)
2. literary quality (Dante, Milton, Blake)
3. mystical depth (Teresa of Ávila, St. John of the Cross)
4. inspirational quality (Pascal, Wesley, Tozer)
5. practical value (Drummond, Tozer, Conway, Nouwen)
6. holistic quality (Nouwen, Fox)
7. progressive quality (McLaren, Spong, Borg, Fox, Rohr)

Since all of us do not read at the same level or with the same comprehension, another factor in my selection is readability, by which I mean accessibility to modern readers.

Of course, many of these authors meet more than one criterion, and some might be found to meet most if not all the criteria. Hence, the names that appear under each criterion above are merely representative of that category and not limited to it. While all of the authors and works selected meet valuable spiritual goals and needs, few are easy reads, and some will require greater patience and commitment. Because some of this literature is difficult, dense, or lengthy, initially you might consider selecting one or more authors or works you find most compelling or attractive, and obtain copies from an available library, through purchase, or as ebooks. Later, you may wish to add to your list. In this regard, be aware that reading and analyzing great religious literature can be daunting, but if you stay with it, your ability to benefit from this experience will expand your horizons and enrich your life. As with previous volumes in this series, each chapter contains contextual and background material on or more authors, together with summary, overview, or synopsis of the literature in that chapter. In some lengthier works, such as in volumes

---

1. Some authors and works, such as Julian of Norwich's *Revelations of Divine Love*, John Bunyan's *Pilgrim's Progress*, Brother Lawrence's *The Practice of the Presence of God*, and Dietrich Bonhoeffer's *The Cost of Discipleship*, are certainly worthy of consideration in this book. They do not appear here because I have discussed these writers and their works elsewhere.

by Augustine, Dante, Luther, Calvin, and the mystical writings by Teresa of Ávila and John of the Cross, I indicate recommended segments for consideration instead of entire works.

Our study of classic Christian literature begins with an introductory chapter (chapter 1), after which we examine the topic of spirituality in biblical literature (chapter 2), followed by select writings of the early medieval theologian Augustine (chapter 3), the early Renaissance author Dante Alighieri (chapter 4), and foundational works by the great Protestant Reformers Martin Luther and John Calvin (chapter 5). Next, we examine the great mystical tradition, focusing on the writings of Reformation-era Spanish mystics Teresa of Ávila and St. John of the Cross (chapter 6), followed by the private writings of George Fox and Blaise Pascal (chapter 7) and the contributions of Enlightenment-era thinkers John Milton and William Blake (chapter 8).

The next two chapters feature the contributions of devotional writers Andrew Murray, Henry Drummond, and A. W. Tozer (chapter 9), Henri Nouwen, Russell Conway, and Brian McLaren (chapter 10), followed by a chapter featuring pioneering works by the Catholic writers Matthew Fox and Richard Rohr (chapter 11), the former a convert to the Episcopal Church following his expulsion from the Catholic Dominican Order and the latter a Franciscan priest and longtime director of the ecumenical Center for Action and Contemplation in Albuquerque, New Mexico. The final chapter features progressive writings by the recently deceased Protestant writers Marcus Borg and John Shelby Spong (chapter 12).

Each chapter concludes with questions for discussion or reflection. Write the answers to each question in your journal, in addition to the questions below, which are appropriate for each chapter. If you are reading this book in a group setting, be prepared to share your answers with others in the group. If your study is private, I encourage you to write answers to each question in your journal for review and further reflection. Leaders may select questions from these lists that they deem most helpful to group discussion.

1. After reading this chapter, what did you learn about spirituality?
2. In your estimation, what is the primary insight gained from this chapter?
3. *For personal reflection*: Does this chapter raise any issues you need to handle or come to terms with successfully? If so, how will you deal with them?

Chapter 1

Introduction

REBUILDING THE TEMPLE, my third volume on spirituality and great literature and the fourth on spirituality and the arts,[1] assumes the interrelationship of spirituality and theology. Viewed from our perspective as human beings, this interrelationship comes to mean that while we can speak of secular humanism, whereby we see our lives as reducible to naturalistic or materialistic elements, we cannot speak of secular spirituality.

If, as the world's religions teach, God is everywhere, then humans cannot not be in God's presence. The principle here is this, "To go deep in any one place is to meet the infinite aliveness that is God, for God is everywhere!" As I noted in *Wading in Water*, my initial volume on spirituality and the arts, spirituality is the journey of life "from God, to God, and with God." As a result, it is also a journey toward the self. In other words, the process of coming to know or to experience God is also the process of knowing oneself.

Viewed globally and interreligiously, the central defining characteristic of spirituality is an individual's connection to a greater whole. At its heart, spirituality involves an emotional experience of awe and reverence, an experience natural to most of our human ancestors. They had a wonderful idea of God because they lived in an awesome world. They wondered at the magnificence of whatever it was that brought the world into being. This led to a sense of adoration. This adoration, this gratitude, we call religion. Now, as the outer world is diminished, our inner world is drying up. The task of spirituality is to help us regain our sense of awe

---

1. The volumes in this series include *Wading in Water*, *Deep Splendor*, and *Deeper Splendor*.

and reverence, beginning with a profound commitment to nature and continuing with an equal commitment to the whole of humanity and every living creature. If we do not love what is visible around us, how can we love God, whom we cannot see? (1 John 4:19–20).

In Christian usage, the word "God" is a both verb and a noun. Because God is active and dynamic, God is relational. As "Father, Son, and Holy Spirit," God is three "relations," understood as formlessness (Father), as form (Son), and as the divine energy binding Father and Son (Holy Spirit). At its heart, spirituality, traditionally defined by Christians as "life in the Spirit," envisions the journey of life from a distinct perspective. In my estimation, the Christian notion of God as Trinity is foundational to spirituality, for this understanding views God as both singular and plural, as "being" yet also as "nonbeing," simultaneously personal, impersonal, and transpersonal.

Using the analogy of love, the medieval theologian Augustine of Hippo viewed the Father as Lover or subject of divine love, the Son as Beloved or object of divine love, and the Spirit as the bond of love between Father and Son, as the divine energy binding God and all reality. Defining theology (God) and spirituality (Spirit) as Relationship moves us away from vague abstraction and opens conversation with the world of science, for it helps us to understand the cohesive mystery permeating all reality, from atoms, to ecosystems, to galaxies. If the nature of God is the nature of everything, then everything in the universe is in relationship and nothing stands alone.

The word that emerges in all the great world religions for that deepest connection is *soul*, the essence of things. People around the world use this word, and yet it seems that the more science and society develop, the more we ignore or come to doubt the existence of soul, not only within ourselves, but also in everything else. Soul implies a symbiotic relationship; once we find it in ourselves, we also find it in others. If we cannot see it in others, we probably will not affirm it in ourselves either. One possible reason why so many people suffer from mental and emotional illnesses today is that they are disconnected rather than connected. If science and society tell us we are alone in the universe, how can we overcome loneliness, alienation, and fragmentation?

Believing in God means life has meaning; such belief promotes hope for our future and offers us peace, security, and the possibility of happiness and wellbeing. Such belief affirms our individuality and empowers our humanity. To say "I believe in God" means that we are connected, embraced, affirmed, and loved. It means that Someone knows me better than I know myself, that Someone knows the secret of all mysteries and where all roads lead. It means we are not alone with our questions, doubts, and fears. It means Someone is with me, deep within, affirming my existence, guaranteeing my potential, and accepting me unconditionally.

According to Franciscan theologian Richard Rohr, the God within us is like a homing device, such as found naturally in homing pigeons. No matter where such pigeons are released, they know how to find their way back home. If, as Jesus and all the world's spiritual sages and mystics affirm, human beings are sons and daughters of God, the guarantee of such connectedness is the Holy Spirit, our interior homing device that guides us back "home"—to love, to connection, to meaningful relationship with God and others, to soul. For it is only God in us that knows God; God in us that loves God; God in us that recognizes God in others and in all things. Rohr calls such knowing, loving, and recognizing "Trinity 101," foundational to all healthy and holistic spirituality.

Viewed synthetically and holistically, "Trinitarian" theology and spirituality defeats the dualistic mindset prevalent in "first half of life" living and thinking and invites us into the nondual, holistic conscience central to "second half of life" living and thinking. Trinitarian spirituality replaces the argumentative principle of two with the dynamic principle of three. Such spirituality brings us inside the inviting open space of "not one, but not two either."

In the past, traditional theologians preferred monarchical or hierarchical models of God, with the Father at the top, which then were imitated and promoted ecclesiastically and societally. If, however, as modern physicists such as Albert Einstein have noted, reality is dynamic rather than static, an energy field emerging from Mystery and flowing toward greater abundance and creativity, then spirituality also is an energy field, flowing from God, through us, to others. Such interflowing is the pattern of the universe, from atoms to galaxies, plants to animals, animals to humans, and humans back to everything else, all flowing from and toward God.

Ultimately, spirituality is about one's relationship with God—not with an idea of God, but actually with God. While such a statement might seem mystical or unrealistic, it is both practical and realistic, if we understand God not as a concept or person, but as a stand-in for everything—Reality, truth, and the essence of our universe. What I have in mind, however, is not pantheism but panentheism, the view that God is in all things yet distinct and not a "thing" at all. What this means is that God is not simply another way of speaking of reality, for God is reality with a face—Reality with Personality—which is the only way most of us relate to others. For relationship to occur there must be personality.

It is important that we understand God correctly, because our image of God influences, even determines, our self-image. There is an absolute connection between how we see God and how we see ourselves, between how we relate to ourselves, to others, and to the world around us and within us. This is why good theology, healthy psychology, and holistic spirituality can make a major difference in how we live with ourselves and with others.

In our conception of the nature of God lies the kernel of the spiritual life. Until we discover the God in which we believe, we will never fully accept and understand ourselves. Such lack of acceptance and understanding means that the polarities of our nature will keep us frustrated and fragmented, preventing the wholeness and integration we seek and need for health and happiness. As we develop physically, intellectually, and emotionally, we must also grow toward a mature spirituality that includes reason, faith, and inner experience we can trust. As we shall discover, such resources are valued and heightened in much of the literature discussed in this study.

GOOD BONES

My wife Susan, a retired pastor and an active Gestalt Pastoral Care Minister, enjoys watching programs on HGTV (The Homes and Gardens television network). While many of those shows feature buying and selling fashionable homes, some shows feature demolishing and rebuilding or remodeling older homes, a process akin to what counselors and therapists call deconstruction and reconstruction and theologians and mystics call death and resurrection (rebirth). Occasionally, I join my wife in watching such shows, finding fascinating the concept behind a show called "Good Bones," in which a husband and wife team up with a group of workers to identify and restore old homes that display "good bones," meaning they possess remodeling value or potential.

While the "potential" that an old house displays may be associated with financial worth or profit, this is not always primary. For example, one show features as clients a young couple who wish to restore a New

Orleans home in a neighborhood destroyed by Hurricane Katrina. The couple values this house because it is where the young lady had grown up and where the couple now wish to live. For her it is a home filled with happy memories, but also part of a neighborhood that has been abandoned and which she wishes to restore, a hopeful start to urban renewal.

In the Bible, much of biblical history and imagery revolves around the temple in Jerusalem, a project conceived by King David and built by his son Solomon. As the Bible makes clear, this ancient temple, the center of Hebrew social and religious life, was destroyed in 587 BCE when the Babylonians captured Judah, taking its inhabitants into captivity as exiles. The fall of Judah, with its utter destruction of Jerusalem and the temple, brought to an end political, social, and religious life in Judah. The culture shock caused by deportation, the problem of adaptation, and resentment against God for letting it happen made this the strongest test the Jews had undergone to date. Their survival required nothing less than the reinvention of their identity.

In 539 BCE the Persians under Cyrus defeated the Babylonian army. Cyrus, a tolerant and enlightened leader, issued an edict liberating the Jews from captivity and permitting repatriation. It is a tribute to Jewish tenacity and vitality that the Mosaic faith not only survived the exile but was immeasurably deepened and enriched. Though some Jews must have capitulated to the pressures of Babylonian culture, others were bound more closely to their tradition and community. Surprisingly, the sense of belonging to the covenant community was intensified, rather than weakened, by life under captivity. In the exile the people devoted themselves to preserving the Torah, studying and searching the tradition intensely for its meaning while preserving their scripture in writing for future generations. The exile was thus a time of religious activity and of concentrated and consecrated attention to Israel's religious heritage.

The first task of the returning exiles was to rebuild their temple, then the walls of Jerusalem. A century later, Ezra (a priest and a scribe) inspired the struggling Jewish settlement in Jerusalem to accept the Torah as its constitution. The Torah now proved an indispensable instrument for uniting and governing the Jewish community. Though a priest, Ezra instituted a major reform that stripped the priests of their religious and intellectual leadership, leaving them only in charge of the conduct of the temple ritual. Instead of a hereditary priesthood, which all too often exhibited the marks of decadence and moral corruption, the spiritual leadership of the people became vested in scholars. Recruited from all classes, they represented a non-hereditary, democratic element. The creative impulse in Judaism was henceforth centered in the synagogue, in which all Jews were equal and which became at once a house of prayer, study, and communal assembly.

In the book of Jeremiah, written around the time of the Babylonian Exile, the prophet speaks of two epochs in the history of Israel: the time of the Mosaic covenant, which ended in human failure, and the time of the new covenant, when the divine *torah* (law, teaching) is written on the heart, resulting in such personal knowledge of God that religious teaching would no longer be necessary. When Christianity emerged from Judaism in the first century CE, Jeremiah's prophecy seemed to describe the Christian community's self-understanding as the new Israel of God (Gal 6:16). By the time of the fateful year 70, when the Romans destroyed the Jewish temple and brought the sacrificial rites of Judaism to an end, Christian Jews began to move out on their own, setting the stage for the growth and expansion of Christianity into Gentile circles.

Already in his first letter to the Corinthians, written about 54 CE by the apostle Paul, a Jewish convert to Christianity, we find the notion of the Jewish temple and its rituals personalized and internalized, for Paul speaks of the physical body of each believer as a "temple of the Holy Spirit" (1 Cor 6:19; see also 1 Cor 3:16; 2 Cor 6:16), using the concept of Jesus' death and resurrection as the basis of the spiritual transformation (rebirth) of the self. As Jesus and other great spiritual teachers make clear, there is a self that must be found and another that must be renounced. This teaching is found in each gospel (see Matt 10:39; 16:25; Mark 8:35; Luke 9:24), but is central to John's gospel, where it is coupled with "dying to the self": "unless a grain of wheat falls into the earth and dies, it remains just a single grain; but if it dies, it bears much fruit" (John 12:24).

In one way or another, almost all religions tell us that we must die before we die—and then we will know what dying means, and what it does not mean. What this means, of course, is the relinquishment of selfish, possessive living, of egoic existence. The "ego self" (also known as the False Self) is the self before death; some form of death—psychological, spiritual, relational, or physical—is the only way we can loosen our ties to our small and separate False Self. Only then does it return in a new shape, which we call the soul, the True Self, the image of God, or the Risen Christ.

The role of true spirituality, of mature religion, is twofold: to help speed up the process of dying to the False Self, and to lead us to ever new experiences of our True Self (of who we are in God, and who God is in us). Whatever one calls it, true spirituality is the form of living embodied by Jesus and taught by ancient spiritual sages such as the Buddha. Such calm, egoless approach to life is invariably characteristic of people at the highest levels of doing and loving in all cultures and religions. These are the ones we call sages or holy ones. My hope and prayer is that by studying this book and reading recommended volumes in the canon of the great classical Christian literature, you too may join this group, thereby enhancing your God-given spiritual potential. If the fallen "temple" of God's body (the universal people of God; see Acts 15:16–18) is to be rebuilt as God's New Creation (see 2 Cor 5:17), it must begin with the restoration of our own inner temple. The restoration of wonder is the beginning of the inward journey toward the awaiting God. Such restoration, we will discover, is the goal of classic Christian literature.

QUESTIONS FOR DISCUSSION AND REFLECTION

In addition to the questions listed at the end of the preface, answer the following questions, writing your answers in a journal. If you are in a group study, be prepared to share your answers with those in the group.

1. Explain and assess the author's statement, "while we can speak of secular humanism, whereby we see our lives as reducible to materialistic or naturalistic elements, we cannot speak of secular spirituality."

2. After reading this chapter, how would you define the term "spirituality"? In your estimation, what is the defining characteristic of Christian spirituality? Explain your answer.

3. In your estimation, how is the Christian notion of God as Trinity foundational to Christian spirituality?

4. What meaning do you associate with the term "soul," and how would you distinguish between the human soul and the human spirit?

5. Explain and assess Richard Rohr's analogy of the Holy Spirit as our interior homing device.

6. This chapter introduces the term "panentheism" to describe God, an expression we encounter in later chapters of this study. Briefly

define the term, and assess its usefulness. In your understanding, can a panentheistic God have personality? Explain your answer.

7. Assess the usefulness of this book's subtitle "Rebuilding the Temple" as an description of the spiritual life or the spiritual journey.

8. Explain and assess the meaning of the idea that "humans must die before they die," and of the role of spirituality in this process.

Chapter 2

Biblical Spirituality[1]

THERE IS NO BETTER place to begin a study on spirituality and classic Christian literature than the Bible, for while most Christian literature originates in personal experience or as a response to historical events, in profound and essential ways, all Christian literature arises from biblical thought. While the Bible is not a text on spirituality, it contains many paradigms of the spiritual life of individuals and communities, none more important than the life and teaching of Jesus, his disciples, and the apostle Paul.

The Bible is perhaps the world's greatest and best resource for spirituality. It provides a two-thousand-year record of humanity's relationship with God, including numerous examples of the human quest for transcendence. Intended initially for corporate worship but gradually, as literacy grew, for individual spirituality as well, the Bible, in its entirety, provides one continuous liturgical resource. Think of the accounts of creation in Genesis. The original setting of those passages—widely gleaned by modern creationists for historical and scientific truths—is not a laboratory, a classroom, or private study, but rather corporate worship.

The setting of the creation-faith within worship is clearly evident in Psalm 24, a three-part liturgy once used during great pilgrimage festivals celebrating Yahweh's kingship. The Psalm was undoubtedly used originally in connection with a processional bearing of the ark of the covenant into Jerusalem. The opening words of the Psalm, which announce that Yahweh is creator, function as an introit: "The earth is the Lord's and all

---

1. This chapter is adapted and abridged from chapter 2 of my *Second Journey*, 19–41.

that is in it, the world, and those who live in it; for he has founded it on the seas, and established it on the rivers" (24:1–2). The second part, in question-and-response format (24:3–6), is a liturgy for admission to the temple, and the third, an "entrance liturgy" (24:7–10), is to be sung antiphonally in the presence of the ark, understood to be Yahweh's throne-seat. In this liturgical setting, the function of creation language is to set the stage for praising God. Thus in the book of Psalms, known as the hymnbook of Judaism, the affirmation that God is the creator is a call to worship.

Psalm 8, related to the Priestly creation account in Genesis 1, is an eloquent witness to the meaning of creation-faith in the liturgy of Israel's worship. This hymn begins and ends with an exclamation of praise to God's glory and majesty, which, to the eye of faith, are evident in nature. The psalmist knows that we sometimes take this world for granted, and yet he knows too that praise is the sign that we are alive, that we are fully human. Creation-faith focuses upon the relationship between God and humanity: "When I look at your heavens, the work of your fingers, the moon and the stars that you have established, what are human beings that you are mindful of them, mortals that you care for them?" (Ps 8:3–4). It is not simply that humans, in contrast to God, are finite. As the book of Ecclesiastes shows, the awareness of the gulf fixed between creature and creator can prompt a feeling of futility and desolation (Eccl 1:12-14; 3:16-22; 6:1-2). Rather, creation-faith provides context for understanding existence, the awareness that our relationship with God is one of incomprehensible grace.

Including the Psalms, about one third of the Hebrew Bible is poetry. Awareness of this feature of Israel's liturgical and literary expression is invaluable for reading and interpreting scripture. The same can be said about the book of Revelation, which ends the Bible. Worship and doxology are central to this book. Revelation contains at least fifteen hymns and songs of praise. No other book of the Bible, except perhaps the Psalms, has shaped Christian music as much as has Revelation. Framed in liturgy, from the opening setting "on the Lord's day" (1:10) to the Eucharistic closing (22:17), Revelation overflows with songs and heavenly choruses praising God and exhorting worshippers to sing through their struggles. The conflict of sovereignties is often portrayed in Revelation by references to worship. In the conflict of sovereignties, the lines are drawn between those who worship the beast (a form of political, social, and economic idolatry from which more narrowly religious idolatry is inseparable) and those who worship God. In Revelation, every stage of God's victory in chapter 7 through 19 is accompanied by worship in heaven.

The New Testament contains numerous letters, written by Paul and other early Christian leaders, primarily to churches. Given the low level of literacy in the first century,[2] we may assume that most early Christians experienced the New Testament only through public readings, primarily in the context of worship. In time, much of the New Testament, as is the case for the Jewish scriptures, acquired a liturgical function.

Viewed traditionally, the Bible represents divinely inspired truth. According to Christian tradition, the Bible consists of two testaments—two covenants between God and believers—one reflecting the ancient Hebraic-Jewish experience and the other the primitive Christian experience. The Hebrew scriptures—known by Christians as the Old Testament—came first. They represent the foundation—historically, ethnically, and culturally—upon which the first Christians build their faith and understanding of God, the cosmos, and the human experience. While it is possible, as Gentile Christians posited, to view the Old Testament's role as purely anticipatory or promissory, fulfilled by Jesus and the New Testament church, our contention is that the New Testament, like the Old, represents both promise and fulfillment—beginnings, endings, and new beginnings.

According to this perspective, the good news of early Christianity was not supersessionist (meaning that a new religious and cultural institution was born to replace an earlier religious and cultural institution—the church instead of the synagogue or temple), but rather that Jewish and Christian religious and cultural institutions are valid when they embrace as vital this possibility of ongoing newness and growth.

The Hebraic religion, represented by the Old Testament, contains both promise and fulfillment, but when it focuses organizationally on the former, for reasons of identity, security, and control, it produces figures such as Moses and David, whose task it is to build lasting theocratic institutions. However, the holistic impulse within these institutions gives birth to mystical, prophetic, wisdom, and apocalyptic figures and movements such as Jeremiah, Isaiah, Daniel, the authors of counter-cultural

---

2. In the first century, the literacy rate was around 10 percent for the Roman Empire and around 5 percent in Judea. Literacy was limited mostly to the governing class, scribes, and the wealthy in the empire, and primarily to the priestly class in Judea. In rural Judea and Galilee, the literacy rate approached zero percent.

wisdom writings such as Job and Ecclesiastes, the Essenes, Philo, and the Zohar, but also Jesus and Christianity.

Today, the Western Christian church is in decline, both numerically and in social influence. Like the cosmos, there are signs of newness and growth in some circles, but overall, the Western church seems caught in a vast entropy, a loss of energy and vitality. I believe this loss can be slowed and even reversed, not by a return to institutional and dogmatic conservatism, but by institutional and individual rediscovery of their progressive heritage.

Acknowledging that no one in the modern world reads the Bible in a "pure" way, since people can only assimilate its insights through their own interpretative traditions and lenses, we select four Old Testament topics and two from the New Testament. From the Old Testament we examine the account of creation, the call of Abraham, the Exodus, and the encounters of Moses and Elijah with God on Mount Sinai. From the New Testament we examine specific teachings of Jesus and the apostle Paul.

OLD TESTAMENT SPIRITUALITY

If by spirituality we mean the spiritual life of individuals, rather than the corporate expression of religious practice better classified as "liturgy," then we find that much of our study of spirituality in the Old Testament is extremely limited. While the Bible introduces numerous noteworthy individuals, the emphasis is not on individualism but on "corporate personality." The Bible portrays Israel as God's people, not simply as a collection of individuals but as a divine company ("a priestly kingdom and a holy nation"; Exod 19:6; 1 Pet 2:9). Out of families, clans, and tribes God forms a nation, with a corporate personality. When one person suffers, everyone suffers; when one person is blessed, the people enjoy the benefits; when one person sins, the whole nation participates in the judgment; when one person receives a promise, he or she does so on behalf of the nation.

Americans today live in a pluralistic society, with diverse cultures, religions, and societal values, and we are taught to be tolerant. Ancient societies were quite the opposite; they were homogeneous, with little tolerance or diversity, and with no such thing as freedom of religion. The concept of corporate personality provided Israel with stability, solidarity, and unity during the period of its ascendency. These qualities enabled

Israelites to maintain social and religious cohesion in a sea of paganism. Their laws, rituals, and values provided them with a distinctive way of life, which has preserved them to this day.

To understand the biblical concept of community, we must go back to the story of Abraham: God started with one family, declaring a promise so wondrous yet absurd as to engender laughter, creating something in Sarah's womb when she was unable to conceive: "Is anything too wonderful for the Lord?" (Gen 18:14). From Isaac came Jacob, and from him the twelve tribes of Israel. They took his name, his personality, his style of life, and the covenant he had with God. They called themselves "*bene* Israel," sons of Israel. The doctrine of election reminded them that they were beloved, God's intentional creation. They were not one nation *out of* many, but one nation *for* many. In such unity there is resolve, resilience, and strength.

Despite this emphasis on corporate personality, the God Israelites worshipped was concerned for the needs of the individual as well as the group; powerful enough to grant their requests; angry with sin yet willing to forgive it; amenable to reasoned argument; glorious yet terrible, deserving of praise but dangerous to behold; reliable, yet not predictable; merciful but just. Above all, they portrayed and worshipped God as a person, though clearly as a larger-than-life person, whose absence was acutely painful even if his presence could be far from comfortable.

1. *The God-Shaped Vacuum in Every Human Heart: The Garden of Eden.* Religion involves the sense of God, of the human, and of creation. These aspects belong together, and they cannot be treated separately. We would have no sense of the divine without creation. Speculatively, we could talk about God as being prior to or outside creation or independent of creation, but in fact there is no such being as God without creation.

There is something very important about the origin of the universe as we now know it: everything is derived from the same source. Science indicates that, and so does theology. If that is so, then everything in the universe is cousin to everything else. There is literally one family in the universe, one bonding. And if our planet is a single community of existence, then all living beings are interconnected and all things are vital. In a universe where everything is related by origin, nothing is unimportant, nothing is marginal.

The book of Genesis begins with the well-known words: "In the beginning God created the heavens and the earth." And God creates without compulsion, for no reason other than love. Therefore, the Bible might well begin with the words: "In the beginning was... Love!" Love is the act of will that at the beginning of time brings forth life. Love—God, energy, Being—is the primal force in the universe. Without love, nothing can exist; however, with love, all is possible.

In the second account of creation (found in Genesis 2–3, the so-called "J account of creation"), the author focuses on two sets of relationships: theological (issues related to the vertical relationship between humans and God) and sociological (issues related to the horizontal relationship between humans). The primary thrust of the story is vertical, having to do with the rule of God and the nature of human destiny. Both agendas belong together.

The first part of the story, the "pattern of creation" (described in Genesis 2:3b–25 and central to the theological agenda) represents harmony between humans and God, nature, others, and self. The second part of the story, the "pattern of the fall," (described in Genesis 3:1–24 and central to the sociological agenda), shows the distortion of human community that comes from human autonomy, that is, human rebellion against the pattern of creation. The result is disharmony with God, nature, others, and self. Disobedience (the "pattern of the fall") represents a reversal of the pattern of creation, disharmony between humans and God, nature, others, and self. The Bible describes the nature of the human spiritual condition thus: God creates us for love and freedom, attachment hinders us, and grace is necessary for our salvation (by "salvation" we mean the transformation necessary to release us from attachment to egoic thinking and living).

The famous French mathematician and philosopher Blaise Pascal spoke inspirationally when he declared: "There is a God-shaped vacuum in the heart of each person that cannot be satisfied by any created thing but only by God the Creator, made known through Jesus Christ." Psychiatrist Gerald May agreed with Pascal when he wrote, "I am convinced that all human beings have an inborn desire for God. Whether we are consciously religious or not, this desire is our deepest longing and our most precious treasure... Some of us have repressed this desire, burying it beneath so many other interests that we are completely unaware of it. Or we may experience it in different ways—as a longing for wholeness, completion, or fulfillment. Regardless of how we describe it, it is a longing for love. It is a hunger to love, to be loved, and to move closer to the

Source of love. This yearning is the essence of the human spirit, the origin of our highest hopes and most noble dreams."[3]

There is a pathetic grandeur in the picture of Adam reaching to taste the fruit of the tree of knowledge of good and evil. Knowledge is humankind's capacity. Freedom to leave the innocence of childhood is precisely what elevates humans above the animals. But when humanity's capacity for knowledge becomes the occasion for arrogant power and self-exaltation, inevitably it results in a fall from the life of trust and goodness that God intends. We cannot recover the mythological innocence of Adam, nor can we return to a Garden that is a figment of the religious imagination. Nevertheless, through revelation humans know there is a better way, the way life can and should be.

While the pattern of the fall ends with the expulsion of Adam and Eve from the Garden, there is good news here. Graciousness appears in the narrative in 3:21, where God clothes the hapless couple, mercifully shielding them from their shame and giving them a new start, for they get to live and try anew. The ending is hopeful, for it represents a new beginning.

2. *God's Love for All Humanity: The Call of Abraham.* In the Bible, the prototypical model for the journey of faith is found in the patriarchal stories of Genesis 12–50, starting with the story of Abraham. For ancient Jewish readers and listeners gathered for worship in synagogues to hear these accounts, the underlying significance of chapters 12–50 was not the accounts of the individual patriarchs and matriarchs but the story of Israel's self-understanding. At the time this material was put into writing, the main question was not, "Who are Abraham, Isaac, Jacob, and Joseph?" but "Who is Israel?" Israel was grappling with her identity, her self-understanding as a people called by God. The theological answer was found in the doctrine of election, the notion that the people of Israel are chosen by God.

But what does election mean? Is God racist, favoring some people over others? The Bible answers this question with a resounding "No." The covenant God established with Israel should not be regarded as an expression of divine preference for Jews over others, or as divine commission for one group to rule others, or as reward for good conduct on Israel's part. As the history of Israel demonstrates, the establishment of the covenant was not followed by good conduct. Moreover, the Bible portrays

---

3. May, *Addiction and Grace*, 1.

the covenant people as sinful, stiff-necked, stubborn, and singularly inept at learning from their experiences. In fact, in the Bible the Israelites are punished repeatedly, and more severely than others are. Nevertheless, God did not nullify the contract or make it void. The biblical answer to election is given in the portrayal of Abraham, Isaac, and Jacob, patriarchs whose lives were characterized by the following traits:

a. They *lived by faith in God*. In Abraham, Israel understood something about herself, that she had been called into existence by God himself, that she had been created by God's initiative and preserved by God's grace.

b. They were *called to be a servant people*. Election did not mean that some people were chosen because they were better than others, but rather that they were called to spread God's grace. God's purpose is seen in Genesis 12:3 ("in you all the families of the earth shall be blessed"); it is a universal purpose, one that moves from particulars to universals, from individuals to communities and nations. In Abraham, God brought one person of faith into existence in order that God's blessing might be extended to all humanity. This is the Bible's stress on election, that when God calls a people, they are called to service, and the rest of the Old Testament, and then the gospels and epistles, show what it means to be a servant people. In the Bible, the election of a people becomes the basis for good news, what the New Testament calls "gospel." This is the message of Genesis 12–50, and it is transported to a higher key in the New Testament.

c. They were *called to a life of pilgrimage*—a life of mobility, movement, and change. Biblical faith is a calling faith, a calling to go forth, to be on the way, to be moving in God's direction, to be pioneers of faith. Abraham was told to break his ties with his land and his former security, a way of life that up to that point had been deeply rooted to the land. Like Abraham, God's people are called to a nomadic consciousness. We see this clearly in the prophetic consciousness, a stance that could be counter-cultural in the sense that one could be both an agent of change and a critic of the established order. The prophetic message is that God is doing a new thing. As we see in Abraham, faith is not so much consent or agreement as something dynamic, manifested in movement. The story of Abraham and the patriarchs is the story of God on the move with his people.

3. *God's Presence with Humanity: Moses and the Exodus*. The presence of God is one of the central themes of the Old Testament. The Torah

(the first five books of the Bible) sets out the terms on which God will be with the people of Israel; the historical writings show from concrete examples how God's presence can be forfeited, and how gracious God is, who never allows absence from an unworthy people become permanent; the prophetic writings look forward to the day when God will never seem absent again; and the Psalms reflect on all aspects of presence and absence as they affect both the worshipping community and the individual at prayer.

The earliest global civilizations, whether Asian, Indian, or Middle Eastern, were religious, and their religions preceded and gave rise to their cultures. This principle particularly exemplified the Egyptians and the ancient Semitic empires of the Middle East. From the first, these cultures conceived of the problem of life on earth as dependent on the larger reality of the cosmos and the transcendent. We know of no time when humans in this region were conscious of themselves but not yet of the divine. As early as the fourteenth century BCE there was an Egyptian monarch (Akhenaton; also known as Amenhotep IV) who conceived of a god who was the creator of the world and of all humankind.

About a century later, an Israelite named Moses led a captive people out of slavery toward a new land of settlement. This event, known as the Exodus, was marked by a wilderness encounter with deity that resulted in a new self-understanding and identity for the people. Moses and his Israelite followers defined their religion in terms of that experience. Their God is the one "who brought them out of the land of Egypt, out of the house of bondage" (see Exod 20:2). This became the first statement of belief in the Judeo-Christian tradition; like those that beliefs that followed, it is an affirmation that something significant happened in the past.

When we seek to understand the meaning of our individual life stories, we do not actually begin with birth or infancy, even though written autobiographies might start there. Rather, we view early childhood in the light of later experiences that are formative or pivotal. Likewise, Israel's life story did not begin with the time of Abraham or even the Creation, although the Old Testament starts there. Rather, Israel's history had its true beginning in a crucial historical experience that created a self-conscious historical community—an event so decisive that earlier happenings and subsequent experiences are seen in its light. That decisive event—the great watershed of Israel's history—is the Exodus from Egypt. Through the ages, the story of the deliverance of slaves from bondage, and their march through the wilderness toward a Promised Land, has had a powerful appeal to the religious imagination of many oppressed groups and individuals. It is the paradigmatic biblical story of salvation and deliverance.

Exodus 1–24, a passage that speaks of the Exodus and the birth of the nation of Israel, is less concerned with what happened historically and more concerned with the meaning behind these events. This is not to say that the narrative does not describe actual events, but to emphasize that it describes them theologically. While providing interesting stories about Moses and the Israelites, the exodus account focuses not so much on Moses as liberator of the people but on God's redemptive role. God, not Moses, is the primary actor. The broader story—beginning with the classic account of deliverance from Egyptian slavery and including the covenant enacted on Mount Sinai and the subsequent wilderness experience that led to the conquest of the Promised Land—is not recorded for its own sake. Rather it provides a clue to who God is and how God acts toward humanity, particularly toward those who are downtrodden and oppressed.

Despite his upbringing in Pharaoh's court, Moses identified with the Hebrew slaves, an impulse that led to his slaying an Egyptian taskmaster. Forced to flee, Moses took refuge in "the land of Midian," an area of the Sinai Peninsula occupied by shepherds. There he married the daughter of a Midianite priest. While tending the flocks of his father-in-law, Moses came upon "the mountain of God." His encounter with the God of the ancestors (Exod 3:13) in that sacred place and his role in the ensuing encounter with the Pharaoh is one of the masterpieces of religious literature. It is in the Midianite wilderness that God disclosed essential aspects of the divine nature, including (1) God's personal name (Yahweh), which, literally untranslatable, has come to be associated with *God's creative activity* ("I am", "I cause to be") and (2) *God's redemptive activity* ("I will be with you"; see Exod 3:12) on behalf of Israel.

Yahweh appeared to Moses with memorable words: "I have observed the misery of my people . . . I have heard their cry . . . I know their sufferings, and I have come down to deliver them . . . and to bring them to a good and broad land, a land flowing with milk and honey . . ." (Exod 3:7–8). In a fundamental declaration of faith, the ancient Israelites affirmed that their history originated in a marvelous liberation from oppression, declaring climactically the mighty deeds of God on their behalf. The verbs of the narrative sweep to a climax: God heard, God saw, God rescued.

The primary purpose of the Exodus narrative is to glorify the God of Israel, the "divine warrior" whose strong hand and outstretched arm wins the victory over Pharaoh and his armies. The text heralds five interlocking biblical themes: (1) *divine love* (when things on earth get bad, God's love is greater still); (2) *divine mercy* (God is always "for us," never "against us"); (3) *divine initiative* (God always takes the initiative in restoring that which is broken, forgotten, or lost); (4) *divine sovereignty* (God is completely in control, even to the point of hardening Pharaoh's heart); and (5) *divine freedom* (while disclosing the divine name, God nevertheless retains the divine freedom that eludes human control: "I will be gracious to whom I will be gracious, and will show mercy on whom I will show mercy. But you cannot see my face; for no one shall see me and live"; Exod 33:19-20).

4. *The Hiddenness of God: Moses and Elijah.* Biblical talk about God is paradoxical. Because God is a person who is alive and active and yet has an awesome, even overwhelming personality, friendship with God is both a privilege and yet elusive. While it is difficult to live with God, it is impossible to live without God. Yet the hiddenness of God—perhaps even God's absence—seems the dominant reality for many seekers throughout history.

A helpful place to examine this conundrum is 1 Kings 19, a passage that records a memorable experience of the prophet Elijah on Mount Sinai. Elijah (his name means "Yahweh is my God"), persecuted by Jezebel (King Ahab's Phoenician wife) for his faithfulness to Yahweh, flees to Mount Sinai, where he prepares for an encounter with the divine: "Now there was a great wind, so strong that it was splitting mountains and breaking rocks in pieces before Yahweh, but Yahweh was not in the wind; and after the wind an earthquake, but Yahweh was not in the earthquake; and after the earthquake a fire, but Yahweh was not in the fire; and after the fire a sound of sheer silence" (1 Kgs 19:11-12; these last few words are traditionally translated "a still small voice").

Elijah's experience on Mount Sinai reminds us of the climactic experience of Moses with God at the same location, the vision of God in darkness described at Exodus 33:17-23. If even Moses saw only God's back, is there any hope that anyone else can see God's "face" and live? For practical purposes, the God of the Old Testament is a hidden God, hidden yet everywhere present. Yet, according to the prophet Isaiah, the God who is hidden can be known by the person who does not seek to "see" God, but rather to obey God's will: "I dwell in the high and holy place," says the Lord, "and also with those who are contrite and humble in spirit" (57:15).

In the book of Jeremiah, the prophet speaks of two epochs: the time of the Mosaic covenant, which ends in human failure, and the time of the new covenant, when the divine Torah (law, teaching) is written on the heart, resulting in such personal knowledge of God that religious teaching would no longer be necessary. This vision of the restored community of Israel is profoundly expressed in Jeremiah's prophecy of the new covenant (Jer 31:31–34), a prophecy that eventually gives the name to the canon of Christian writings ("New Testament" means "New Covenant"). In the New Testament, God is said to be fully with us in Jesus. As we read in John 1:18, "No one has ever seen God. It is God the only Son, who is close to the Father's heart, who has made him known."

NEW TESTAMENT SPIRITUALITY

For Christians, the relationship between the Old and New Testaments is one of continuity and discontinuity. Like two partners joined in marriage, neither is a substitute for the other, nor are they independent of one another. Rather there is relative independence, whereby they complement one another. For Christians, the gulf between the testaments is bridged by Jesus Christ, whose person and work establishes a deep discontinuity with Israel's scripture and, at the same time, a deep continuity in the purpose of God.

Until the emergence of the historical and critical study of the Bible in the eighteenth and nineteenth centuries, the Bible was revered as sole authority for Christian practice and belief. For a time, Christians sought to identify "*the* theology of the New Testament" behind all the writings, believing that scripture contained one divine revelation, which was inspired and therefore not contradictory. Modern scholarship reveals a quite different picture, recognizing a plurality of theologies within the New Testament. Consequently, less attention is placed on "spirituality," except as it is implicit in "theology," but it is now equally clear that we can no longer expect to find only one spirituality or *the* spirituality of the New Testament, and have every reason to detect many. In that respect, we can speak of a Markan spirituality, but also of a Matthean, Lukan, Johannine, and Pauline spirituality.

When we read the Bible, there are two dangers we cannot avoid but must guard against, namely (1) to interpret it uncritically, that is, subjectively or out of context, and (2) to read it as a rule book or as an easy-step instruction book. When we let it go as a modern answer book, we get to discover it for what it really is, a book that tells us who we are and what our story is. While the Bible provides individual wisdom and guidance, it calls us to create a community that becomes a catalyst for doing God's work in the world.

1. *Jesus and Spirituality*. The central theme of the New Testament is a person, Jesus of Nazareth, a wandering preacher of the first century who changes the course of history. Whether Christian or not, all who live in the Western world are influenced by the teachings and life of this individual. Early disciples envisioned Jesus as the climactic historical figure, the Messiah who brought the long-awaited messianic kingdom of God, a rule that by ending evil and suffering ushered in an age of bliss. Later followers and even unbelievers understood Jesus' historical role as pivotal, representing its midpoint. Ernst Renan, famous nineteenth-century scholar, affirmed this view when he wrote: "All history is incomprehensible without Christ"; also Napoleon, who confessed toward the end of his life: "This man, Jesus, vanished for eighteen hundred years, still holds the character of men as in a vise"; and H. G. Wells, who declared, "I am an historian. I am not a believer. But I must confess, as an historian, that this penniless preacher from Galilee is irresistibly the center of history."

As we examine the gospels, the sources for the life, teaching, and character of Jesus, we recognize that these are entirely *Christian* documents. They were not the work of neutral observers, but of those already committed to Jesus as the Christ and Son of God, and above all, to his resurrection. Though they record pre-Easter events, they are post-Easter documents. And they were written, not for a purely historical purpose, but for the edification and instruction of fellow-believers.

When we think of Jesus, I suggest we think of the historical human being who represents for Christians the ideal universal person, the embodiment of the highest and best in us all. At this point in our discussion, then, we focus on the Jesus of history, the one who bears the ideal of normality and universality simultaneously.

The human Jesus must have been a figure of great power and originality. In him a force of immeasurable magnitude began to operate in this world, unleashing a movement that lasted through twenty centuries and is on the rise globally. When a person of such eminence appears, who can apprehend that person totally? One observer sees one aspect, another a different aspect; and even the collection of their observations cannot yield the whole person. Of course, no one can know another person completely. Even after years of marriage, husbands and wives often discover aspects of one another's being of which, up to that moment, they are ignorant. This being so, it is not surprising that, when Jesus of Nazareth appeared, no single mind could encompass the whole of him, no single artist could paint the definitive portrait. What we have in the New Testament is a collection of fragments of memory and interpretation concerning Jesus, extruded through longstanding Jewish hermeneutical processes. Early Christians, believing that in Jesus all of God's promises are fulfilled (2 Cor 1:20), added to this tradition, searching the Hebrew scriptures for passages that could be interpreted christologically.

Like the Hebrew prophets, Jesus claimed knowledge of God, from which his teaching derived and upon which it was based. What he heard from God—more on the level of inner experience than on the level of head knowledge—was his to pass on. For that reason, he adopted the term "Amen," a beautiful and powerful expression of Jewish affirmation placed at the end of prayer. Yet Jesus, a devout Jew, put it at the beginning of everything important he said. When Jesus said "Amen, Amen" (often translated as "Truly" or "Verily"), he seemed to be making two affirmations: (1) that his teaching was based on what he heard from God, and (2) that his message was based on divine authority.

Like good disciples, in loving relationship with God and in communion with Jesus, we too must live in confidence to also say, as it were, "Amen, Amen." What Jesus heard from God is now ours to pass on. "Let the same mind be in you," Paul writes in Philippians 2:5, "that you have in Christ Jesus." This is the truth of the Christian tradition, what it truly means to be a disciple of Jesus. We are called to recognize, surrender to, and ultimately be identified with the mystery of God utterly beyond understanding.

We need to acknowledge that Jesus says nothing to us that he hasn't somehow heard from God. Jesus had a familial relationship with God, whom he called Abba, and it is out of that relationship that he taught, healed, blessed, and nurtured the spiritual family we call the church. To be disciples of Jesus, we need to let ourselves be loved as he did. It is in receiving that love that we find our insight and strength.

For Jesus, discipleship is about being in an intimate, loving, and challenging relationship, much like that between parent and child. There is a unique nature to the healthy parent-child relationship, and each person has a role to play. Ideally, the parent employs the gifts of experience and knowledge to care for, nurture, and protect the child. In turn, the child depends on and trusts the parent for sustenance, well-being, and guidance in a world of unknowing. Discipleship follows that sequence. First, we learn how to be God's children, allowing ourselves to receive love, to be loved, to be cared for, and believed in, so that we can be entrusted to go about our "Father's business" as Jesus did (Luke 2:49 KJV).

In the beginning, Jesus stepped into his ministry as a child of God, not as the parent or authority figure. Rather, he let himself be the recipient, and he trusted God to lead him. Because Jesus was always listening to God and experiencing God's presence, God continually taught him. Jesus didn't begin his life full of power and authority. He was born helpless and vulnerable, like all of us, but throughout his life he continued to grow in love, wisdom, and maturity (see Luke 2:52). Like every true disciple, Jesus came into the fullness of his being by faithfully following and listening to his divine Teacher, who is forever true, the source of all wisdom and knowing.

Had Jesus no other legacy, he would be remembered as one of the world's master teachers. Jesus, however, did not come on the scene to conform to anyone's preconceived expectation about sages, or for that matter, about prophets or messiahs. His subject, essentially, was threefold: he made known something about God, something about humankind, and something about their interrelationship.

Apart from the tradition of Judaism, however, the life or teaching of Jesus is incomprehensible. In Jesus' day there was a vast human quest for God, wrapped up in piety and legalism (Judaism), and in idolatry and superstition (Gentiles). The Jews were monotheists and had a central temple in Jerusalem, dedicated to sacrifice and rituals. Much of their worship was motivated by duty and regulated by tradition. However, no code of laws can deal with the variety of human beings. While Jesus affirmed the value of Jewish law in many of his actions and teachings, he regularly pointed beyond the law. According to Jesus, each of us has individual value and our own unique journey to God.

While Jesus changed the way we understand God, the God of the Old Testament had been speaking to humanity through an entire history of dialogue with Israel. As Walter Brueggemann indicates in his *Theology of the Old Testament*, the God that Jesus incarnated was already seen to be "merciful, gracious, faithful, forgiving, and steadfast in love" (Exod

34:6–7). This "credo of adjectives," positive and relational in nature, announces the character of God, indicating God's intense solidarity, loyalty, and commitment to those with whom he is related.[4]

Much as we need to unlearn harsh and damning views of God, we also must unlearn many of the ways we have been taught about dealing with other human beings. There seems to be only one demand that this God of love lays upon those who receive love and forgiveness, namely, to treat those around them as they have been treated by God. That is the litmus test of all spiritual transformation.

When the institutional element dominates religion, there is often an obsession with the organization and with the details of its regulations. Blind obedience is required. This often results in institutional rigidity and sterility. When religion becomes only a matter of outer rules and rituals, then those who deviate from the accepted practices and beliefs are not tolerated. Such religious prejudice drives thoughtful people away from the institutional church. The implications of Christian teaching can be ignored if we accept tradition by rote. Hence, it took eighteen hundred years before Jesus' teaching of the equal value of all human beings resulted in the abolition of slavery. It took even longer before women were accorded the place that Jesus gives them. Cultural accretions quite at variance to a religion often creep into religious tradition to corrupt and dilute it. For that reason tradition needs ongoing experiences of God, continuous reflection on what makes us human, and transformative love. Without them religion becomes destructive and oppressive.

2. *Paul and the Second Journey.* One of the heroic figures in the life of the early church, the apostle Paul emerged from being an arch-persecutor of Christians into an unrelenting missionary of the gospel. The impact of Paul upon the church was both widespread and permanent. As the first great theologian of the church, he was both a practical theologian—in that he addressed specific needs arising in the church—and a task theologian. To him belonged the unique task of developing or disclosing a theology for the Gentile church, indicating how Gentiles are brought into full participation in the fellowship of Christ, what Paul refers to as "the body of Christ" (Rom 12:5; 1 Cor 12:13, 27; cf. Col 1:18; Eph 4:4) and "the Israel of God" (Gal 6:16; cf. Rom 11:25–26).

The first full-time missionary to the Gentiles, Paul helped bridge the gap as the church became less Jewish and more Gentile in its makeup.

---

4. Brueggemann, *Theology of the Old Testament*, 215–28.

Jesus had performed a revolution in religion, recognizing in Judaism a rich spiritual treasure, resulting in a distinct system of worship, a religious way of life, and a high ethical outlook. Yet that treasure was not available to everyone, for Judaism was an ethnic and deeply exclusive faith. As Paul saw it, Jesus was not simply a teacher of truth but the Messiah, through whom God's eternal purpose for Israel and the nations were fulfilled. Up to that point, Jesus' task of liberating the spiritual treasure of Israel's faith for humanity was limited to Jews, and his faithfulness to God led to the cross. Now, the work of Christ was entrusted to his followers, who were empowered by the Holy Spirit to continue the mission Jesus has begun. It is in Paul and his work that we see the task being accomplished. Paul took the work of Christ and set it free from possession by any one ethnic group, sect, or clique. In so doing, Paul remains the classic exponent of the idea of freedom in Christ and of the universality of God's plan for all humanity (see Rom 3:29–30; Gal 3:14; 5:1; cf. Eph 3:6).

Paul also founded new congregations during his missionary travels, providing exhortation, encouragement, and support through letters and personal visits. He helped heal doctrinal and moral difficulties in his churches, providing a form of moral instruction known as *paraenesis* (see, for example, 1 Thess 4:1–12), such as one might expect to see in the philosophical letters of his day. His letters to the church of Corinth deal with numerous practical issues they were facing, helping later Christians more fully understand the nature of the Christian life. While Paul had no idea he was writing scripture, there is no denying that he considered his writings to be invested with special authority, and furthermore, that he expected his readers generally to recognize this as factual (1 Cor 2:16; 7:17; 14:37–38; cf. 2 Thess 3:14).

Aside from Jesus, Paul is the most distinctive individual in the New Testament. While it is easy to focus on his many unique insights, he was not entirely idiosyncratic. Though a pioneer of the church's Gentile mission, he was an apostle with the other apostles (see 1 Cor 15:1–11), and he sought to work in fellowship with church leaders in Jerusalem (Gal 1:18––2:10). He was not antinomian, despite his strong rejection of the Jewish Torah when regarded as a means of self-justification, for he asserted its moral precepts and Jesus' summary of them (Gal 5:14; Rom 13:8–10). In his writings, when he speaks of the role of the Old Testament and its relation to the "law of Christ," he means the law of love: "The whole law is summed up in a single commandment, 'You shall love your neighbor as yourself'" (5:14).

As Paul indicates in 1 Thessalonians, believers should live with hope and courage, progressing in love for each other and to all (3:12–13), for a life of love, as modeled by Christ, never fails (see 1 Cor 13:8, regularly translated as "never ends"). Already children of light (1 Thess 5:5), believers must not be restless or neurotic, but calm and industrious (4:11–12; see also 2 Thess 3:6–15). While outward affliction can affect our external and false self, our focus should be on the renewal occurring within (the resurrection of our True Self), for what is being born is eternal rather than temporal (2 Cor 4:16–21).

QUESTIONS FOR DISCUSSION AND REFLECTION

In addition to the questions listed at the end of the preface, answer the following questions, writing your answers in a journal. If you are in a group study, be prepared to share your answers with those in the group.

1. If the Bible was originally intended for liturgical use, assess the advantage (or disadvantage) of reading it privately or studying it in small-group settings?
2. If the Bible consists of two sets of scripture, one Jewish and the other Christian, how do they relate?
3. In your estimation, does the modern emphasis on individualism distort the intended biblical message? Why or why not?
4. Assess the merit of Blaise Pascal's statement concerning the "God-shaped vacuum in the human heart."
5. Assess the biblical emphasis on election; what did it mean then, and what does it mean for us today?
6. If you were to write the story of your spiritual journey, where would you begin and end, and what event would you consider most decisive, that is, your watershed event?
7. Assess the meaning of the following statement: "While it is difficult to live with God, it is impossible to live without God."
8. What do you consider Jesus' greatest teaching on spirituality? Explain your answer.
9. What do you consider Paul's greatest teaching on spirituality? Explain your answer.

Chapter 3

Augustine's *Confessions* and *Enchiridion*

IN THE HISTORY OF EUROPE, the medieval period (the thousand-year period said to last from the fall of the Western Roman Empire in 476 to the fall of Constantinople in 1453) altered the Western and Middle Eastern worlds profoundly. However, the start of the fourth century, beginning with the Edict of Milan in 313, changed the fortunes of Christianity forever. With the conversion of Constantine to Christianity in 312, state persecution of Christians ceased, and Christianity was on its way to becoming the official religion of the Roman Empire (an event made official by Emperor Theodosius in 380).

This dramatic change of church-state relations, with Christianity no longer endangered but established, had a profound effect upon prayer and spirituality. On the one hand, it led to an impressive display of liturgical worship. Spacious churches were built and richly decorated, where the Eucharist could be celebrated in formal splendor. At this time there was also a rapid development of pilgrimages, the cult of the saints, and devotion to the Virgin Mary. On the other hand, ascetic piety, present in Christianity from the start, assumed a more articulate form with the emergence of monasticism as an organized movement, distinct from the life of the parish. Both the "way of affirmation" and the "way of negation" became sharply differentiated.

In our thinking of early medieval theology, we focus on the contributions of Augustine (354–430), the single-most influential Christian thinker outside of the Bible, although his influence is more in the Western Church (Catholicism and Protestantism) than in the Eastern Church

(Eastern Orthodoxy). While there are many things in medieval spirituality that modern people find extreme or self-deprecating, medieval Catholic spirituality is not all excess and abuse. There is also a wonderful spiritual legacy here, from which we have much to learn. Medieval spirituality is about a journey to God. Being with God is regarded as the destiny of believers, our heritage, our home. For this we are created, and here we belong. The journey, called by Augustinian scholar Phillip Cary "The Augustinian paradigm of spirituality," goes back to Augustine, who lived during the church's conciliar age, near the end of the Roman Empire. Augustine's thought established the fundamental theological categories for medieval thought, meaning that all medieval church theologians lived and thought in an Augustinian framework. Despite notable exceptions, for one thousand years the Augustinian spirituality was nearly every Christian's paradigm.

For Augustine, the essential process of the spiritual life was the reformation of the "image of God" in the human person, a twofold process requiring both the grace of God and human freedom. Transformed into a friend of God, the soul enters into union with God not merely as creature with Creator but as friend with Friend. God offers this form of friendship to all human beings through Christ. Unique to Christian spirituality is the centrality of Christ, whose signs are humility and love. The unity of minds and hearts in the church is the beginning of the pilgrimage toward unity with the risen Christ. Christ is present in the church in Word and Sacrament. This unity is nourished by Sacrament and is manifested in love toward all. Since God is Love, the doorway to spirituality is love, the Spirit's gift. In his letters, Augustine speaks of friendship as a necessity of life, indeed as the very goal of human existence. Hence, spirituality is not a solitary affair. This common love of truth unites friends, and the common love of Christ unites all Christians. Augustinian spirituality is opposed to naturalism but not to nature, and opposed to individualism only when it divides people from one another.

Communal spirituality is a friendship in Christ that liberates and develops all that is best in human beings. Within this Christian spirituality, the dominant characteristics are a thirst for God, a delight in searching for God, joy in truth, commitment to contemplation, responsiveness to the neighbor's need, participation in the church's worship and mission, and above all, unity with all in love. Through rightly ordered love—the love of generosity—humans participate in the Trinitarian mystery and enjoy a foretaste of eternal life.

For medieval Christians, the goal of the spiritual journey was finding happiness, often called "beatitude," "bliss," or simply "the blessed life." In this context, ultimate or eternal happiness meant finding God, or, as Augustine put it, "seeing" God. Of course, this did not happen with one's physical sight, but with what Augustine called inward or "intellectual" vision, seeing with one's mind and heart. Such vision is what we experience when we struggle to understand something before we finally "see" or "get" its meaning. That intuitive way of knowing, that recognition, is what Augustine meant by "seeing" or experiencing God, who, we might add, is not only final and absolute truth, but the Truth at the center of the universe from whom come all other truths. Imagine having this knowledge, this certainty, this relationship, at the center of your life! Imagine living within the context of the eternal "Aha! Now I get it!" That happiness, joy, and bliss, seeing God with your mind's eye, is what Augustine's spirituality had as its goal. This, for Augustine, is what it means "to see God eternally," and also what it means to speak of "heaven."

This, of course, is the end of the journey. During the journey, we might have glimpses of God, but there is yet no finality. The journey is long and arduous, and what we need for the journey are values, morality, and commitment. What we need for the journey is not vision—that comes at the end—but faith, hope, and love, moral characteristics of the soul that power the soul on its journey. The journey begins with faith, which means, essentially, believing what you are told. Then there is this long road to travel, a road we travel by love—of God and others. For Jesus and Paul, this is the summation of the religious law, which goes back to the Old Testament, and Augustine puts it at the heart of Christian ethics. Love is like gravity—a force of attraction—but it pulls us upward, not downward. Love for God attracts us to God, pulling us upward, like sparks from a fire, ultimately uniting us with God.

Whenever a conversation arises concerning Christian doctrine, invariably Augustine is cited. Everyone has heard of Augustine, often in connection with his *Confessions* or his *City of God*, two monumental works that broke new ground in the areas of Christian autobiography and church history. Additionally, people credit Augustine for his contribution to the doctrine of the Trinity, particularly for his perceptive use of psychological analogies to affirm both the unity and the plurality of the Godhead. In addition to his *Confessions*, written early in his theological career, an excellent introduction to Augustine's writings is his brief treatise known as the *Enchiridion* (the Latin word means "handbook" or "manual"), a lucid and accessible work that represents the summation of Augustine's entire Christian teaching in the briefest possible form. It is on these two works, his *Confessions* and his *Enchiridion*, that we focus in this chapter. In these two works—the nearest equivalent to summation in the whole of the Augustinian corpus—we can find all his essential themes and can sample the characteristic flavor of his thought.

Augustine regarded himself as much less an innovator than a summator. He was less a reformer of the church than the defender of the church's faith, centered on the biblical scriptures. While Augustine cannot be said to have a theological or philosophical system, he did have a stable and coherent Christian outlook. Moreover, he had a consistent and ardent concern: the salvation of men and women from their hopeless plight, through the gracious action of God's redeeming love. To understand and interpret this was his one endeavor, and to this task he devoted his considerable genius. In addition to his theological and philosophical prowess, he was far and away the best—if not the first—psychologist in the ancient world. His observations and descriptions of human motives and emotions, his depth analyses of will and thought in their interaction, and his exploration of the inner nature of the human self—these have established one of the main traditions in Western conceptions of human nature, even down to our own time. Augustine is an essential source for both contemporary depth psychology and existentialist philosophy. His view of the shape and process of human history has been more influential than any other single source in the development of the Western tradition that regards political order as inextricably involved in moral order. His metaphysical explorations of the problems of being, the character of evil, the relation of faith and knowledge, of will and reason, of time and eternity, of creation and cosmic order, have not ceased to animate and enrich various philosophic reflections throughout the succeeding centuries. At the same time the hallmark of the Augustinian perspective is its insistent demand that reflective thought issue in practical consequence; no contemplation of the end of life suffices unless it discovers the means by which human beings are brought to their proper goals. In sum, Augustine is one of the few thinkers who simply cannot be ignored or dismissed in any estimate of Western civilization without serious distortion and impoverishment of one's historical and religious understanding.

Whereas first-century Christians, including authors of the New Testament documents, tended to perceive a sharp contrast between emerging Christian theology and Greek philosophy, in the second and third centuries, Christian apologists and other educated thinkers came to believe that great insights from other cultures or pagan philosophers could be used to support and advance biblical ideas. Of course, some of this methodology was already evident in the composition of the biblical documents themselves, as we see in Paul's quotation from pagan philosophers in his speech to the Athenian elders in Acts 17:22–29, his use of natural theology in Romans 1:19–20, and the borrowing of Logos ideology in John's prologue. Beginning already in the first century and continuing through the Middle Ages, the Renaissance, and into modern times, specific Christian thinkers sought to weave biblical and nonbiblical ideas together, manipulating competing traditions in a multitude of ways to render them more compatible.

Throughout much of Christian history, certainly from the fourth through the fifteenth centuries, prominent Christian theologians attempted to combine or synthesize biblical and Greek ideas, particularly ideas associated with Plato and Aristotle. For them, all truth was God's truth, independent of origin. Prior to 1250, Platonic ideas exerted the primary influence on church theologians, while after that period, beginning with Thomas Aquinas's *Summa Theologica*, Aristotle's influence became predominant.

Most important among Christian thinkers who significantly shaped Western society and history are Aquinas, Luther, Calvin, and John Wesley. Their interpretations and commentaries on Judeo-Christian theology established major patterns for Western thought and culture. In profound ways, all were impacted by Augustine, a colossal figure who gave Christian thought much of its formative character.

BIOGRAPHICAL CONSIDERATIONS

An African by birth, Augustine was born and raised in Thagaste, Algeria. His father, a non-Christian, was unconcerned about morality and allowed his son to do whatever he wished. Augustine's mother, Monica, in contrast to her husband, was a devout Christian who dearly loved Augustine. At the age of twelve, the precocious youngster was sent to a school for intellectually gifted children. There he furthered his education by reading Virgil and other Greek and Roman poets. As a teenager, his sensuality took over, and he indulged in sexual affairs. When he was sixteen years old, his father died, at which time Augustine went to Carthage, continuing his schooling at the expense of a wealthy benefactor.

Carthage, a seaport on the Mediterranean Sea, had an ethical reputation for being one of the most corrupt cities of the Roman Empire. Monica, Augustine's Christian mother, advised him against fornication, but unable to heed her advice, in Carthage he took a mistress and fathered a son. Meanwhile, his intellectual growth continued. In his late teenage years he was influenced by Cicero, who argued that people find true happiness only in the pursuit of wisdom, that is, in philosophy. Augustine was inspired to seek true wisdom, but he ran into two problems. First, according to Monica, Christianity was the highest form of wisdom, but when Augustine turned to the Bible, he found that it was not particularly well written and that many of its characters were clearly immoral. Second, though inspired by Cicero's claim that true happiness comes from philosophy, Augustine found it difficult to give up material forms of happiness, such as sex and other sensual pleasures.

Disillusioned with Christianity and the Bible, during his twenties Augustine joined a sect called Manicheism. It founder, Mani (216–274), raised an Elchasaite Christian in a village near Babylon, worshipped Jesus but placed great emphasis on ritual purity. The recipient of visions and inspired revelations, he became convinced of his role as the seal of all prophecy and therefore as the one destined to unite all existing religions into one Truth.

Mani taught a view of reality that was thoroughly dualistic, positing an eternal conflict between two antithetical kingdoms, a cosmic kingdom of light forever waging war against a cosmic kingdom of darkness. This conflict extends to human beings, themselves a combination of good and evil, fragments of light trapped in material, bodily, prison houses of darkness. Salvation comes from awareness, right thinking, and an ascetic rejection of physical appetites and desires. The Manichean myth was quite complicated, but it had widespread appeal due to its clear explanation for the existence of evil and suffering, and for why people often feel torn between good and evil.

According to Mani, evil is real because it exists from the beginning. God did not create evil or even allow it to come into being. Instead, evil, in the form of a realm of darkness, always existed, and humans now find themselves trapped in that realm, particles of light, spiritual in essence, trapped in physical bodies, evil by nature. Manicheism explained why humans are attracted to both good and evil. Evil impulses arise from our bodies, which are composed of darkness. While our bodies of darkness draw us to evil deeds and keep us in ignorance, our souls, composed of light, prompt us to want to do the good. As Paul indicates in Romans 7, there is a war within each of us, and for Mani, that war was also in the natural realm. For Manichees, salvation comes from awareness (right understanding) coupled with an ascetic rejection of physical appetites and desires.

Adherents of Manicheism were divided into two classes: the few, called the Elect, led celibate and mostly pure lives, while the many, designated the Hearers, led normal married lives. Attracted to its emphasis on rational demonstration of wisdom, its rejection of the Old Testament, and its rigorous spirituality, Augustine remained a Hearer for ten years.

On one of his visits to his home, Augustine told his mother of his interest in cosmic dualism and the Manichean plan of salvation. Upset that this abstract system made no room for Jesus' redemptive activity, Monica tearfully ordered her son to leave her house. Restless and troubled, the thirty-year old Augustine decided to move from Carthage to Rome. Disenchanted with Manicheism, he became a skeptic in search of a new faith. While in Rome, his search for a new faith led him to Neoplatonism. A year later, he moved to northern Italy to take a teaching position in rhetoric. Upon arriving in Milan with his mistress and son, he rented a villa, and when he was not teaching, he studied Neoplatonism. For a while he was fascinated by Neoplatonism, which had certain similarities with Manicheism. However, under the influence of Monica, who came to live with him, he began to attend church, where he listened to the sermons of Bishop Ambrose. These stirred his heart and mind and interested him in Christianity. He learned he need not interpret the Bible literally, and this helped overcome many of his reservations with scripture.

When he was thirty-two years old, a friend challenged him to answer the question, "What am I doing on this earth?" After his friend left, Augustine went to his garden and heard the voice of a child playing nearby. When the child cried, "Take up and read," Augustine found the nearest book, a Bible, and opened it at random to read Paul's words, "Not in reveling and drunkenness, not in debauchery and licentiousness, not in quarreling and jealousy. Instead, put on the Lord Jesus Christ, and make no provision for the flesh, to gratify its desires" (Rom 13:13–14). Instantly he was converted. The following Easter he was baptized by Ambrose.

Shortly thereafter Augustine returned to Africa, and in response to a need in the coastal town of Hippo, he went to serve the Christians there.

Four years later, amid great jubilation, Augustine was ordained a priest and a year later, bishop. For the next thirty-three years, until his death in 430, he remained in this small town, addressing the doctrinal questions of his time. After converting to Christianity, he continued synthesizing Greek and biblical thought, but as he grew in understanding, he differentiated more and more between these teachings until his mature theological thought became more consistently biblical.

When serving as the bishop of Hippo, his goal was to minister to individuals in his congregation in ways that would lead to their salvation, much as he had experienced in his conversion. As a bishop, he believed that it was his job to interpret the work of the Bible, and he chose the passages that were to be read in the churches of his diocese every week. He became a famous preacher (he preached around ten thousand sermons when he was alive, some five hundred of which are accessible today). When he preached his sermons, they were recorded by stenographers. Some of his sermons lasted over one hour, and he would preach them multiple times throughout a given week.

Augustine was one of the most prolific Latin authors in terms of surviving works; the list of his works consists of more than one hundred separate titles, including apologetic works against the views of the Arians, Donatists, Manichees, and Pelagians, considered heretical. He also wrote exegetical works such as commentaries on Genesis, the Psalms, and Paul's letter to the Romans, many letters, and the *Retractations*, a review of his earlier works that he wrote near the end of his life. Augustine's writings covered diverse fields including theology, psychology, philosophy, sociology, and church history. His theological subjects are vast and comprehensive, covering such topics as creation, eschatology, sin, salvation, predestination, free will, the nature of evil, natural law, sexuality, ethics, Trinitarian theology, and sacramental theology, all informed by his concept of grace. Many Protestants, especially Calvinists and Lutherans, consider Augustine one of the theological fathers of the Protestant Reformation due to his teachings on salvation and divine grace.

Believing the grace of Christ was indispensable to human freedom, Augustine helped formulate the doctrine of original sin and made significant contributions to the development of just war theory. In the middle of his active ecclesiastical career, when the Western Roman Empire began to disintegrate, Augustine imagined the church as a spiritual "City of God," distinct from the material Earthly City. In the *City of God*, written over a period of fourteen years and the work Augustine considered his masterpiece, Augustine wrote to restore the confidence of his fellow Christians, which was badly shaken by the sack of Rome by the Goths in 410 CE. One persistent rumor was that Christianity had sapped the strength of Rome. The officials and citizenry of Rome were still divided into Christians and pagans.

The *City of God* was well planned in advance. Of the book's twenty-two chapters, the first ten constitute Augustine's response to the pagan charge against the Christianizing of the Empire. In this section Augustine shows that the greatness that was Rome's was not due to its pagan past. He studies at great length the powers and functions of the many pagan deities in order to convince his readers that these mythological beings benefitted the Roman people neither physically nor morally. In the tenth book, Augustine begins to expound the worldview of Christianity and to contrast it with paganism. Books 11 and 12 offer a positive interpretation of human society, in which the protagonists are not Rome and its enemies but two radically different cities, each characterized by opposing loyalties, one by the "love of God," the other by the "love of Man." For Augustine, all human history and culture may be viewed as the interplay of the competing values of these two loves.

THE CONFESSIONS

Augustine began work on the *Confessions* around the year 397, when he was forty-three years old and shortly after he became bishop. His precise motivation for writing his life story at this point was twofold. First, his contemporaries were suspicious of him because of his classical, pagan-influenced education, his public career as a teacher of rhetoric, and his status as an ex-Manichee. Maintaining a prominent role in the Donatist controversies, he was suspected both by Donatists and by wary Catholic allies.

Those unfamiliar with Donatism need to know that in Augustine's day, African Christians were polarized over the idea of the church. Viewed as the divine Mother of all believers, the church was thought of as a haven of safety and purity. It existed to protect believers from the forces of darkness, and it served as an alternative to things hostile and impure. Since 311, African Christians had been divided on the distinction between the ideal holiness of the church and the actual purity of its members. The Donatists, following Donatus, a bishop of Carthage, claimed that the church could only survive if it remained pure, meaning that prayers and sacraments performed by unworthy bishops (whether through private sin or through compromise in times of persecution) were ineffective. Augustine's Catholicism, by contrast, reflected a broader and more benevolent attitude, confident of the church's powers to absorb the world without losing its identity or spiritual vitality. Prior to Augustine, public sentiment favored the Donatist stance. Augustine, steeped in Neoplatonic thought, viewed the Christian life as dynamic rather than static—a process of "becoming" rather than a state of "being"—and the visible church as an imperfect shadow of eternal reality. For Augustine, Christians are a work in progress, and the church a place of healing, welcome, and reconciliation, a microcosm of the re-established unity of the human race. Clearly, the church had to abide by standards, but always through friendship, forgiveness, and love.

One purpose of the *Confessions*, then, was to defend himself against criticism by fellow Christians, by explaining how he had arrived at his Christian faith and by demonstrating that his beliefs were truly Christian. Another motivation was the request by a notable Christian convert, Paulinus, Bishop of Nola, a Roman aristocrat who had converted to Christianity and who, after reading some of Augustine's works, wished an account of his life and conversion. While Augustine had many external reasons for writing his spiritual account at this moment in his career, he was also entering his midlife, an auspicious time to write an autobiography.

Around 397, Augustine had reached a watershed in his life. Since 391, he had been forced to adjust to a new existence as a priest and bishop. This change had affected him deeply. The humanistic ideals on which he had hoped to build his life had been set aside, and the original optimism of his conversion had disappeared, leaving him in a state of anxious self-examination. The kind of life he had set himself to live in his prime would not last him into old age. The past still haunted him, and writing the *Confessions* became an act of therapy for Augustine, forcing him to come to terms with himself. Despite their antiquity and dogmatic nature, the *Confessions* are unmistakably current, glowing with deep spiritual insight. Above all, they are holistic, for they illustrate that mystical spirituality can be compatible both with the life of the intellect and also with the practical affairs of everyday life.

The *Confessions* are about spiritual passion and love, particularly about loving God foremost. Previously, Augustine's loves were disordered, for as he discovered in his conversion to the Christian faith, in his pre-conversion state he loved created things more than the Creator: "Late have I loved you, O Beauty, so ancient and so new, late have I loved you! And behold, you were within me and I was outside, and there I sought for you, and in my deformity I rushed headlong into the well-formed things that you have made. You were with me, and I was not with you. Those outer beauties held me far from you, yet if they had not been in you, they would not have existed at all" (10.27).[1] This citation, chosen because it brings together vividly Augustine's early struggles and his mature faith, in a sense provides the key to that which was to make him a foremost figure in history.

As a Christian, Augustine learned that love of God leads to love for created things. He also discovered that, unlike the philosophies of Manicheism and Neoplatonism he once embraced, the Christian worldview upholds the goodness of God, the Creator, and, as a result, the goodness of created things. Moreover, Christianity offered Augustine two things he sought in his philosophical and spiritual quest: a divine origin of the universe and life and a hopeful eschatology, rooted in an all-powerful and all-loving God.

Structurally, the *Confessions* falls into three segments: books 1 through 9 recount the first thirty-three years of Augustine's life and his spiritual journey. Book 10 reveals the spiritual state of Augustine after his conversion and at the time he was writing this book. Books 11 through 13, a meditation on the first chapter of Genesis, contain reflections on time and eternity, creation and reconciliation, and transfiguration and the restoration of all things.

While modern readers may not find time or wish to read the *Confessions* in their entirety, I recommend that you read books 7 to 10. Book 7 records Augustine's intellectual conversion through the reading of Neoplatonist books. Book 8 describes the moral influence of fervent Christians on Augustine that led to his dramatic personal conversion. In book 9 he describes the influence and final days of Monica, his Christian mother, and recalls a moving mystical experience they shared before her death. In book 10 Augustine explains his motivation in writing the *Confessions* and provides a penetrating analysis of memory, which later he uses as a foundation to his doctrine of the Trinity. After exploring the meaning and mode of true prayer, he confesses the temptations to which

---

1. This translation is Mary T Clark's, found in The Classics of Western Spirituality volume on selected writings of Augustine, 144.

he remains subject, understanding the teachings of 1 John 2:16—"the desire of the flesh, the desire of the eyes, [and] the pride in riches (worldly ambition)"—as anticipating the three Neoplatonic vices: *libido*, *superbia*, and *curiositas*. In book 10, Augustine also admits to moment of experiencing God, though he places his hope not in transitory religious experiences but rather in Christ, "the true Mediator" (1 Tim 2:5).

The *Confessions* is a story of conversion. As an adult, Augustine actually underwent several conversions: to Manicheism; to the pursuit of moral truth, influenced by Cicero's *Hortensius*; to an intellectual acceptance of Christian doctrine; and finally to an emotional acceptance of Christian faith. Yet the term "conversion" is somewhat misleading, for never did Augustine truly doubt the existence of God. Although he dabbled briefly with the radical skepticism of the rationalists, he was always certain, even as a Manichee, that Christ was the savior of the world.

In one sense, the *Confessions* is Augustine's story, but it is also a story with an almost universal or archetypal quality. Augustine is a kind of Everyman, representing a lost and struggling humanity trying to rediscover the divine, the only source of lasting peace and satisfaction. As in a fairy tale, the outcome of the *Confessions* is never in doubt; its hero is predestined, as Monica foresees, to find what he seeks.

The *Confessions* is one of Augustine's three major works, the other two being *On the Trinity* and *The City of God*. Augustine's *Confessions*, a literary, theological, and philosophical masterpiece, is the most studied of all Augustine's works in the modern era, attracting not only the attention of theologians and philosophers, but also of psychologists. Because of this work, the facts of Augustine's youth are better known than those of any other figure in antiquity. Though many works lay claim to the title of first "modern" literary work, the *Confessions* stakes its claim to this title on the fact that it is the first work to explore extensively interior states of the human mind and the mutual relationship of grace and free will, themes dominant in the history of Western philosophy and theology.

The question of a unifying theme or of the precise nature of the *Confessions* has been the subject of intense debate, particularly in modern times. Clearly, Augustine has not given us an autobiography in the contemporary understanding of that term, for he writes selectively, not exhaustively or comprehensively. In it, he omits a great deal, for he is recalling only those crucial episodes and events in which he can witness and celebrate the actions of God's prevenient and provident grace.

The *Confessions* is very much a book of a person who had come to regard his past as training for his present career. It is the story of the journey toward conversion, an odyssey of a soul. The fall and return of the soul to God, a theme frequently found in ancient literature, especially in Neoplatonism, as well as in Luke's story of the prodigal son, dominates the account. Human life, for Augustine, is the product of free decisions guided by God's grace to its proper conclusion. He returns to this thesis in *City of God*, where he applies it to all creation and provides what has often been termed his philosophy or theology of history.

Many have sought the unifying principle of the *Confessions* in the several meaning of the word "confession," among which are admission of one's sins, which Augustine does with gusto, confessing not only his sexual lust but also his ambition and intellectual pride. Confession also means a statement of belief, and this aspect is reflected in Augustine's detailed account of how he arrived at this Christian beliefs and his knowledge of God. Finally, confession means a statement of praise, and in the *Confessions*, Augustine constantly gives praise to the God who mercifully directed his path and brought him out of misery and error. In many ways, the *Confessions* is one long prayer of thanksgiving and praise.

Prior to Augustine, prayer had long been a recognized vehicle for speculative inquiry. Augustine had begun one of his first philosophical works, the *Soliloquies*, with a prayer, and he would end his historical masterpiece, *The City of God*, with another. The *Confessions* are to be read in this spirit. They are a prolonged exploration of the nature of God, written in the form of a prayer. However, while prayers had regularly been regarded as part of the preliminary stage in the lifting of the philosopher's mind to God, they had never been used, as Augustine would use them throughout the *Confessions*, to strike up a lively conversation with God.

The *Confessions* is a manifesto of the inner world. This is made clear in the opening paragraph of the book, for it contains what is perhaps Augustine's best-known quote, "Thou hast made us for thyself, and restless is our heart until it comes to rest in thee" (1.1.1).[2] This affirmation establishes his frame of mind: he is entirely focused on God, as evidenced in the first sentence, which is comprised of not one but two scripture references: "Great art thou, O Lord, and greatly to be praised" (Ps 47:2); "great is thy power, and infinite is thy wisdom" (Ps 146:5). Moreover, as one reads the *Confessions*, one gets the sense that Augustine "thinks in

---

2. Unless otherwise noted, all citations from the *Confessions* are taken from Outler's translation in the Library of Christian Classics.

scripture," especially through the Psalms. Furthermore, a person cannot hope to find God unless he first find himself, for this God "is more inward to me than the most inward part of me; and higher than my highest reach" (3.6.11). Above all, it is a person's tragedy to flee "outwards," to lose touch with his own heart and the God within: "There thou wast, before me; but I had gone away, even from myself, and I could not find myself, much less thee" (5.2.2).

Had Augustine written his autobiography at the time of his conversion in 586, it would have been a very different book; it would have contained much information that is passed over as irrelevant in his *Confessions*—more precise details of the books he had read, of the views he had held, of the fascinating people he had met in Milan. It may well not have included the minor story of the robbing of a pear tree, and likely not the emotional upheaval in the garden in Milan. What was important to Augustine as a Christian are the emotions of the convert, conjured up with classic authenticity. In the *Confessions*, the evocation of Augustine's feelings forms part of the wider study of the evolution of his will. Every step Augustine takes in his career is now analyzed for its motives. Here we are faced with the full force of Augustine's new awareness of the limitations of human freedom. The gratuitous act of vandalism can no longer be viewed as an isolated incident, but as a sad paradigm for free will. Humans are free, but only to their own downfall, for when they will the good, they find themselves bound by the "iron chain" of their previous actions.

In book 8 of the *Confessions*, the problem of the will leaps into focus, for here we find Augustine still trapped in the habits of a lifetime: "The enemy held fast my will, and had made of it a chain, and had bound me tight with it. . . . By these links . . . a hard bondage held me in slavery" (8.5.10). The somber preoccupation of Augustine with the manner in which people can imprison themselves in the "old nature" makes the *Confessions* a very modern book. In many ancient and medieval biographies, we meet heroes described in terms of the ideal qualities, but here we meet Augustine in his weakness, firmly held in his past. For Augustine, a person's past is very much alive in the present; humans are different from each other precisely because their wills are shaped by the sum total of their past experience.

A few years earlier, when Augustine had written *On Free Choice of the Will*, defending the freedom of the will against Manichean determinism, he had posed the problem differently. At this time, Augustine was, at least on paper, as Pelagian as Pelagius would be. Pelagius would later quote from Augustine's book in support of his own views. Now, humans must start with their need to be healed, and this comes to mean that they must accept responsibility for what they are and yet, at the same time, welcome dependence on a therapy beyond their control. The need to confess now determines his thinking. Earlier, particularly during his Manichean phase, "it gratified my pride to be beyond blame, and when I did anything wrong not to have to confess that *I* had done wrong" (5.10.18). In the garden in Milan, it was different, for by that time, Augustine had come to accept responsibility for his actions (7.3.4). Now, if denial of guilt is the first enemy, self-reliance is the last.

Augustine wrote the *Confessions* in the spirit of a physician committed to a new form of treatment. In the first nine books, he illustrates what happens when this treatment is not applied, how he had come to discover it, and, skipping a decade, he demonstrates in book 10, its continued application in the present. Augustine's age demanded a dramatic story of conversion, which might have led him to end the *Confessions* at book 9. Instead, Augustine added four more, long books, for conversion was no longer enough. The peace of the convert was still subject to temptations, his "harbor" still troubled by storms. For Neoplatonists, the real self of an individual lay in his depths; and this inner self was divine, having never lost touch with the ideal. For Augustine, by contrast, the inner world is a source of anxiety as much as of strength: "Yet there is a little light in men. Let them walk—let them walk in it, lest the darkness overtake them" (10.23.33).

Like the apostle Paul in Romans 7, in book 10 of the *Confessions*, Augustine finds himself in a lamentable darkness in which his motives and latent capabilities are hidden even from himself. A decade earlier, he had believed in the possibility of attaining the full enjoyment of the absolute and true good. Now he is resigned ever to know more than glimpses of this estate. Earlier, he had interpreted Paul as a Platonist, sharing in Paul's sense of triumph: "see, everything has become new!" (2 Cor 5:17). Now, he sees in Paul a simple, unresolved tension between "flesh" and "spirit" (Gal 5:17; Rom 8:5–7), and the Christian life as characterized by utter dependence on divine grace (Eph. 2:8). Only after this life would the moral tension be resolved, when "death has been swallowed up in victory" (1 Cor 15:54).

While pagan writers regularly exposed and subordinated their souls (their minds and inner motives and wills) to the commands of deity, it was most unusual to insist, as Augustine now does, that no person could ever sufficiently know his whole personality: "I beseech thee now, O my God, to reveal myself to me also" (10.37.62); "our sole hope, our sole confidence, our only assured promise," he notes, "is thy mercy" (10.32.48).

After the distant storm of the garden in Milan, after this anxious peering into dark potentialities, the remaining three books of the *Confessions* are a fitting ending to Augustine's deepest insights. The hard refrain of "Command"—"Command what you will"—gives way to "Give"—"Give what you command and command what you will" (10.29.40; Clark translation).

THE *ENCHIRIDION*

At age sixty-six, in the middle of writing the *City of God*, Augustine wrote a manual on the Christian life called *Enchiridion on Faith, Hope, and Love*. Of Augustine's ninety-three major written works, this small handbook represents Augustine's fully matured theological perspective and displays his most integrated picture of life before God. Though brief, the *Enchiridion* certainly deserves its position as a classic in Christian writing. In 122 brief chapters, Augustine thoughtfully examines the needs of daily Christian living in the light of biblical teaching and the Apostles' Creed.

In 421, Augustine received a request from Laurentius, a Christian layperson who was the brother of the tribune Dulcitius, for whom Augustine had written an earlier work. Laurentius wanted a handbook (enchiridion) that would sum up the essential Christian teaching in the briefest possible form. Augustine notes that the shortest complete summary of Christian wisdom is piety, or the worship of God, and that "God is to be worshiped in faith, hope, [and] love" (1.3). In other words, Christian wisdom is not simply knowledge of the basics of what Christians believe (what Laurentius seems to have expected), but a way of life characterized by love. As a summary of faith, Christians have the Creed, and as a summary of hope and love, the Lord's Prayer. Augustine does not use a common term for faith, hope, and love, but these three, wholly interdependent, constitute a way of life that is true worship, the "faith that works by love" (1.5; see Gal 5:6).

Augustine spends most of the treatise discussing faith, with short subsequent sections on hope and love. This is not to underestimate the importance of hope or love, but only to emphasize that correct faith engenders the appropriate hope and love. In speaking of faith, hope, and love (Paul's famous supernatural virtues; see 1 Cor 13:13), we cannot overlook grace, which, though not mentioned in the Apostles' Creed, receives a high profile in Augustine's theology. In fact, the *Enchiridion* may be one of the most illuminating defenses of Augustine's doctrine of grace precisely because in this short doctrinal summary grace's links to all other doctrines is most visible.

According to Augustine, the "foundation of the Catholic faith is Christ" (1.5), the Word of God who "emptied himself" (Phil 2:6) by becoming human, uniting his own person with a human being, Jesus. This incarnation is, for Augustine, the supreme instance of grace, since there is no question of antecedent merit on the part of the human Jesus (10.35–11.36). The glory of the incarnation is the glory of God's grace. This supreme instance of grace is also the supreme instance of humility, the humility of God, who elected to become human.

As we consider the mystery of the Mediator (28.108), we are considering the "fount [source] of grace," for as Augustine proceeds to show, all benefits of God's redemption come from this "mystery of the Mediator," (28.108), laid out here in creedal order: the Creator and the Goodness of Creation (3.9–5.16), the Fall and Sin (5.17–8.26), Redemption (8.27–14.55), the Holy Spirit and the Church, Communion of Saints, the Forgiveness of Sins, Judgment, and the Resurrection (15.56–29.113).

For Augustine, the perfection of Christian life is attained practically, not doctrinally or theoretically, particularly by those who love their enemies, but barring that, by those who forgive their enemies for wrongs done (19.73). Awareness of the great gift of God's humility in Christ, and placing hope in that and not in oneself, one's sins progressively give way to love, for love is the fulfillment of every commandment. Love, in this context, naturally includes both the love of God and the love of neighbor (32.121) for, as noted earlier, God does not command what God does not give. The source and goal of all obligation is love, for God is love. All of God's imperatives "are rightly obeyed when they are measured by the standard of our love of God and our love of our neighbor in God" (32.121). Such love, displayed practically and actively, best describes Augustine's understanding of spirituality.

QUESTIONS FOR DISCUSSION AND REFLECTION

In addition to the questions listed at the end of the preface, answer the following questions, writing your answers in a journal. If you are in a group study, be prepared to share your answers with those in the group.

1. Identify and explain the main concepts associated with "the Augustinian paradigm of spirituality."
2. Explain the role of friendship in Augustine's understanding of spirituality.
3. If, for Augustine, finding happiness is the goal of the spiritual life, what does happiness mean?
4. Explain the role of faith, hope, and love in Augustine's understanding of the spiritual journey.
5. Explain why Augustine is considered the premier psychologist in the ancient world. In your estimation, what evidence can we gather from Augustine's *Confessions* to support that claim?
6. Explain the role of conversion in Augustine's life, and the obstacles—intellectual, social, and personal—he had to overcome to arrive at this decision.
7. Explain the role Manicheism played in Augustine's understanding of good and evil and the change in his thinking that occurred when he became a Christian.
8. Explain the role pagan philosophy played in Augustine's conversion to Christianity.
9. Explain the meaning of the statement, "As one reads the *Confessions*, one gets the sense that Augustine 'thinks in scripture.'"
10. After reading the segment on the *Enchiridion*, what role does the concept of grace play in Augustine's theology?
11. In your estimation, what was Augustine's greatest contribution to Christian theology? Support your answer.
12. In your estimation, what was Augustine's greatest contribution to Christian spirituality? Support your answer.

Chapter 4

Dante Alighieri's *Divine Comedy*

WHILE THE WRITINGS OF Dante Alighieri (1265–1321) may not appear on any of our lists of top books to read or devotional books to consult, his masterpiece, known as the *Divine Comedy* or simply by its Italian name, *Commedia*, is one of Western spirituality's most intriguing and influential works of literature. Dante's depictions of Hell, Purgatory, and Heaven provided inspiration for Western art and literature in general, and specifically on such English writers as Geoffrey Chaucer, John Milton, Alfred Tennyson, T. S. Eliot, and C. S. Lewis, among many others. Christened "*Divina*" by the great Renaissance poet Giovanni Boccaccio, Dante's epic poem is considered one of the most important poems of the Middle Ages and the greatest literary work in the Italian language. Written in vernacular Italian at a time when most Western poetry was written in Latin and accessible only to the most educated readers (in the Middle Ages, Latin was not only the language of liturgy, history, and scholarship, but also of lyric poetry), made it available to a wide audience. In addition, Dante's use of the Tuscan dialect for works such as *La Vita Nuova* (*The New Life*, 1295) and the *Divine Comedy* (1320) helped establish the modern-day standardized Italian language.

Dante was born and lived his early life in Florence, during a time of change and great economic and cultural expansion. Not much is known about Dante's education; he presumably studied at home or in a school attached to a church or monastery in Florence. Dante was critically aware of developments in Florentine poetry and painting. It is known that he studied Tuscan poetry, in addition to the Provençal poetry of the troubadours and such Latin writers of classical antiquity as Cicero, Ovid, and especially Virgil. Dante was more aware than most early Italian writers of the variety of Italian literary dialects and of the need to create a literature and a unified literary language beyond the limits of Latin writing. In that sense, he was a forerunner of the Renaissance, with its effort to create vernacular literature in competition with earlier classical writers. He wrote his *Comedy* in a language he called "Italian," in some sense an amalgamated literary language mostly based on the regional dialect of Tuscany, but with some elements of Latin and other regional dialects. By creating a poem of epic structure and philosophic purpose, he established that the Italian language was suitable for the highest sort of expression. While Dante was not immediately read widely by European authors of his time, his status was secured during the Romantic era. To the Romantics, Dante, like Homer and Shakespeare, was a prime example of the "original genius" who set his own rules, created characters of great stature and depth, and went far beyond imitating the patterns of earlier masters. Throughout the nineteenth century, Dante's reputation grew and solidified, and by 1865, the six hundredth anniversary of his birth, he had become established as one of the greatest literary icons of the Western world.

Like most Florentines of his day, Dante was involved in the political life of his city, particularly in the long-lasting conflict between the Guelphs and the Ghibellines. Dante's family was loyal to the Guelphs, a political alliance that, while subsequently dividing into Black and White Guelphs, broadly allied themselves with the Papacy and sought to further the local interests of their city-state. The Guelphs were involved in complex rivalry with the Ghibellines, who backed the Holy Roman emperor and the imperial cause. To further his political career, Dante became a pharmacist. He did not intend to practice this profession, but only to follow a law issued in 1295 requiring nobles aspiring to public office to be enrolled in one of several recognized professions, and so he obtained admission to the Apothecaries' Guild. Even at this time, Dante must have been aware not only of the political realities of his day, which later the *Comedy* consistently reflects, but also of economic realities in a city divided into competing classes. Internationally, too, the old order was changing. The Holy Roman Empire was losing what power it had to extend a *pax romana* over the Italian peninsula, while the church, expanding to fill the political vacuum left by the empire, displayed an increasing concern with temporal rather than spiritual advancement.

After defeating the Ghibellines in the Battle of Campaldino in 1289, the Guelphs divided into two factions: the White and the Black Guelphs.

Although the split was along family lines at first, ideological differences arose based on opposing views of the papal role in Florentine affairs. The Blacks supported the Pope and the Whites (Dante's party) wanted more freedom from Rome. The Whites took power first and expelled the Blacks. In response, Pope Boniface VIII planned a military occupation of Florence.

In 1300, Dante served as one of the six priors elected to govern the republic. The following year, all the pressures brewing politically and economically were unleashed against him. While he was absent from Florence on a mission to Rome to ascertain the pope's intention, Charles of Valois, brother of King Philip IV of France and the pope's legate, entered Florence with the Black Guelphs, who in the next six days destroyed much of the city and killed many of their enemies. A new Black Guelph government was installed that in 1302 condemned Dante to exile for two years on charges of corruption and financial wrongdoing and ordered him to pay a large fine. Dante did no pay the fine, in part because he believed he was not guilty and in part because all his assets in Florence had been seized. On this account, he was condemned to perpetual exile.

Over the years, Dante took part in several attempts by the White Guelphs to regain power, but these failed due to treachery. Bitter at the treatment he received from his enemies, he grew disgusted with the infighting and the ineffectiveness of his former allies and vowed to become a political party of one. In 1310, Holy Roman Emperor Henry VII of Luxembourg marched into Italy at the head of a large army. Dante saw in him a new Charlemagne who would restore the office of the Holy Roman Emperor to its former glory and also retake Florence from the Black Guelphs. Mixing religion and private concerns in his writings, during this time he wrote *De Monarchia* (1313), a treatise on religion and secular power, proposing a universal monarchy under Henry VII. In 1312, Henry assaulted Florence and defeated the Black Guelphs, but Henry died in 1313, and with him any hope for Dante to return to Florence.

De Monarchia, written while he was working on his *Comedy*, represents Dante's original contribution to medieval philosophy. Here, arguing from first principles, Dante demonstrates that peace and order are possible on earth through the restoration of a universal empire. God had providentially ordained the Roman Empire and its future permutations to establish a realm of justice and to banish all greed, and therefore dissension, from the world. While the church is instituted to lead human beings to eternal happiness, God also intends humanity to enjoy happiness in this life, and it is the function of a just emperor to secure temporal happiness.

Dante stayed with friends and patrons during his exile. He spent the remaining twenty years of his life turning—with increasingly forlorn hopes—to the Empire for justice, and (from around 1307) writing the *Comedy*, as if that could be a remedy. It is known that the *Inferno* was published by 1317, but there is no certainty as to whether the three parts of the *Comedy* were published in full or a few cantos (chapters) at a time. *Paradiso* seems to have been published posthumously. Dante spent his final days in Ravenna, where he had been invited to stay by its prince. He died there in 1321, of malaria contracted while returning from a diplomatic mission to the Republic of Venice. He was attended by his three children and likely by his wife Gemma Donati, along with friends and admirers in the city.

In addition to *De Monarchia* and the *Commedia*, Dante's important works include *Convivio* (*The Banquet*; 1307)), a collection of his longest poems, with an allegorical commentary, and *On the Eloquence in the Vernacular* (1302–1305) written in Latin to support the merits of vernacular literature. While much of Dante's literary work was composed during his exile, a major exception is *La Vita Nuova* (1294), a collection of lyric love poems with commentary in prose, written entirely in the Tuscan dialect.

In addition to lyric poems, *La Vita Nuova* also contains—or constructs—the story of Dante's love for Beatrice, who later serves as a symbol of salvation in the *Comedy* and Dante's guide through Paradise. As we learn in the *Comedy*, it is Beatrice, Dante's "beloved," who sends Virgil to Dante to guide and protect him through Inferno and Purgatorio, and it is Beatrice who takes over as Dante's guide in the four cantos of *Purgatorio* and who guides Dante on the final leg of his journey to God. Dante informs us that he first met Beatrice when he was nine (and she about eight), and with whom he claims to have fallen in love "at first sight," apparently without ever talking with her. When he was twelve, however, he was promised in marriage to Gemma Donati, member of the powerful Donati family. Dante claims to have seen Beatrice frequently as a young adult, exchanging greetings with her but never telling her of his love. Years after his marriage to Gemma, he claims to have met Beatrice again. Though Beatrice died when she was only twenty-five, Dante wrote many beautiful poems dedicated to her, praising her beauty and love. Significantly, Dante never mentioned Gemma in any of his poems.

Dante's interactions with Beatrice set an example of so-called "courtly love." While Dante's experience of such love had been developed in French and Provençal poetry, his expression of it was unique. It was in the name of this love that Dante left his imprint on the *dolce stil novo* (sweet new style), a term Dante coined, and he would join other contemporary poets and writers in exploring never-before-emphasized aspects of *Amore*. Such human love, when understood as wholesome, pure, and altogether natural and uncontrolled, came to be considered a form of divine love, which undergirds and inspires all other loves, loyalties, and commitment. Love for Beatrice, together with social and political ideals, would be Dante's reason for writing poetry and for living.

THE DIVINE COMEDY

Dante's *Commedia* describes his journey through Hell (*Inferno*), Purgatory (*Purgatorio*), and Paradise (*Paradiso*). He is first guided by the Roman poet Virgil and then by Beatrice. Dante is the protagonist and main character of all three parts of the poem. His journey is an autobiographical portrayal. In it he includes many of his enemies and historical figures of the past, whom he portrays in the complicated world of Heaven and Hell. Of the three books, *Inferno* is most read, *Purgatorio* arguably the most lyrical, and *Paradiso* the most mystical, beautiful, and heavily theological.

In the middle of his life, Dante found himself spiritually lost and in need of divine guidance. While the *Comedy* is his story, there is more than a touch of Everyman in it, as the first words show: "Midway in the journey of *our* life I found myself in a dark wood, for the straight was lost." The *Comedy* explores the relationship that Dante believed to exist between God as Creator of the universe and human beings as creatures of God. In common with other Christians, Dante held that this relationship was a personal one in which God, far from being some indeterminate cosmic force, could be known—because of the incarnation of Christ—as a distinct being, loving and conceiving purposes for each of the beings he had brought into existence.

Representing himself as the protagonist in his story, Dante writes of a journey that is simultaneously inward and outward. Inwardly he sets himself to explore both the worst and best of which human beings are capable. Outwardly he aims to investigate nothing less than the whole of the physical and spiritual universe. At every stage, the storyteller dramatizes the shock or pleasure of discovery, and at every stage, he produces words and images appropriate to each new development in experience.

Dante's *Divine Comedy* is one of the most impressive poems ever written. It is cosmic in scale, for Dante travels through the entire universe, from the deepest, coldest pit of Hell to the very summit of Heaven, where God dwells in endless glory. The journey described in the *Comedy* begins with a descent into Hell; and in Hell, no less than through the *Purgatorio* and in the final moments of the *Paradiso*, Dante sets himself to deal with the reality of God. The journey concludes when—within the perfect circle that until then has represented divine activity—God, now relatable and graspable by mortals, is altered into a human image, and Dante finally sees God "face to face."

THE DIVINE COMEDY: OVERVIEW

Dante's journey begins with the pilgrim in a dark wood of error. As he is about to succumb to despair, he is met by the poet Virgil, who tells him that he must go by another route if he is to escape his condition. His journey, he learns, must take him through Hell. If he is journeying toward God, we wonder, why does he need to go through Hell? As we discover, Dante must descend in order to ascend. His journey through Hell will teach him not only the nature of sin but also how to overcome these tendencies within himself. Thus, the sinners with whom he will spend the most time will be those who have the most to say to him personally as well as in terms of his own moral development.

When Dante and Virgil enter Hell, they see an inscription on its gate that ends with the words, "Abandon every hope, you who enter." These words increase Dante's initial fear, for he doesn't think he can survive a trip through Hell, though he knows that he must do this in order to get back on the straight path to God. Nevertheless, he is encouraged by Virgil, who convinces him that his journey is overseen by God.

Hell, the place where unrepentant sinners dwell, consists of nine concentric circles inside the earth, each smaller than the previous one. The order of the nine circles and its underlying logic are based loosely on a pattern found in Aristotle's *Nicomachean Ethics* (7.1).[1] As Dante traverses the levels of Hell with Virgil as guide, he learns that each level is

---

1. Aristotle's ethics make no mention of limbo or heresy, for both involve deficient faith and hence have no place in Aristotle's system.

its own kind of hell and is divided by types of sin. The worse the sin, the greater are the consequences each soul has to face. As Dante and Virgil descend deeper into Hell, they see suffering increasing and punishments worsening, for each successive concentric circle reveals the nature of ever more serious sins.

The first circle, Limbo, consists of unbaptized souls who either lived before Christ or never got baptized. Technically an inferior form of Heaven, this is a place where virtuous pagans remain for eternity. Here, Dante and Virgil meet Greek and Roman philosophers, poets, and artists such as Homer, Ovid, Socrates, Cicero, and Julius Caesar. As we learn, Virgil is one of their number. The remaining circles—lust, gluttony, greed, anger, heresy, violence, fraud, and treachery—are more typical of Hell, for they involve ever more serious sins and increased suffering.[2]

The geography of Hell is significant, for it is a moral geography as well as a physical one, reflecting the nature of the sin. Hell is divided into three major categories of moral failure—incontinence, violence, and fraud. Taken from classical sources, these divisions are inversions of the classical versions of moderation, courage, and wisdom. The fourth classical virtue, justice, is also inverted in Hell, which is constructed of unjust inhabitants. The sinners that Dante meets are from many times and places; some are great figures from history, literature, or mythology, and some are "local figures" from Dante's own time and place. The sinners have in common a desire to justify themselves and to put the blame for their actions elsewhere.

The sins of incontinence (circles two through five) are sins of impulse, brought about by immoderate passion rather than by habit; they are lust, gluttony, avarice, and anger. The seventh circle houses the violent, while the eighth and ninth circles contain the fraudulent. Violence is divided into three subsets—against one's neighbor, against the self, and against God. The sins of malice cause injustice and harm to others, either by force or by fraud. Injurious acts achieved by fraud are considered more sinful than those achieved by force because fraud requires the misuse of reason, humanity's peculiar gift.

The eighth circle contains those who practiced fraud on the untrusting, and the ninth and lowest circle of Hell contains traitors, that is,

---

2. The disposition of the offenders here is not according to the traditional Christian seven deadly sins, as we might expect, but from classical sources. Dante reserves the Christian list of deadly sins for the *Purgatorio*, partly because that canticle allows for occasions that are more introspective.

sinners who practiced fraud on those who trusted them. In circle eight we meet two famous individuals, the classical warrior Ulysses (the Latin name for Odysseus) and the Christian pope Boniface VIII. For Ulysses, whom Dante knows only from Latin sources, including summaries of Homer's *Odyssey* and particularly Ulysses as he appears in Virgil's *Aeneid*, Dante creates a "sequel" to the *Odyssey* by sending Ulysses on another journey after his return home from Troy, a journey that reveals his sin. This part of the story is Dante's own invention, a sequel to the story of Odysseus's homecoming in the *Odyssey* (which Dante does not know). In his sequel, Dante portrays Ulysses as having inverted the classical virtue of *pietas* (piety) through disloyalty to father, son, and wife. Likewise, among the sinners in circle 8 is Pope Boniface, Dante's political enemy, an example of fraud in failed leadership and of the evil it works on individuals and communities.

The travelers stop and speak with many lost souls along the way. Dante grows ever more fearful as the journey continues until finally it is time to make his way out of Hell and continue his journey through Purgatory. After leaving Hell, the travelers find themselves at a place where they can look down at earth and up to heaven. Purgatory, the place where souls come to do penitence, is a place between heaven and earth, a place of hope and redemption. Purgatory, viewed by Dante as earth at its very best, is a cone-shaped mountain with seven terraces, each terrace representing one of the seven deadly sins, viewed as sins against others, oneself, and against God.

Before the travelers enter Purgatory, an angel puts seven "P's" on Dante's forehead. They correspond to the seven deadly sins—pride, envy, wrath, sloth, greed, gluttony, and lust. The angel tells Dante that every time a terrace is surpassed, a "P" will be removed. On the first terrace Dante and Virgil see penitents carrying heavy weights up the mountain of humility to cure them of their pride. As the poets reach the stairway to the second terrace, the Angel of Humility salutes them and brushes Dante's forehead with his wings, erasing the letter "P" corresponding to the sin of pride, and Dante hears the beatitude, "Blessed are the poor in spirit" (Matt 5:3). On the second terrace, envious penitents are treated by having their eyelids sewn shut with iron wire. Here, Dante and Virgil hear voices telling stories of generosity, the opposite virtue, and the beatitude, "Blessed are the merciful" (Matt 5:7). As the poets reach the stairway to the third terrace, the Angel of Charity brushes away another "P" from Dante's brow. On the third terrace, wrathful penitents are treated with black smoke that makes them blind. On this terrace, examples of meekness (the opposite virtue) are given to Dante as visions in his mind. When the visions have passed, the Angel of Peace greets the poets and brushes Dante's forehead, erasing the third "P." Then follows the pronouncing of the beatitude, "Blessed are the peacemakers" (Matt 5:9).

On the fourth terrace, slothful penitents are punished by running without stopping or resting. Examples of zeal (sloth's opposite virtue), are called out by souls as they run around the terrace. The beatitude for this terrace is "Blessed are those who mourn" (Matt 5:4). Upon awakening from his second night's sleep, Dante is visited by the Angel of Zeal, who removes another "P" from his brow. On the fifth terrace, greedy and avaricious souls are tied by their feet and arms, face down on the ground. In order to rid themselves of these sins, they must shout examples of poverty and generosity. The beatitude for this terrace is "Blessed are those who hunger and thirst for righteousness" (Matt 5:6). At the end, the Angel of Moderation directs the poets forward after brushing another "P" from Dante's forehead.

In the sixth terrace, gluttons clean their souls by experiencing extreme hunger and thirst. At the end, Dante is greeted by the Angel of Temperance, who removes another "P" from his brow and pronounces Matthew's fourth beatitude in paraphrase, "Blessed are they who are so illumined by grace that the love of food does not kindle their desires beyond what is fitting" (see Matt 5:6). On the seventh and final terrace, lustful penitents walk in flames and shout out examples of chastity. Two groups of souls, homosexuals and heterosexuals, run through the flames calling out examples of lust. The homosexuals run counter to the sun, from west to east, while the heterosexuals run from east to west, with the sun. Dante's depiction of homosexuals as souls capable of salvation is particularly lenient for the time period, a departure from Inferno, where Dante represents sodomy as sin of violence instead of one of excessive love.

At sunset Virgil and Dante reach the exit of the last terrace and Dante's last "P" is removed by the angel. The beatitude for this terrace is Matthew's sixth, "Blessed are the pure in heart" (Matt 5:8). In order to proceed, Dante must go through a wall of flames that separates Purgatorio and Paradiso. He is frightened and hesitates, but Virgil convinces him to cheer up and be brave, because once he is through this obstacle, he will see Beatrice, his true love, and this hope encourages Dante to continue his journey. Eventually the travelers arrive in the Garden of Eden, where

Virgil takes his leave. There Dante sees Beatrice, and he is overwhelmed with emotion. Beatrice promptly reprimands him for having straying so far from the path in life that he had to travel to the depths of Hell to regain what had been lost.

Dante's third and final realm, Paradise, consists of nine spheres. Each sphere represents a state of mind that all Christians should possess, culminating in faith, hope and love. Divided into thirty-three cantos like *Purgatorio*, *Paradiso* traces the pilgrim's ascent through the nine celestial spheres of Dante's Ptolemaic cosmos. The first three spheres, the Moon (the home of those who lack courage), Mercury (the home of those who did good deeds for fame and glory), and Venus (the home of lovers and the place where Dante learns about the importance of inclusion and social diversity), contain souls who are defective in the virtues represented by those spheres: faith, hope, and love. In so doing, Dante wishes to show that perfection on earth is by no means necessary for salvation.

Other spheres include the Sun (here Dante meets medieval sages such as Aquinas and Bonaventure and the biblical King Solomon, and learns about wisdom, poverty, and humility, conditions essential to prudence, by hearing of the lives of Saint Francis and Saint Dominic, founders of great mendicant orders), Mars (the home of warriors who died for their faith and God), Jupiter (the home of kings who displayed justice), Saturn (the home of those who lived by temperance and who were faithful in prayer), and the Fixed Stars (here Dante finds the Virgin Mary and biblical characters such as Adam, Peter, James, and John). In *Paradiso* 6 (Jupiter) we meet Roman Emperor Justinian, This is the only canto in the *Divine Comedy* that has only one speaker from beginning to end. In Justinian's fascinating discourse, Dante continues the discussion of politics that he had begun in *Inferno* 6 and continued in *Purgatorio* 6. In this speech, we see the poet's take on world politics, a connection between politics on the world stage and Dante's own exile, and an important lesson on the proper response to exile in the figure of Romeo of Villeneuve (d. 1250), a character described by Justinian at the end of the canto. Romeo had been a statesman in a Provençal court, and like Dante, had been punished for good work by exile. The first part of Justinian's discourse is a rewriting and retelling of the history of Rome that is presented in Book 6 of the *Aeneid*, the history of empire from Troy and Aeneas to Rome and Emperor Augustus. In this story, we see a paradigm of the right relationship between the political and the religious spheres, attained in the codification and dissemination of Roman law in the Code of Justinian. The larger context of empire presented in this canto helps Dante deal with his own exile.

The ninth heavenly sphere is the Primum Mobile or Unmoved First Mover (the source of all movement in planetary time and space and, according to Aristotle, the outermost sphere of the created universe), and the tenth sphere Dante calls the Empyrean, where the angels, saints, and beatified souls repose, basking in the radiance of God for all eternity. The Empyrean, a realm beyond space and time, is the goal of Dante's journey, because it is the "dwelling place" of God.

Dante's journey through Heaven is largely dedicated to the elaborate preparations that are necessary for a mortal to partake in a vision of God that, by definition, surpasses human capabilities and understanding. In this realm, the pilgrim's task is to move from seeing God "through a mirror dimly" to encountering God "face to face (1 Cor 13:12).

Beatrice and Dante traverse the heavens one by one. Beatrice's role is that of guide and teacher. Her aim is to strengthen and sharpen the intellectual vision of her charge so that he will be able to pass an examination on the cardinal virtues of faith, hope, and love, administered by Peter, James, and John in the Heaven of the Fixed Stars, and, having passed this exam, to proceed onward and upward. Like Virgil, Beatrice is fated to disappear once she accomplishes her mission, leaving Dante under the guidance of Bernard of Clairvaux, an appropriate choice for many reasons. Bernard is both a mystic and a writer on mysticism, but he was also an ardent crusader and reformer. Like Dante, he was also a poet, who is responsible for interceding on Dante's behalf with the Virgin Mary, in order to ensure that the final face-to-face vision with God is granted. On his journey, Dante sees the Trinity as three rings of different colors all sharing the same space and reflecting upon each other. Everywhere he sees light, and in the light is beauty. Eventually he sees Jesus and the Virgin Mary and finally looks upon the face of God.

Marian piety is an important part of Dante's poem. *Paradiso* 33, the *Comedy*'s final canto, begins with a hymn to the Virgin Mary. Here, only the language of paradox can convey the central mysteries that Dante "sees," for here he learns that the Virgin is the daughter of her son, and that she is simultaneously the most humble and the most exalted of creatures. The hymn is characterized by the language of paradox, for it is the only language that makes sense at this point in the journey. Previously, in *Paradiso* 32, Bernard of Clairvaux, a Cistercian monk, showed Dante the structure of the mystical rose, the white rose that is "home" to the souls in

Paradise. The rose represents complementarity, for in it male and female are juxtaposed, as are young and old, circular and linear arrangements, and even the Old and New Testaments. It is to her place in the rose that Beatrice returns when her role as Dante's guide is taken over by Bernard of Clairvaux.

Marian piety plays a central role in Cistercian piety. For example, every monk in this order has "Mary" as his second name. In its emphasis on meditation and grace, and in its poetic power, Dante's mystical poem or poetic prayer in his closing canto can be seen as recapitulating the entire *Comedy*, reminding the reader of the beginning of the poem with Mary's intercession on behalf of the pilgrim. Now, at the end, it is the Virgin, "Empress" of Heaven (combining the pagan role assigned to the Mother Goddess and the redemptive role she was assigned by Roman Christians as "Mother of God" and co-redeemer with Christ), who intercedes for Dante so that he may see God face to face.

At the end, as Dante reflects on the mysteries of the Trinity and the Incarnation, he becomes part of what he sees, for while he does not—indeed cannot—understand, he *experiences*. The "love which moves the sun and the other stars" (*Paradiso* 33.145) is now moving his desire and his will. The poem ends not with understanding but with harmony, for Dante, in harmony with the Creator and the Creation, is now experiencing the Christian mysteries. The final vision crystallizes much of what is distinctive about *Paradiso*. It offers furtive glimpses of divinity, a divinity that necessarily exceeds the powers of human language and imagination.

As regards love, Dante collapses the distinction between thinking and loving from *Paradiso*'s opening to its closing verse. In the course of the journey, we learn that it is love that binds together Creator and Creation, inasmuch as love causes the nine orders of angels to spin furiously around God and, in so doing, to turn the nine heavenly spheres. Love is also the force that drives the blessed to descend in order that the pilgrim may ascend. Finally, it is love that serves as *Paradiso*'s system of propulsion. In *Inferno*, Dante's motion spiraled downward, and little more was required of him than to give in to his fallen body's natural tendency to gravitate downward toward Satan and sin. In *Purgatorio*, Dante had struggled to undo the effects of original sin and to transform this pull into levitation toward God. In *Paradiso*, the transformation is complete. It suffices for Dante to gaze into the eyes of his beloved, eyes in which the vision of heaven is reflected, and the effect is sudden. Together, Dante and Beatrice rise up, as if disembodied, to the next heaven, effortlessly drawn toward their Creator, the true center of the universe.

POINTS TO PONDER IN *THE DIVINE COMEDY*

Despite being autobiographical, Dante's epic poem addresses human concerns and questions that are valid for all times, issues of our day as well as of Dante's time. Among these are ethical concerns such as the nature of justice, civic concerns such as the nature of good government, artistic concerns such as the nature of art in general and poetry in particular, and the necessity of transformation in the spiritual life.

Strictly speaking, the *Divine Comedy* is not a comedy, though in this case, the word "comedy" implies a story with a successful ending after a difficult beginning. As Dante tells his patron, his purpose for writing is moral, namely, "to remove those living in this life from a state of misery and to bring them to a state of happiness."[3] In this respect, Dante's purpose was to show people the horrors their souls would encounter if they did not obey God's laws or live righteous lives.

There is a great deal of symbolism in the *Comedy*, particularly in its use of numbers. For example, the number three is quite common. In the first part of the *Comedy* we encounter three beasts, a three-headed dog, and a three-faced Satan. Evil, for Dante, thrives on deception. As three is the number of the Trinity, so evil imitates and masquerades as good. Another number significant to the *Comedy* is seven; there are seven deadly sins and seven terraces in *Purgatorio*. Another symbolic number is the number nine, used for the nine circles of Hell and the nine spheres in Heaven. Following the medieval way of reading scripture, Dante indicated that his work should be read both literally and allegorically. Beyond the literal, Dante also distinguished three types of secondary meaning, called allegorical, moral, and anagogical: what is to be *believed*, what is to be *done*, and what is to be *striven for*.

Clearly, Dante was deeply concerned about personal religion. However, he also had a social purpose, for his belief was that God intends happiness for us here and beatitude hereafter. According to Dante, God had provided two rulers, Emperor and Pope, and when they ruled together in concord, God's will would be done on earth. However, in Dante's estimation, the emperors had forsaken Italy, and the church had become

---

3. Cited in Jones, *Study of Spirituality*, 309.

opportunist and corrupt. By the time the *Comedy* was written, the papacy had abandoned Rome for Avignon.

Unjustly exiled, Dante chose to assert his innocence and to proclaim his faith through a poem that mingled imagination and autobiography. He imagined a vision during Holy Week in 1300 as the time when he, a living man, descended into Hell to learn God's justice, climbed the mountain of Purgatory to prove God's mercy, and was carried to the height of Heaven to see God's glory. To relate his account, he regularly quotes scripture, at least some two hundred times, including numerous liturgical prayers and beatitudes in his narrative.

In this story, Dante the traveler embarks on an ominous journey for the sake of his own soul. He has lost his way in life by straying from the path of righteousness, but is fortunate that he has a guide to lead him by encouragement, knowledge, and care. The guide is Virgil, a great Roman poet whose major work, the *Aeneid*, recounts the wanderings of Aeneas, fashioning the account into a compelling founding myth or national epic that ties Rome to the legends of Troy, explains the Punic Wars, glorifies traditional Roman virtues, and legitimizes the Julio-Claudian dynasty as descendants of the founders, heroes, and gods of Rome and Troy.

Despite the *Aeneid*'s focus on Rome, Dante understands Aeneas's epic voyage as an image or representation of human life. Already in *The Vita Nuova*, Dante had envisioned the pursuit of truth as a pilgrimage. However, an epic journey models the notion of pilgrimage more precisely, for it emphasizes the pilgrim's ability to conceive an ultimate goal. To travel like Aeneas is to experience skill in maintaining momentum, negotiating hazards, and in plotting direction until one arrives at the port or city one is meant to reach. In *Purgatorio*, Dante's emphasis falls less on the experience of arrival and more upon the process, labor, and commitment to the journey. The canticle is concerned with transition, and here Dante examines means rather than ends.

The *Aeneid* clearly inspired Dante's *Comedy*, for while traveling to Italy, Aeneas visits the underworld, where he receives a vision of his and Rome's future. In Tartarus, Aeneas is shown the fate of the wicked and is warned to bow to the justice of the gods. After visiting Tartarus, Aeneas visits the green fields of Elysium, the afterlife home of heroic and righteous individuals and of others chosen by the gods. In Elysium, Aeneas speaks with the spirit of his father and receives a vision of the destiny of Rome. It is easy to see why Dante chose Virgil as guide, for the *Aeneid* served as a cornerstone of Latin education and became a canonical text for people like Dante, who were educated in Latin-Christian culture. In the Western world, the *Aeneid* would be considered the pinnacle of Latin literature, much as the *Iliad* was seen to be the pinnacle of Greek literature.

Because Dante's *Purgatorio* may be the least read section of his *Comedy* and because it contains material significant to spiritual life on earth, our focus in these concluding pages will be on this canticle.[4] Purgatory, unlike Heaven or Hell, is a place of change and hence, a place that resembles earth. Great themes of Dante's second canticle include the passage from time to eternity; the overcoming of sin; the redemptive potential of poetry, imagination, and art; the role of Virgil and Beatrice as guides; the mending of broken relationships in families and communities; the political, moral, and spiritual roles of just rulers; the nature of free will; and the role of Amore (human love as depicted in Beatrice) and Agape (divine love as depicted in the Virgin Mary) in salvation.

While the idea of purgatory, a symbolic representation of the penitent Christian life, goes back much further than Dante, it was Dante, through his *Purgatorio*, who was most responsible for the church's imagery of purgatory. Though the doctrine of purgatory is not explicitly defined in the Bible, it evolved from what was seen as the implied meanings of texts such as 1 Corinthians 3:11–15, which states that less serious sins will be tested, punished, or canceled by fire on the Day of Judgment, and apocryphal texts such as 2 Maccabees 12:40–46, used to support belief in prayers for the dead.

The crucial concept underlying the traditional Catholic doctrine of purgatory is that of the obligation to make satisfaction for sins after they have been forgiven. This is based on the distinction between venial and mortal sins. When a person repents, God removes the guilt (*culpa*); however, in the case of mortal sins, the debt of temporal punishment (*poena*) remains and must be paid off by penances, namely, acts of satisfaction imposed by priests in confession, voluntary penances, and the acceptance of sufferings sent by God. Purgatory is therefore the place where punishments not yet satisfied in life are paid off after death, and in the case of unrepented venial sins (which do not carry the obligation to

---

4. In terms of practicality and functionality, the choice of *Purgatorio* as a model applicable to our lives on earth currently may be seen in Thomas Merton's choice of title for his autobiography, entitled *The Seven Storey Mountain*, clearly a reference to Dante's seven-circled mountain of Purgatory.

eternal punishment in Hell), Purgatory removes the guilt as well as the punishments.

According to Dante, Mount Purgatory consists of three parts: (1) Ante-Purgatory, where the excommunicate and late-repentant wait because they made God wait; (2) Purgatory proper; and (3) the Earthly Paradise at the top of the mountain, which is the Garden of Eden, where human beings had been created in the image of God. If sin may be compared to layers of soot and varnish that, over time, diminish the beauty of an artistic masterpiece, then purgation strips away these accretions and restores the human image to its original divine splendor.

Below the entrance into Purgatory proper is Ante-Purgatory, where the excommunicate are detained for a period thirty times as long as their period of earthly insubordination, and the late-repentant, which includes three groups: those too lazy or too preoccupied to repent, those who repented at the last minute without formally receiving last rites, and negligent rulers. Such souls will be admitted to Purgatory on account of their genuine repentance, but they must wait outside for an amount of time equal to their lives on earth. Here Dante encounters the troubadour Sordello, who explains the "Rule of the Mountain": that after sunset, souls are incapable of climbing any further. Progress in Purgatory, like spirituality on earth, is a combination of action and contemplation, work and rest. Allegorically, the sun represents God, meaning that progress in the penitent Christian life can only be made through divine grace.

For Dante, purgation assumes the form of a dynamic process. Souls in Purgatory are on the move, and their mobility accounts for the sense of urgency, for time is precious here. For Dante, pilgrim time is precious, because he has been granted only a three-day stay in Purgatory. Significantly, Purgatory's pilgrims measure out their sentences in the same units that mortals do their lives: units defined by the circling of the stars and planets. Daytime is for circling and climbing; nighttime is for sleep. This explains why astronomical references abound in Dante's account of his spiral ascent as nowhere else in the *Comedy*. Purgatory, like life on earth, consists of trials and tests, of loss and recovery of "original blessing."

Prayer is a dominant theme in *Purgatorio*. Many of the souls Dante meets are depicted in prayer, with multiple liturgical references to psalms and hymns throughout the terraces. Prayers by the living on behalf of the dead also play a large role in *Purgatorio*, with some souls the pilgrim meets along the way requesting prayers from living relatives and even from the pilgrim himself.

In discussing the nature of sin, examples of vice and virtue, as well as moral issues in politics and in the church, Dante's *Purgatorio* theorizes that all sins arise from love—either perverted love harmful to others, or deficient, disordered, or excessive love of good things. Unlike *Inferno*, *Paradiso* is hopeful, for it represents not finality or dead ends but new beginnings, buoyed by willful momentum upward and onward toward God, the ultimate goal. In this characterization of the Christian life, we are reminded of Paul's imagery in Philippians 3:13–14 and in 1 Corinthians 9:24–27, where he uses athletic imagery to speak of spirituality and the Christian life.

The theme of *Purgatorio* is freedom. Therefore, in *Purgatorio* 16–18, we find three cantos that are at the exact structural center of the *Commedia* and that deal with free will. If the topic of freedom is central to *Purgatorio*, we need first define what Dante meant by freedom. The *Inferno* shows what freedom does not mean: freedom is not the breaking of bounds, still less irresponsibility toward others. In the third terrace of Purgatory, that of wrathful penitents, Dante encounters Marco Lombardo, and the two discuss the nature of free will. Dante wonders why the world is unfair and disordered, and attributes its cause to fate. Marco disparages Dante's suggestion that our actions are determined by external factors and launches into a discussion on free will, because without free will, he notes, the rewards and punishments of the afterlife make no sense. This leads Marco to the necessity and nature of law, and he cites faulty leadership as a cause of inequality and injustice in the world.

In *Purgatorio* 17 and 18, the discussion continues, only it moves from free will to the nature of love. Because love is the goal of the *Comedy*, a poem that ends with "the love which moves the sun and the other stars" (*Paradiso* 33:145) makes these cantos central to Dante's vision. The discussion reveals how the absence of love, or misdirected love, leads to sin. Choosing the wrong object for love, or choosing to love a good object in the wrong way, Dante learns, is the essence of sin. The discussion then moves to the nature of the seven deadly sins as examples of wrong ways to love.

The whole organization of Purgatory is mapped out in canto 17, beginning with the worst sins. The three lowest levels are where pride, envy, and wrath are purged; the middle level is where sloth (loving without proper zeal) is cured, and the top three levels are where avarice, gluttony, and lust are cured. Canto 18 continues the discussion by developing the nature of freedom. There Virgil tells Dante that he will take him as far as reason will allow. However, because reason is limited, the final answer awaits Beatrice as his guide, for in matters of freedom, love has the final say.

Over time, Dante recognizes that the disciplines of purgation are not mere restrictions but rather are the means by which individuals place themselves in relation to other beings, both human and divine. Law becomes Love, and freedom finally is seen to reside in that interdependence of all beings that is fully enjoyed in Paradise.

Taken as a whole, *Purgatorio* 16–18 can be seen to form the structural center of the second canticle, with its system of seven deadly sins. However, these cantos also form the center of the entire *Commedia*, with its system of punishments and rewards. Retrospectively, *Purgatorio* instructs us on the nature of the souls in Hell: they are not being punished by God, we learn, but rather are living out the consequences of choices they made in their mortal lives.

We end our discussion of Dante's *Comedy* with the topic of Virgil and the importance of poetry (but also of literature in general) for spirituality. In *Purgatorio* 21, Dante and Virgil encounter the Roman poet Statius. To place Statius in Purgatory and on his way to Heaven, Dante invents the account of Statius's conversion, revealing that the pagan poet had become a Christian through the influence of Virgil's poetry. Because Statius does not know that he is in Virgil's company when he tells his story, the moment when Virgil's identity is revealed is especially poignant. Dante's homage to Statius, and hence to the importance of poetry as a vehicle for salvation and grace, is clear. This homage to Virgil is also poignant because Virgil is about to be superseded by Beatrice as Dante's guide. In the pilgrim's encounter with his own poetic predecessors, we see that his debt to them is not unlike the debt of Statius to Virgil.

Purgatorio 21 opens with two powerful biblical references. The first is the story of the Samaritan woman in chapter 4 of John's gospel, and the second is a reference to the resurrected Jesus appearing to his disciples as told in chapter 24 of Luke's gospel. In Virgil's refusal to let Statius embrace him, we find a reference to Jesus' words to Mary Magdalene, "Do not hold on to me" (John 20:17). Paradoxically, in Dante's "retelling" of the gospel story, Virgil is now in the position of Christ, rather than Statius, who is the figure for Christ at the beginning of the canto. Statius, in an almost shocking revelation, states that the main source of his conversion was none other than Virgil. "It was you who first did light me on to God" (*Purgatorio* 22.65–66), he states, citing Virgil's Fourth Eclogue—the short poem describing how a new age would begin with the birth of a child (that is, an heir to Emperor Augustus), which in the Middle Ages was regularly regarded as a messianic prophecy. Virgil, a pagan, was seen in Dante's time as a "prophet" of the incarnation, his work a "lamp" to make others wise. Virgil, of course, was completely unaware that his work revealed the way to God. As Dante reveals in *Purgatorio* 23 through 26, in which he meets some of his immediate poetic predecessors in the vernacular languages, poetry, particularly love poetry, can convey deep spiritual truth, for the work of "living poetry" such as the *Purgatorio* is that there need be no divergence between fact and myth. However, like classical poetry, pagan truth needs to be "baptized" or "Christianized," for while a valuable guide to wisdom and truth, poetry is limited in nature and scope. In writing poetry and in living his life, Dante recognized that he needed to take what is best from profane poetry, for like prophecy in general, poetry contains more than the writers themselves ever thought or imagined. Dante himself—and all pilgrims throughout history, ourselves included—is to these writers as Statius is to Virgil. From the meeting with Statius in *Purgatorio* 21 through *Purgatorio* 26, what Dante the pilgrim learns in his climb up Mount Purgatory is that literature and poetry, like scripture and salvation, are connected to spirituality and to God.

In the end, Dante's *Divine Comedy* is worth reading and rereading because as a work of art it holds the power to influence us as only the best works of art can. While Dante is a Christian, his poem is meaningful for people of all faiths and convictions. Its central metaphor of a journey from bondage to freedom indicates why biblical accounts of events such as the Exodus and the Incarnation, Death, and Resurrection of Christ continue to inspire so many people. In reading the *Divine Comedy*, the final challenge is not to read the book in its entirety, or even to unravel its complicated imagery, but rather to make Dante's *Commedia* our Commedia.

QUESTIONS FOR DISCUSSION AND REFLECTION

In addition to the questions listed at the end of the preface, answer the following questions, writing your answers in a journal. If you are in a group study, be prepared to share your answers with those in the group.

1. Explain how Dante's involvement in local politics influenced his view of the roles of church and state.

2. Explain the role Beatrice plays in Dante's life and in his *Commedia*.
3. In your estimation, can *amore* be considered a form of divine love? Explain your answer.
4. Explain the role Virgil plays in the *Commedia*, and why Dante chose him as his guide through Hell and Purgatory.
5. Explain the meaning of Dante's notion that one must descend in order to ascend.
6. After reading this chapter, assess the merits of the Catholic doctrine of Limbo.
7. In Dante's Hell, the descending order of moral failures goes from incontinence to violence to fraud. Explain and assess the merits of the notion that distrust and disloyalty are the greatest of sins. In your estimation, what category of sin would you consider most grievous? Explain your answer.
8. Explain and assess the merits of the medieval doctrine of purgatory.
9. According to Dante, what is the purpose and goal of human life? Explain your answer.
10. Explain the roles of Bernard of Clairvaux and of the Virgin Mary in Dante's *Paradiso*.
11. Explain the relevance of Dante's understanding of spirituality to the contemporary Christian understanding of the spiritual journey.
12. Assess the merits of selecting the *Purgatorio* for study by modern Christians. If you were to recommend one part of Dante's *Commedia* for reading by modern Christians, which would you choose? Explain your answer.

Chapter 5

Martin Luther's *Freedom of a Christian* and John Calvin's *Institutes*

THE SPIRIT OF REFORM erupted with surprising intensity in the sixteenth century, giving birth to Protestantism and challenging papal leadership of Western Christendom. Four major traditions marked early Protestantism: Lutheran, Anabaptist, Reformed, and Anglican Christianity. Shortly thereafter, Roman Catholic Christianity regrouped and, led by the Jesuits, recovered its moral zeal. Bloody struggles between Catholics and Protestants followed, and Europe was ravaged by war before it became obvious that Western Christendom was permanently divided.

During the Reformation of the sixteenth century, Protestant thinkers began questioning doctrines and practices established during the medieval period, including ecclesiastical hierarchicalism, the authority of the pope, the estrangement between laity and clergy, sacramentalism, monasticism, the veneration of relics and saints, the emphasis on good works as meritorious for salvation, and the sale of indulgences. In so doing, most Protestants were not rejecting church authority, but rather subordinating it to biblical constraints. While retaining the ancient creeds and the theological formulations of the great ecumenical councils of the fourth and fifth centuries, mainline Protestants rejected those doctrines, practices, and ceremonies for which no clear warrant existed in the Bible, or which seemed to contradict its letter and intent.

According to church sociologist Ernst Troeltsch, Protestantism is a variation of Catholicism, asking four traditional Catholic questions and arriving at different answers. The four questions that Protestantism answers in new ways are: (1) How is a person saved? (2) Where does religious authority lie? (3) What is the church? and (4) What is the essence of Christian living? During the sixteenth century, Protestant Reformers agreed on the essentials, but fresh answers emerged in Martin Luther's conflict with Rome.

The Protestant Reformation brought profound changes to European culture, for the Reformers repudiated the synthesis mentality that had dominated Christian thought for centuries. Many secular historians have argued that political, economic, and social issues inspired the major transformations of the sixteenth century. While these forces influenced the development and course of the Reformation, spiritual and moral issues were primary. Above all else, the Reformers sought to correct the doctrine and life of the church. Their movement represented "a revolt of conscience."

Two major worldviews molded medieval intellectual and religious culture: the Greek and the biblical traditions. The Reformers sought to repudiate medieval thought, with its reliance upon reason. In their opinion, medieval thinkers had made a conscious and thoroughgoing attempt to fuse radically different traditions into one theological system. The Reformers' attack upon extravagances of the papal court, the sale of indulgences and church offices, and excessive church taxation were part of a larger campaign to return the church to its biblical foundation. Their cry became *ad fontes*, "back to the sources," meaning that they wished to return to the scriptures of the Old and New Testaments.

MARTIN LUTHER: BIOGRAPHICAL CONSIDERATIONS

The son of a peasant miner, Martin Luther (1483–1546) had every intention of becoming a lawyer until one day in 1505 he was caught in a thunderstorm. Struck by a bolt of lightning, he prayed to the patroness of miners, "St. Anne, save me, and I'll become a monk." He kept his vow and two weeks later entered an Augustinian monastery. Obsessed with his own sin, he tried austere acts of penance such as prolonged fasting, sleeping outdoors in freezing weather, and self-flagellation. The purity and wrath of God, however, proved to be too great, and no amount of penance soothed his spirit.

The troubled monk was assigned to the chair of biblical studies at the recently established Wittenberg University, where he found a different view of God. He wished, above all, to live in a state of grace, and he knew that to live in this state meant to love God. In 1515, while pondering Paul's epistle to the Romans, Luther came upon the statement that "the just shall live by his faith" (1:17). Here was the key to his dilemma. The answer lay in Christ's identity with sinful humanity. Luther understood clearly now the gospel message: salvation is only by faith in Christ. As a gift of God's grace, it cannot be earned, but merely affirmed by an act of faith. Luther had come by his famous doctrine of justification by faith alone. He saw how sharply it clashed with the Roman Church's doctrine of justification by faith and good works. The implications of Luther's discovery were enormous. If salvation comes through faith in Christ alone, the intercession of priests, masses, and prayers to the saints was unnecessary. The mediation of the institutional church, through hierarchical, sacramental, and monastic means, was superfluous.

As his 1516 lecture notes on the epistle of Romans reveal, his search for a deeper understanding of love led him to the writings of the twelfth-century mystic, Bernard of Clairvaux. In his writings Bernard revealed a progressive spirituality of love, moving from (1) loving self for self's sake, an initial state of selfishness, to (2) loving God for self's sake, a deeper but still immature state in which one relates to God by wanting something from God, to (3) loving God for God's sake, a mature relational state of love, to (4) loving self for God's sake, an advanced state of grace, whereby the believer loves God by loving what God has made, understanding oneself as an instrument of God's love.

In his early professional life, Luther struggled to make his love increasingly less self-willed, or, as he put it, less "curved in on itself." At this time, he thought of impure motives as evil. He was still tormented by sin, for he had not yet been freed from the late medieval mindset to discover what he later called "the gospel." His understanding of salvation came close to what we might call "self hatred," for it was only in despising himself that he could hope to be acceptable to God.

Young Luther was not yet in a good place, for his spirituality was all law and no grace. What grace he sought, he sought only in law. It is as if good works come before grace, something alien to Augustinian spirituality but which Luther found in late medieval spirituality, a form of spirituality still alive in traditional Christianity. "Do the best that you can," it taught, "and learn to love God by sheer will, after which you can hope for God's grace." That approach, Luther discovered, does not work. Love works by delight, he learned, and not by demand or by sheer force of will. Good deeds can be done that way, but that is not how spirituality works. Spirituality *starts* with grace, lives by grace, and reaches its goal by grace. In a manner of speaking, God does it all. Like a great tide, love lifts all lives. Living by the confessional and by penance only confirmed the premise that we are sinners, unacceptable to God. Such an approach does not lead to joy, peace, and the other benefits of love, but only to begging and sighing, always seeking and never finding acceptance, grace, or righteousness.

At this point, Luther believed that God was more concerned with judging and condemning than with loving and forgiving. This form of spirituality, masochistic in nature, never focuses on what is good and right, but emphasizes what is sinful and wrong. According to this theology, God is Judge and Accuser, not Friend or Lover. The bottom line of young Luther's spirituality was this: To love God is to hate oneself. His confessor at the time, a priest named Staupitz, had to bring Luther to his senses by telling him, "Martin, you say that God is angry with you, but it is you who are angry with God."

Such an approach never works, for as Jesus regularly declared, we are not made to hate ourselves, but to love ourselves, and to love God and others with appropriate self-love. As we learn from the biblical and Augustinian paradigms, we must want good things, not bad things, for ourselves and for others. What we want and truly need is a loving God; nothing else will do. Martin Luther had yet to discover the transformative element in spirituality. He was seeking condemnation, but what he needed was acceptance.

In 1510, young Luther had visited Rome, which was under Pope Julius II, known as Julius the Terrible. Luther was an unknown priest at the time, and he found Rome to be worldly, cynical, and even atheistic. Italian priests were more secular that religious, more opportunistic than believing. Their word for a "faithful" Christian was a "fool." Luther was shocked by their behavior, for these priests kept the "red light district" going; many had mistresses, prostitutes, or both, bearing numerous illegitimate children. In this environment, Luther was attempting a religious pilgrimage, seeking God's grace for deceased relatives in purgatory. For his deceased grandfather, he climbed the sacred steps on his knees. These were the steps supposedly of the Jerusalem house of Pilate, where Jesus had been on trial, moved to Rome. According to church tradition, if penitents climbed these steps one at a time, pausing at each step to recite the Lord's Prayer, when they reached the top, the departed soul was released from purgatory.

Much of the wealth of Renaissance popes came from pilgrims or parishioners from other European nations. Their spirituality was based on the late medieval piety of fear and anxiety about divine punishment in the afterlife, a condition exacerbated by the clergy. Average parishioners had little peace in this life, for death came suddenly, and if you died with unconfessed venial sin, you were destined for punishment. However, if you died with unconfessed mortal sin, your soul would go straight to hell with no chance of escape. Of course, if you died and went to purgatory, your punishment could be reduced, but this required financial and penitential acts by concerned relatives or friends.

Of course, such activity proved lucrative for the church. To supplement this income, the church devised a practice known as indulgences, whereby devout believers could pay money in exchange for a written guarantee that the souls of their loved ones would be released from purgatory or their punishment in the afterlife lessened or reduced. An entire economy was built on religious anxiety and superstition, much of it manufactured by greedy and cynical clergy in search of financial gain.

Luther, like other Reformers, had no desire to start a new religion, denomination, or sect, but rather to reform the church of its excess. He had no idea where his spiritual discovery was leading, but he knew it was important. It took flagrant abuse of church finances through the sale of indulgences to propel him into confrontation with papal authority. Luther's displeasure increased noticeably during 1517, when the Dominican John Tetzel traveled throughout Germany on behalf of a papal fundraising campaign to complete the construction of St. Peter's basilica in Rome. In exchange for a contribution, Tetzel boasted, he would provide donors with an indulgence that would free souls from purgatory. "As soon as the coin in the coffer rings," went his jingle, "the soul from purgatory upward springs."

The Reformation is said to have begun on October 31, 1517, when, protesting the sale of indulgences, Luther nailed his 95 Theses to the bulletin board on the door of the Castle Church at Wittenberg. While these theses did not present his theology, they proposed theological debate. Copies of Luther's theses were published and republished all over Europe, sparking a theological revolution. Luther came to regard the printing press as one of the great gifts of God.

In this context, Luther's gospel hit like a bombshell. Sincere parishioners in Germany became unhappy with this state of affairs, and they erupted in protest, with Luther at the center of the revolt. In the midst of this debate about the afterlife, Luther announced that believers could have certainty of God's grace. The guarantee, he declared, is in scripture. Instead of paying money or performing deeds of penitence, wondering whether they made any difference, one could go to scripture and simply trust in God's promise of love and forgiveness.

Luther's stress on the gospel not only gave believers peace of mind, it also had enormous economic and political consequences. It meant parishioners were no longer dependent upon clergy and the sacraments for divine grace. Through prayer, believers had direct access to God. No longer were penance, indulgences, or payments to the papacy needed. The gospel was free, for payment had been made on our behalf by Christ. That is what Jesus meant when he told his followers, "This is my body, given for you."

In part, the situation at the start of the Reformation could be characterized as a disagreement between German and Italian Catholics. Germans were anxious about the afterlife, and they were paying dearly for promises they could not trust. Meanwhile their money was being used by cynical priests to fund wars, extravagant buildings, and artistic projects in Rome. Pious Germans, with Luther as their spokesperson, were fed up. They discovered they didn't need all their religious baggage. All they needed was Jesus Christ and the gospel. Once they heard that, tremors resulted, and the earthquake came to be called the Reformation.

Within a short time, German Dominicans denounced Luther to Rome as preaching "dangerous doctrines." The Vatican issued a series of counter-theses, arguing that anyone who criticized the sale of indulgences was guilty of heresy. Luther decided to put his case before the German people. Utilizing the printing press, his reply came through a vast literary production. In one year alone (1520) he published five major works, relying on biblical arguments for support. His *Treatise on Good Works* demonstrated how faith in Christ was the only good work that God expected from repentant sinners. In *The Papacy of Rome* he attacked the pope directly, calling him Antichrist because he kept people from understanding and heeding the message of the gospel. His *Address to the Christian Nobility of the German Nation* called on the princes of northern Europe to throw off the tyranny—economic and political as well as spiritual—that bound them to Rome. His *Babylonian Captivity of the Church* examined the sevenfold system of sacraments, claiming to find only baptism and the Lord's Supper (and perhaps confession) as authorized by Christ in the New Testament. In contrast to the sharp polemics of these works, Luther published *Freedom of a Christian*, a conciliatory effort explaining how saving grace results in doing good works.

Among the ideas in these writings, three gained emphasis: (1) the supremacy of scripture as the only source and rule for Christian faith and practice (*sola scriptura*), (2) justification by grace received by faith alone (*sola gratia/sola fide*), and (3) the priesthood of believers (all church members are called to be "priests" to one another, the keys of the kingdom having been granted to the entire faith community and not only to the clergy [see Matt 18:18]). Known as the "three principles of Protestantism," these ideals countered essential aspects of medieval Catholicism: (1) "scripture alone" opposed Roman emphasis on the twofold authority of scripture and tradition, which made the decrees of popes and councils the only legitimate interpreters of the Bible; (2) "grace alone" opposed the Roman theory that faith and good works cooperated as sources of justification; (3) "the priesthood of believers" opposed the theory of the church as a vast hierarchy, which made ordained priests the necessary mediators between God and humanity.

In June 1520, Pope Leo X issued a decree condemning Luther and giving him sixty days to turn from his heretical course. Luther received his copy in October. At the end of his sixty-day period of grace, he led a throng of students outside Wittenberg and burned copies of medieval church documents, adding for good measure a copy of the decree condemning him. That was his answer. In 1521, the pope declared him a heretic, making complete his excommunication. The problem now fell into the hands of Charles V, a young man of twenty-one who, in addition to serving as king of Spain, had recently been elected Holy Roman Emperor. He summoned Luther to the imperial Diet (assembly) meeting at the German city of Worms to recant. Before the assembly Luther again insisted that only biblical authority would sway him: "I will not recant, for to go against conscience is neither honest nor safe. Here I stand, I cannot do otherwise." With these words, Protestantism was born. Protestants would obey the Bible before all other authorities. Europe—and the church—would never be the same.

Charles V gave Luther twenty-one days before the sentence fell. It never came. Luther was saved from arrest and death by the prince of Saxony, Duke Frederick the Wise, whose domains included Wittenberg. The duke gave Luther sanctuary at Wartburg Castle, where he remained for nearly a year, disguised as a minor nobleman. During this time, he translated the New Testament into German, an important step toward reshaping public and private worship in Germany.¹ Meanwhile the revolt against Rome spread and new reformers appeared on the scene. Princes, dukes, and electors defied the condemnation of Luther by giving support to the new movement. In 1522 Luther returned to Wittenberg to put into effect the spiritual reform that became the model for much of Germany. He called for the abolition of the office of bishop, arguing that the churches needed pastors, not dignitaries. He advocated for the abandonment of celibacy for monks and nuns, and in 1525, married Katherine von Bora, a former nun.

The last twenty years of his life were not as dramatic as the years between 1517 and 1525, which had made him both the most revered and the most hated person in Europe. Among his favorite writings he singled out the Small Catechism of 1529, which through simple questions and answers explained the Ten Commandments, the Apostles' Creed, and the Lord's Prayer. In that same year, Luther engaged in a momentous debate with Ulrich Zwingli, a distinguished preacher from the Swiss city of Zurich. The two reformers found that they could agree on most points of doctrine and practice, but not on the meaning of the Lord's Supper. Luther held that Christ was truly present in the Supper, Zwingli that he was present only symbolically. Inability to resolve that troubling issue indicated more clearly than any previous event that the reform movement would lead to Protestant churches rather than to a reform of the one Western church.

By 1530, when a summit conference of Reformation leaders convened in Augsburg to draw up a common statement of faith, leadership of the movement had begun to pass from Luther. The Reformer was still an outlaw and unable to attend. The task of presenting Lutheranism fell to Philip Melanchthon, a young professor of Greek at Wittenberg and Luther's closest colleague. The Augsburg Confession, signed by several important princes in attendance, became the doctrinal standard for the Lutheran churches that were emerging in Germany, Scandinavia, and Eastern Europe. After 1530, Emperor Charles V made clear his intention to crush the growing heresy. In defense, the Lutheran princes banded together. The combatants reached a compromise in the Peace of Augsburg (1555), which allowed each prince to decide the religion of his subjects and ordered all Catholic bishops to give up their property if they turned Lutheran. The effects of these provisions were profound. Lutheranism

---

1. In 1534 Luther completed his translation of the entire Bible, on which he worked with the help of colleagues for over a decade.

became a state religion in large portions of the empire. Religious opinions became the private property of the princes, and individuals had to believe whatever form of Christianity their prince wanted them to believe.

Luther's greatest contribution, however, was not political but religious. He took four Christian concerns and offered radically new answers. To the question, How is a person saved? Luther replied, "not by works but by faith alone." To the question, Where does religious authority lie? he answered, "not in the institutional Catholic church but in the Word of God found in the Bible." To the question, What is the church? he responded, "the whole community of Christian believers, since all are priests before God." And to the question, What is the essence of Christian living? he replied, "serving God in any useful calling, whether ordained or lay." To this day, any classical description of Protestantism must echo those responses.

MARTIN LUTHER'S *ON THE FREEDOM OF A CHRISTIAN*

On the Freedom of a Christian, sometimes called *A Treatise on Christian Liberty*, was the third of Luther's major reforming treatises of 1520. The work appeared in a shorter German and a more elaborate Latin form. This tract was written to attempt to persuade Pope Leo X and Roman Catholics in general that the theology of the Reformation was not a novelty in the faith, but a pure confession of the Word of God and consistent with the truth of the Christian scriptures. Out of his affliction, Luther wrote one of the most enduring treatments on Christian freedom.

Luther opens his letter to Pope Leo X with a respectful and admiring greeting. He details the rumors of his personal attack of Leo X, explaining that he meant to let these rumors quiet down. However, he now feels that he must write to Leo and personally renounce these lies. Luther denies ever resorting to personal attacks of the pope, but does apologize for any unintentional slander. He then states clearly his support for attacking ungodly teaching. Luther believes he must speak out against "ungodliness" because Jesus provided that example throughout the Bible. It is for this reason that Luther then condemns the papal structures and functions. He believes Christian believers are being deceived into committing wrong and even sinful actions. Luther goes so far as to charge Leo X and his cardinals with worsening the hurts and issues within the Roman Church rather than healing them. Luther asks the pope to consider these things and turn from the sinful traditions of the church.

Luther's tract begins with two seemingly contradictory propositions: (1) A Christian is a perfectly free lord of all, subject to none; and (2) A Christian is a perfectly dutiful servant of all, subject to all. Among the ancients, Aristotle had stated the obvious about lords and servants: "If there is a lord, then there is (also) a servant. And if there is a servant, then there is also a lord." Luther's paradoxical teaching of Christian freedom, following Jesus and Paul, joins lord and servant in one person. By faith alone, God sets a person utterly free in Christ. That person is lord of all, subject to none. Love, however, binds him as an utterly dutiful servant to the neighbor, subject to everyone. The paradox of Christian freedom then plays out in faith and love.

Luther introduces his tract with a brief discussion of the themes of Christianity. His main point is that faith is the defining characteristic of a believing Christian. The issue is that faith is learned only through trials and hardship. Those who do not experience those trials cannot understand faith, and those who have experienced those trials only want to experience more. This true experience of faith then leads to two themes of Christianity: freedom and service. These themes may seem contradictory but are in fact in perfect agreement.

Luther cites the apostle Paul to illustrate the nature of agreement between the ideas of freedom and service. Paul explains that a believer is made free from the consequences of sin through faith in Jesus Christ. The believer no longer lives under the condemnation of the law but is free in faith. Similarly, a believer is bound by love to serve other people. This paradox is lived out perfectly in the life and death of Jesus Christ. Luther further explains this contradiction by explaining the dual nature of human beings. Every human has two parts: the spirit and the flesh. The spirit or soul is the inner person and craves the things of God. However, the flesh is the outer person or the body and the part of humans that craves the things not of God. These two parts of humans are in conflict and fight against each other.

Luther considers freedom first as it relates to the inner person. The inner person becomes righteous, free, and a pious Christian in Christ. For Luther, the Word—by which he means the gospel of God concerning Christ—does all the work, accomplishing all that God commands. By faith alone, the Christian receives all that Christ gives. Thus, a person is justified by faith alone. Later in the tract, Luther considers the outer person. Luther's liberty is not a liberty of ease, as Roman Catholic opponents declared. Insofar as Christian are servants, they perform all kinds of good deeds. Against those who resent human autonomy, arguing that the church always knows what is best for people, Luther is a vigorous advocate of Christian liberty. However, against any reduction of this freedom to an opportunity for license, self-preoccupation, or indifference to the needs of others, Luther makes the service of others the hallmark and goal of how Christian liberty is to be used.

In speaking of how faith alone, without the "works of the law" (that is, the laws and ceremonies required in the Jewish Torah), can justify the believer and confer so many spiritual benefits, Luther introduces the distinction between command and promise (law and gospel). Of the commands, Luther says they function "to teach us about ourselves."[2] They show us what we ought to do but they do not give us the power to do it. Faith, according to Luther, has a threefold power:

- *Faith frees us from the law.* Christian freedom does not lead Christians to live lazy and wicked lives, but makes the law and works unnecessary for salvation.
- *Faith honors God.* Saving faith honors God by trusting in God alone. To trust in the promises of God is the highest worship of God, for to regard God as truthful and righteous is to honor God.
- *Faith unites the soul with Christ.* This aspect of faith Luther calls the "blessed exchange." Just as a groom is united with his bride by a solemn vow, so "Christ and the soul become one flesh."[3] This is the great exchange, where the property of the groom becomes that of his wife and vice versa. Luther describes faith as the exchange of wedding vows. In exchanging rings, promises are given, but underlying the vow is the promise of the giving of self by each individual to the other. Everything that is ours (our debts, wounds, anguish, and loss) is Christ's, and in exchange, everything that is Christ's (his righteousness, holiness, and blessedness) is ours. In proclaiming the gospel, Luther makes it clear that by faith Christ takes our sin and in return, gives us his righteousness.

Luther's tract on freedom has been called the most perfect expression of the Reformation understanding of the mystery of Christ. In his

2. Lull, *Luther's Basic Theological Writings*, 600.
3. Lull, *Luther's Basic Theological Writings*, 603.

conclusion, Luther reminds his readers that there are two kinds of freedom. One is a worldly freedom, the other a spiritual freedom, which he calls "the freedom of love."[4]

The Freedom of the Christian is a confession of Christian grace in a nutshell. Christian freedom is a gift from Christ himself, "For freedom Christ has set us free" (Gal 5:1). What Christ did to win salvation he then gives to those who bear his name. God justifies sinners by faith alone, changing both their inner and outer person after his likeness. Christians are at once utterly free in faith and a servant to all in works of love. This paradoxical Christian freedom, Luther insisted, is lived between the twin poles of faith and love.

JOHN CALVIN: BIOGRAPHICAL CONSIDERATIONS

If one thinks of the Protestant Reformers along a spectrum running from conservative to truly radical, we would place Luther along the conservative end. Despite his bold new ideas, he still affirmed many elements of Catholic worship. If we continue moving left on the spectrum, we come next to a group we call Reformed Christians, epitomized by the personality and views of John Calvin. Reformed Christians wanted even greater change than Luther, and their ideas had major implications for politics. To the far left are the Anabaptists (Radical Reformers), for their notions of society were the most far-reaching and extreme.

Two years after Luther posted his theses on the parish door, Ulrich Zwingli (1484–1531) became pastor of the Great Minster Church in Zurich. Unlike the fiery Luther, Zwingli came to the fore as a pastor. Because his primary concern was with worship and devotional practice, he became an early exponent of the "Reformed" branch of Protestantism. Like Luther, Zwingli had a Renaissance education, and he read ancient church theology in Latin and Greek. Under the influence of the famous humanist scholar Erasmus (1466–1536), the Catholic linguist who compiled and edited the Greek New Testament, Zwingli had come to revere the language and message of the New Testament. A patriot, Zwingli resented the power of Catholic bishops in Switzerland. They were often corrupt and more interested in secular than religious power.

Zwingli became critical of Catholic veneration of saints, the ritual of the Mass, and all the rules about feasting and fasting. He wanted to

---

4. Lull, *Luther's Basic Theological Writings*, 621.

reform Christian practice so that it was closer to the instructions provided in the New Testament, at least as he read them. Zwingli's understanding of the Lord's Supper is important. Luther, you might recall, held that Christ was truly present in the Supper, whereas Zwingli held that he was present only symbolically. This helps us see that the starting point of the Reformed break with Catholicism was a critique of idolatry, not a critique of religious law, as it was with Luther. Moreover, Reformed Protestants generally had more confidence that God used grace to perfect Christians over time, to enable them to better follow the commandments. From this perspective, Zwingli found Luther's explanation of justification too individualist. He was worried about how it would work in practice, in a Christian community.

In 1523, Zurich politicians decided to reform the churches in their territory, with Zwingli's help. He started with worship, not a university curriculum, as did Luther. Zwingli urged the officials to moderation, but they wanted radical change. They wanted to destroy icons and all suggestion of idolatry. By 1525 the Swiss Reformation turned violent when Zwingli participated in a civil war that pitted Protestants against Catholics. In 1531, Zwingli died on the battlefield, and the Reformed torch passed to John Calvin (1509–1564), the second-generation Reformer who consolidated Protestant gains and became the Reformation's most important scholar. Like Luther, he attempted to reform doctrine and church organization, and like Zwingli, he was concerned with reforming worship and devotional practice. However, unlike both, he also attempted to bring the socio-political order into harmony with the teachings of scripture. A careful and painstaking exposition of the scriptures and a firm disciplinarian in what he believed to be for the glory of God and the right conduct of a Christian community, Calvin became known as the first and perhaps greatest Protestant interpreter and systematizer of Christian theology.

Born in Noyon (Picardy), France, he studied law to please his father. However, his real passion was for ancient languages and literature. After his father died, he trained to be a priest, but he became disillusioned with the French clergy, seeing them as immoral and ignorant. Like Luther, he experienced a dramatic conversion, although he was not driven by guilt or fear as his German counterpart. He began to preach to congregations in the area, and started his career as a prolific writer expounding Protestant ideals. When severe persecution broke out against French Protestants, Calvin found refuge in the Swiss city of Basel, where, at the age of twenty-seven, he completed the first edition of his most influential work, the *Institutes of the Christian Religion*. By the time the final edition was published in 1559, this work had grown from a short exposition of Christian doctrine to the most significant theological work of the Reformation. The preface of the first edition, a letter to Francis I of France protesting his persecution of Protestants, is a masterpiece of apologetic literature. No one had spoken so effectively on their behalf, and with this letter Calvin assumed a position of leadership in the Protestant cause. After its publication, Calvin sought haven in Strasbourg, but warfare forced him to travel by way of Geneva.

The Geneva to which Calvin came was a vigorous, liberty-loving city of some ten thousand inhabitants. Under William Farel's leadership, the small independent republic had recently become nominally Protestant. Its churches had been seized for Protestantism and its four monasteries and a nunnery closed. The Council in charge of political affairs had taken drastic measures to regulate private morals and to compel attendance at sermons. Despite these measures, Geneva's leaders were primarily motivated by political rather than religious consideration. In the city, which was a magnet for exiles and expatriates, the political climate was unpredictable. Because these were perilous times, Calvin wished to travel through Geneva incognito.

When Farel discovered that Calvin was in town, he went to meet him. Farel was then in the midst of a vigorous but unorganized attempt to establish the new Genevan Protestant church. The chaos of the situation required the touch of a master organizer, and Farel was quick to detect in Calvin the helper he needed. Calvin was reluctant to give up the prospect of a quiet life of study at Strasbourg, for he was by nature retiring and studious. But Farel pressed him into service with an argument that was almost an imprecation: "I denounce unto you, in the name of Almighty God, that if, under the pretext of prosecuting your studies, you refuse to labor with us in this work of the Lord, the Lord will curse you, as seeking yourself rather than Christ." Upon hearing these words, Calvin gave up his intended journey and enlisted in the service of Geneva.

In Geneva, Calvin established a system of civic and ecclesiastical governance that rejected papal authority and created a central hub from which Reformation theology could be propagated. Working with unusual dedication throughout his career, he neglected neither the priestly nor the prophetic duties of his office. Theodore Beza, his early biographer, estimates that Calvin preached 286 times a year, while also lecturing 180 times. His growing reputation brought people from far and near to Geneva in search of his advice, and he maintained a voluminous correspondence, of which four thousand letters remain. Any matter arising in one of the Reformed churches, of which there were a great many by this time, was almost certainly brought to his attention for settlement.

The Protestant Reformation, based upon concepts such as the priesthood of all believers, the importance of the individual conscience, and the supremacy of scripture, made widespread literacy important. For a long time Calvin wished to set up a college—a municipal school system for all children—with the academy as the center of instruction for the very best students. Such a school had been founded in the fifteenth century, but no longer suited the requirements of the day. The establishment in 1559 of his academy, with Beza as rector of what soon became a full university, was Calvin's crowning achievement in the building of a Christian state. It provided free instruction for all grades from primary work through high school. Though the need of preparing men for the ministry was an important reason for the establishment of the university, Calvin was also motivated by a profound desire to train an educated Protestant laity. Broadly educated himself, he attracted learned scholars to the school and helped elevate its reputation and extend its influence.

The endeavor flourished. The academy, which attracted students from all over Europe, served as a model for other academies around the world and eventually became the University of Geneva. Lest we think that Calvin was simply founding a university, we must keep in mind that he considered the crown of education to be theology, for which all arts and sciences were a preparation. Students were trained, not for degrees or lucrative employment, but to serve God as preachers or as godly civil servants.

When one examines the life of John Calvin, and the many demands upon his life as a cleric, one wonders how he found the time and energy for education, religious or secular. Yet it was such a priority that in his latter years he is known to have taught ten hours a day, six days a week. Such an emphasis on education, however, is not surprising. The humanism of the Renaissance stimulated unprecedented academic ferment and a concern for academic freedom. Earnest debates took place in the universities about the nature of the church and the source and extent of the authority of the papacy, of church councils, and of princes. The invention of the printing press, while making the Bible increasingly available to the general public, allowed quick broadcasting of ideas. Popular discontent at moral corruption in the church, coupled with the spread of nationalistic fervor, led support for a reformation as never before.

JOHN CALVIN'S *INSTITUTES OF THE CHRISTIAN RELIGION*

The *Institutes*, John Calvin's seminal work of systematic theology, is regarded as one of the most influential works of Protestant, or to be more specific, of Reformed theology. It is one of the few books that have profoundly affected the course of history. It was published in Latin in 1536 and in French in 1541, with definitive (expanded) editions appearing in 1559 (Latin) and in 1560 (French). The book was written to serve a double purpose: it was a "confession" in the sense of being an apology to win immunity from persecution for those who held Calvin's opinions; and it was a book of instruction for religious inquirers, an introductory textbook on Protestant belief covering a broad range of theological topics from the doctrines of the church and sacraments to justification by faith alone and Christian liberty. It vigorously attacked the teachings of those Calvin considered unorthodox, particularly Roman Catholicism, to which Calvin had been devoted before his conversion to Protestantism.

The original publication of the *Institutes* contained a preface addressed to King Francis I of France, entreating him to give the Protestants a hearing rather than continue to persecute them. Six chapters in length, the *Institutes* covered the basics of Christian creeds, using the familiar structure of the Ten Commandments, the Apostles' Creed, the Lord's Prayer, and the sacraments, as well as a chapter on Christian liberty and political theology. The *Institutes* proved instantly popular, with many requests for a revised edition. The fifth and final edition, published in Geneva in 1559 and used by scholars as the authoritative text, consists of four books divided into eighty chapters. It is based on the Apostles' Creed, a traditional structure of Christian instruction used in Western Christianity. Calvin's theology did not change substantially throughout his life, and so while he expanded and added to the *Institutes*, he did not change its main ideas.

The opening chapter of the *Institutes* is perhaps the best known, in which Calvin presents the basic plan of the book. In effect, there are only two general subjects to be examined: the Creator and his creatures. Above all, the book concerns the knowledge of God the Creator, but as it is in the creation of humans that the divine perfections are best displayed, there is also an examination of what can be known about humankind. After all, knowledge of God and of what God requires of his creatures is the primary issue of concern for a book of theology. In the first chapter, these two issues are considered together to show how God relates to human beings (and other creatures) and how knowing God is connected with human knowledge.

The *Institutes* begin with the statement that our best wisdom consists in a knowledge of God and of ourselves: "Wisdom lies in knowing God and knowing oneself" (1.1). In other words, we cannot know either without some knowledge of the other: Wisdom—the right application of knowledge—is the entire point of the *Institutes*. Such wisdom is a gift from God to humans in order that they may come to know the Creator. To know God involves for Calvin far more than intellectual comprehension. Knowing God leads to godliness (*pietas* or reverence joined to love of God) and pure religion (*religio*). God is to be known in order to be worshiped and obeyed. Piety and religion are inseparable in the *Institutes*. Piety leads to faith that enacts true religion in the person changed by God. It is only here that one may offer up true religion to God, for without this change, humans remain in a fallen state. God makes himself known to humans in a twofold revelation: through creation and through scripture. The latter, known as special revelation, reveals God as Redeemer, whereas the former, known as general revelation, reveals God as Creator.

Next, Calvin explains that this knowledge presses us to ask, "What is God like?" We ought not to betray our knowledge by asking, "What is God?" or "Does God exist?" Rather, with a certain knowledge based on evidence and attended by *pietas* and *religio* one may attain to a proper knowledge of God. There are other ways to know God, but they prove ineffectual and ultimately do not help the inquirer but further condemn him. Calvin then proceeds to explain how attaining knowledge of God apart from revelation fails, and that the only way one can truly understand and embrace the reality of the divine mind is by illumination from God.

Following the pattern of the Apostles' Creed, then, the first section of the *Institutes* considers knowledge of God the Father as creator, provider, and sustainer. Next, Calvin examines how the Son reveals the Father, since only God is able to reveal God. The third section of the *Institutes* describes the work of the Holy Spirit, who raised Christ from the dead, and who comes from the Father and the Son to affect a union in the church through faith in Jesus Christ. Finally, the fourth section speaks of the Christian church, and how Christians are to live out the truths of God and the scriptures, particularly through the sacraments. This section also describes the functions and ministries of the church, how civil government relates to religious matters, and includes a lengthy discussion of the deficiencies of the papacy.

While modern readers are often daunted or perplexed reading older books, once people are oriented to Calvin's intention in composing the *Institutes*, they can readily understand most of it without needing recourse to a commentary or guide. The reason is simple: Calvin was a Christian writing to Christians about the most important reality in the universe to them—God, and our need to know and enjoy him. Calvin desired his readers to know and love God through reading his book, a desire that Christians throughout the ages have felt, whether persecuted sixteenth-century French Protestants or twenty-first-century Christians trying to navigate the upheavals of our world. Calvin wanted his readers to come away from his book filled with a passion to know their Lord. This desire drives much of the *Institutes*. Whether you agree with Calvin's emphasis on election, predestination, or the condition of humanity as sinful, the *Institutes* are "must reading" for Christians at all stages of their lives.

While it is hoped that participants in this study on classic Christian literature will endeavor to read major portions of the *Institutes* in the future, for now, you are requested to read Section 2 of Book 3, which discusses the nature of the Christian life. Book 3 of the *Institutes*, which explains the work of the Holy Spirit, describes faith in relation to the third member of the Trinity. Calvin begins Section 1 by explaining the work of Christ through the power of the Holy Spirit. As the community of the saved, believers must be engrafted into Christ, and this is done by the work of the Spirit.

In Section 2, Calvin describes repentance as that which is a product of faith. It does not precede it or follow it necessarily. It is a true turning of the life of a sinner to God based on the work of change wrought in such a person by the Holy Spirit. Such faith (1) is a transformation of the soul; (2) arises out of a serious fear of God; and (3) is a combination of mortification and vivification—mortifying the deeds of the flesh and putting on the "new man."

As a result of regeneration and repentance, the Christian is to engage in a denial of self. Such a denial of life is first toward God and then toward others. Turning toward God means resigning our wills completely to God and following him as Shepherd. This humility is to affect every area of our life before God and every circumstance God may bring into our lives. Life may break the Christian, but in turning to God, our joy is made complete even in suffering. Thus, we are to bear our cross, despise the world, and live to God. Having turned toward God, believers should be as stewards of love acting on behalf of God toward others.

Modern readers may find perplexing the use of the Latin word "*institutio*," translated in the title as "institutes." The same word may also be translated "instruction," a term commonly used in the titles of legal works as well as other summary works covering a large body of knowledge. In its original form, the word "institutes" may not have functioned merely as an exposition of Reformation doctrine; for many, it proved the inspiration to a new form of Christian life. In its treatment of faith and sacraments, the *Institutes* was indebted to Martin Luther; in what it says of divine will and predestination, to Martin Bucer; and in its teaching regarding freedom in the relation of church and state, to the later scholastics.

Calvin was aware that his book served a double purpose. It was a "confession" in the sense of being an apology to win immunity from persecution for those who held his opinions. However, it was also a book of instruction for religious inquirers. The catechetical and apologetic aims of the work remain, because in fact they can never be disentangled. If Calvin spoke *for* French Protestants of his day, he also spoke *to* them, even as he speaks to and for many Christians to this day.

QUESTIONS FOR DISCUSSION AND REFLECTION

In addition to the questions listed at the end of the preface, answer the following questions, writing your answers in a journal. If you are in a group study, be prepared to share your answers with those in the group.

1. In your own words, explain the similarities and differences between mainline Protestants and radical Protestants.
2. In your estimation, how did the Protestant Reformation prepare the West for modernity?
3. In your estimation, could the Protestant Reformation have been prevented, or was it an inevitable component of the change that

burst upon Europe in the late medieval period? Explain your answer.

4. In your estimation, what was Martin Luther's greatest contribution to Protestant Christianity? Explain your answer.

5. In your estimation, what was Martin Luther's greatest contribution to Christian spirituality? Explain your answer.

6. Of the "three principles of Protestantism," which do you consider most important? Why? Which do you consider least important? Why?

7. In your own words, explain the paradox at the center of Luther's *Treatise on Christian Liberty*. In your estimation, did Luther's concept of freedom or of liberty influence the American Revolution? Explain your answer.

8. Explain the meaning of the concept of the "blessed exchange" in Luther's understanding of saving grace.

9. In your estimation, what was John Calvin's greatest contribution to Protestant Christianity? Explain your answer.

10. In your estimation, what was John Calvin's greatest contribution to Christian spirituality? Explain your answer.

11. Explain Calvin's distinction between "general" and "special" revelation.

12. Explain and assess the author's statement that Calvin's *Institutes* "profoundly affected the course of history."

Chapter 6

Teresa of Ávila's *Interior Castle* and John of the Cross's *Dark Night of the Soul*

WHILE MOST CHRISTIANS CONSIDER themselves disciples of Jesus and try to follow his teachings, a smaller number focus on practical acts of service or solidarity. While these can be done in tandem, some Christians feel compelled to pursue a third option, the difficult mystic path. Mystics, of course, come in many forms and express their mystical focus through many commitments and lifestyles. While all mystics seek union with God or Ultimate Reality, some seek union through nature and thus may be called "nature mystics." Others, whom we may call "social mystics," seek union through volunteerism and through commitment to freedom and justice for all. Yet others, whom we may call "intellectual mystics," seek union through reading, silence, discussion, and study. Throughout Christian history, some mystics followed the monastic path, pursuing union and spiritual perfection through self-denial, ascetic practices, and extreme devotion. In this chapter we discuss the lives and writings of "monastic mystics" Teresa of Ávila and John of the Cross. While exemplifying Catholic mysticism in the immediate post-Reformation era, both are regarded as preeminent authorities of Christian spirituality.

Much of organized religion, without meaning to, actually discourages us from taking the mystical path by telling us to trust outer authority exclusively—whether in the form of scripture, tradition, or reliance on specific religious experts—instead of encouraging and supporting the value of inner experience. This first-half-of-life approach—trusting the "containers" instead of the "contents"—blocks access to experiential second-half-of-life spirituality. Discouraging or denying people's actual experience of God can create passivity and lead to the conclusion that either there is no God to be experienced or that such experience is not possible. This approach can result in distrusting our soul, and hence the Holy Spirit within us.

Contrast this with Jesus' common advice, "Go in peace. Your faith has made you well" (see Mark 5:34; also Luke 17:19). He said this to people who made no dogmatic affirmations, did not think he was "God," did not pass any moral checklist, and rarely belonged to the "correct group." They were simply people who trustfully affirmed the grace of their hungry experience, and that, in that moment, God cared about it.

Admittedly, personal experiences are easy to misinterpret, and we cannot assume that our experience is always from God. Most of us—by necessity—see everything, mystical and otherwise, through the lens of our own temperament, early conditioning, brain function, role and place in society, education, personal needs, and cultural biases and assumptions. We must develop filters to clear away our own agenda and ego. Hence, we need a solid grounding in theology, psychology, and sociology, along with good and wise counsel. We cannot forget Paul's reminder, which is meant to keep us humble, "For we know only in part, and we prophesy only in part" (1 Cor 13:9).

Because the mystical path is often described in vague, negative, or extreme terms, it appears unappealing or even inaccessible to most. However, if we define "mysticism" to mean "experiential knowledge of spiritual things," as opposed to head knowledge, book knowledge, church knowledge, or other forms of secondhand knowledge, it appears more compelling.

A LIFE OF PRAYER

If there is a God—as all the world's great religious affirm—who is Creator, Sustainer, and Redeemer, then there must be an afterlife, a place of eternal joy, peace, love, and beauty. If such eternity awaits us, then it must be in the presence of God. As Christianity teaches, the life of blessedness and bliss that awaits us need not be postponed until after death, but can be anticipated and even experienced spiritually in the present, here on earth, through worship, contemplation, and service.

Such a life, lived proleptically, has been characterized as a life of prayer. Prayer is central to a believer's life, but it means different things to different people. Like other spiritual practices, prayer is primarily about paying attention to God. There are three major types of Christian prayer: verbal prayer, meditation, and contemplation. Verbal prayer addresses God with words, whether audibly or silently, whereas meditation and contemplation are not about talking to God, but rather, listening for God.

There are five categories of verbal prayer: adoration or praise, thanksgiving, confession, intercession, and petition. The most common forms of prayer, intercession and petition, focus on asking for something for ourselves or for others. Skeptics sometimes dismiss prayer by thinking the obvious, namely, that God already knows about our needs and deeds, but that misses the point. Our human nature is to share, for sharing is part of all intimate relationships. Our relationship with God deepens through disclosure and conversation. Like adoration, ultimately all prayer is a human way to love God.

For many Christians, prayer is a temporary or momentary form of confession, adoration, thanksgiving, and praise. Such prayer often takes place in church or at home, normally at specified times and places such as at mealtimes, during morning or evening devotions, or in church worship. For others, prayer is primarily petitionary, either on behalf of themselves or of others. People adept at petitionary prayer are known as "prayer warriors." This way of prayer characterized my missionary parents. While they combined intercession with praise, their prayer was primarily verbal, something they practiced regularly, devoting an hour daily to scripture reading and an hour to intercessory prayer, their prayers starting with local ministries and concerns and extending to ministries distinct and distant from their own.

For yet other believers, prayer is a way of life, modeled after Paul's admonition in 1 Thessalonians 5:17, "pray without ceasing." This approach to prayer also describes what Paul had in mind in Philippians 2:12, when he exhorts his followers to "work out your own salvation with fear and trembling," for as he discloses in verse 13, "it is God who is working in you, enabling you to will and to work for his good pleasure."

If knowing and enjoying God is the goal and end of life, as Dante envisioned in his *Divine Comedy* and as John Bunyan allegorized in his *Pilgrim's Progress*, can one "know" God in this mortal life? This question directs our discussion in this chapter. For the majority of Christians, a relationship with God occurs in this life by means of "practicing the presence of God," which means, by living ordinary lives "with, through, and for God," thereby affirming the presence of God in all things. This perspective or spiritual way of living is available to each of us now, no matter our vocation or lifestyle. For a select group of Christians, however, a life with God is best lived in solitude or in a cloistered setting, in common with other believers who choose to love and serve God by living distinct, fully religious lives, either through priestly vocations or in monastic communities.

During medieval times, the mystical journey to union with God was understood to comprise three stages—purgation, illumination, and perfection or union. For the anonymous fifth or sixth-century Greek theologian named Denys the Areopagite or simply Pseudo-Dionysius, as Western Christians commonly know him, human beings know God in three ways or through three "theologies." The first is through the created order, because God is said to pour himself in the creation. Called "symbolic" by Denys, this theology or way of spirituality corresponds to seeing God in material things, and by seeing how material things bear God, either through a natural likeness, by their inspired use in scripture, or by their use in the Christian sacraments. Symbolic theology yields a vision of the natural world as full of God and as bearing God to us. Thus viewed, nature possesses a sacramental quality, which conveys grace as well as discloses deeper reality. For Denys, symbolic theology—like a steeple—points beyond itself to the Creator.

Denys's second way of knowing God, called "kataphatic" theology, is a form of spirituality that approaches God through attributes or names we use of God such as Good, Just, Life, Wisdom, Power, and so forth. Kataphatic spirituality focuses on terms we use in worship and on affirmations we make in our praise of God. However, as Denys reminds us, using such language doesn't limit God, but rather is a way of affirming God as the source of all things, as above them, yet as their origin. In his *Divine Names*, Denys reminds us that all affirmations fall short of God, for no human concepts can describe what is unknowable. This leads to Denys's third way of knowing God, called "apophatic" theology, with its realization that "the most divine knowledge of God" is that known through "unknowing."

Both symbolic and kataphatic theology point beyond themselves to a state where symbols and concepts are transcended and where God is known by unknowing. This is apophatic spirituality—the term in Greek means "negation" or "denial"—the theology of rest. The West picked up some of this way of thinking, speaking of the *via negativa*, saying what God is not, such as immutable (not changing), immortal (not mortal), and incomprehensible (above human understanding). In this respect, the fourteenth-century English work known as *The Cloud of Unknowing*, written in the apophatic tradition, is a masterpiece of negative mystical theology.

Denys identified the Trinity as simple, meaning God has no parts and therefore is above intelligibility. Intelligibility of God is a manner of understanding unavailable to human beings because it is likened to looking directly at the brightness of the sun, something human sight is not designed to view. Looking at God is therefore not like trying to see in the darkness, something human beings can achieve to a limited extent, but rather more like looking at a darkness that is so bright—like looking directly at the sun—which darkens our eyesight through brilliance. There is a divine darkness, says Denys, which is like the dazzling brightness of the sun. It is above intelligibility, above light, above understanding, because, like the sun, God is a brightness too visible to see, too dazzling to understand.

The Christian mystic engages in both kataphatic and apophatic ways of knowing God, fluctuating between affirming things about God and then denying those very things, even to the point of negating one's negations about God. Such theology creates space within the mystic, a place of "unknowing," which God's divine energy can fill. In this form of *gnosis*, we negate our mind and even our egoic self so that God can take over. In apophatic spirituality, the seeker gains *gnosis* of God through a-gnosis—knowledge through non-knowledge. This activity of negation is partly something we do—Denys used the analogy of a sculptor cutting away in order to reveal hidden beauty—but more deeply, in the darkness of unknowing, something God does. By submitting to God, the soul experiences an ecstasy of love, surrounded by God's own ecstatic love of his creation. It is reassuring that even when talking of darkness, Denys relied on the Christian definition of God as love.

Ultimately, there are not three "theologies," three ways to experience communion and union with God, potentially in conflict with one another, for all spirituality is rooted in Denys's conviction that God, who creates *ex nihilo* (out of nothing), is a totally different order of reality from creation and thus unknowable. Moreover, since God is unknowable, God is "known in all things, and also apart from all things . . . Therefore, everything may be ascribed to [God] at one and the same time, and yet [God] is none of these things" (*Divine Names* 7.3.872A).

The Spanish language—in which both Teresa of Ávila and John of the Cross spoke, thought, and wrote—uses two different words for knowing someone or something: *saber*, meaning to know intellectually, with one's head, and *conocer*, meaning to know experientially, with one's heart. To those reared in a Christian or religious manner, faith is the means by which people know, honor, love, and obey God. To unbelievers, faith seems like a more rational or epistemological choice, and an odd one at that, so that they cannot understand why God does not manifest himself in a way that would make faith unnecessary. This line of thought is deceptive, for it fails to recognize the inadequacy of misguided belief in the omnicompetence of reason, or is due to a crude or misguided understanding of deity.

For mystics and other believers seeking to know God experientially, faith is not some arbitrary intellectual choice, but rather a necessary means for uniting the human soul to God, as in unitive spirituality, the soul transcends dependence on its lower faculties. The common caricature of faith as belief without evidence misconstrues faith as an ordinary epistemology (way of knowing), when in reality faith is apprehension of God without cognition, imagination, or sensation. As the latter faculties are inadequate to the task of contemplating God to anyone with spiritual maturity, it is evident that faith, which involves the shedding of the lower faculties of knowing and has little or nothing to do with the presence of absence of evidence, is necessary for union with God.

In an earlier writing,[1] I noted that prayer is fundamental to the Christian life, quite possibly the first religious act one performs. There, building upon a perspective developed by Episcopal Bishop John Shelby Spong,[2] I suggested that prayer is more attitudinal than verbal, and more active than passive, by which I meant that true prayer should be more oriented to service in the world than to solitude in one's heart. Later, I came to understand prayer through the eyes of the Russian existentialist writer Fyodor Dostoevsky, who encouraged his readers to view the world with agape love, for by so doing they would come to love all things, and in so doing, comprehend the divine mystery more every day.[3]

1. Vande Kappelle, *Refined by Fire*, 160–61.
2. Spong, *Christianity Must Change*, 143–48.
3. Vande Kappelle, *Deeper Splendor*, 54.

Now, after reading the Spanish mystics Teresa and John, I realize the inadequacy of these views. They represent a good foundation for understanding prayer, but they stop short of the goal, which is intimacy with God. To say one loves God by loving others or by communing with God through nature is commendable, splendid, and even biblical. However, it is not sufficient. Imagine falling in love and eventually marrying your beloved, only to tell him or her that your love will be expressed through loving others or by committing fully to a vocation or lifestyle that will provide wonderfully for his or her financial needs. The beloved would refuse such a relationship, for while caring and responsible, it would not be direct love. To be effective and complete, marriage requires romance, sharing, intimate communication, and time together. Daily phone calls, weekends at home, annual vacations—all are valuable, but they are add-ons and never substitutes for the joys and priorities of togetherness. The same applies to one's love for God, which cannot take place apart from a total commitment of heart, mind, soul, and strength (see Mark 12:28–31). Such commitment may be manifested indirectly through deeds of kindness and compassion for others, through public worship and growth in religious knowledge, or by sustaining nature through ecological activities, but these are always secondary and can never substitute for the joys and priorities of "alone time" with God, where one shares daily and intimately one's hopes and fears, but above all, where one spends time simply abiding with God.

Teresa and John are major figures in the history of Christian mysticism. Teresa is regarded as one of the foremost writers on mental prayer, which stem from her personal experiences, thereby manifesting considerable insight and analytical gifts. Like Teresa, John's studies on the soul and its journey to God are considered the summit of mystical literature. If, as Teresa and John taught, the spiritual life is a path to divine union, then the journey requires purgation, followed by illumination, and then union. In her writings, Teresa describes the ascent of the soul to God in four stages:

- The first, *Devotion of the Heart*, consists of mental prayer and contemplation. As a Catholic, she felt this step required penitence and devout meditation on the passion of Christ.
- The second, *Devotion of Peace*, is where one's human will is surrendered to God. This occurs through God's grace. While worldly distractions still occur, the prevailing state is one of quietude.

- The third, *Devotion of Union*, concerns absorption in God. At this level, reason is surrendered to God, and only memory and imagination are left to wander. This state is characterized by blissful peace and by a consciousness of being enraptured by the love of God.
- The fourth, *Devotion of Ecstasy*, is where bodily consciousness disappears. In this state, regarded as the culmination of mystical experience, temporary trance-like ecstatic states occur, sensory faculties cease to operate, and memory and imagination become absorbed in God.

In *Dark Night* 2.19, John of the Cross describes ten steps on the ladder of mystical love, steps introduced earlier by Bernard of Clairvaux and Thomas Aquinas as representing the development of spiritual growth:

- *First step*: the soul languishes in temporal and emotional aridity, for it desires nothing but God.
- *Second step*: the soul seeks God unceasingly.
- *Third step*: the soul receives the fervor necessary for this pursuit.
- *Fourth step*: the soul suffers for God, but disregards such suffering, since the will is not enkindled with divine love.
- *Fifth step*: the soul impatiently yearns for God, so that it is afflicted by every moment without union with God.
- *Sixth step*: the intellect receives its first touches of divine illumination, though the soul remains driven by divine love infused in the will.
- *Seventh step*: charity and hope increase, leading to unbounded faith and hope. This is the faith that moves mountains, and is received only by divine favor.
- *Eighth step*: here union with God is experienced, but only briefly in most cases. If one could remain this state, it would be heavenly glory.
- *Ninth step*: here the soul is perfected, sweetly ablaze in God. This is the highest state available to mortal flesh.
- *Tenth step*: those who die in the ninth step ascend immediately to the Beatific Vision.

TERESA OF ÁVILA AND JOHN OF THE CROSS: LIVES AND LEGACY

Because the lives of these Carmelite mystics intertwine in obvious ways, and because of their close collaboration in Ávila from 1572 to 1577, it seems best to discuss their lives and spiritual contributions together. Teresa de Cepeda y Ahumada, better known as Teresa of Ávila (1515–1582) or by her Carmelite name Teresa of Jesús, was born of a wealthy family in Ávila, Spain, a family, as is now known, with hidden Jewish roots. Recoiling from the Inquisition of fifteenth-century Spain, Teresa's wealthy Jewish grandfather purchased the title of *hidalgo* to buy his children access to the noble classes. Many *conversos*, as they were known, were actually crypto-Jews who publicly professed adherence to Christian dogma yet privately practiced their ancestral faith.

Teresa, reared as a traditional Catholic, was twelve when she lost her mother, and she was devastated by her death, for she had been unusually close to her mother. Teresa appealed to the Virgin Mary to be her mother now, a prayer that burned in her heart for the rest of her life. Initially, however, she spent some time out of control, for she was a wild child. When she was sixteen, the attractive girl became involved in a forbidden romance, and she was banished to a nunnery. The hope was that a convent education might straighten her out. To her amazement, the high-spirited Teresa found herself developing a taste for the life of prayer and solitude to which she had been banished. After a process of rigorous self-examination, she decided on an ascetic life as a nun. To her dismay, her father did not agree to her plan, for he wanted her to come home and find a decent husband, like other girls.

Teresa's decision to renounce the world coincided with a rapid plunge in physical health. She began suffering from fainting spells and inexplicable fevers. At one point, she even suffered a fit of paralysis from which it took her many months to recover. However, her decision to take vows was finalized after she read a treatise on contemplative prayer by Francisco de Osuna. As she dedicated herself to the cultivation of interior silence and began to grow in spiritual wisdom, her health continued to decline. At one point, she slipped into a coma, but opened her eyes as she was about to be pronounced dead. Her recovery was deemed miraculous, and her devotion to God deepened.

In 1536, at the age of twenty, she entered the local Carmelite convent at a time when the rule of the order was lax. Her zeal for mortification caused her to become ill again, and she spent almost a year in bed, causing huge worry to her community and family. She nearly died, but recovered, attributing her recovery to the miraculous intercession of St. Joseph. At this point, she began to experience bouts of religious ecstasy, which sometimes involved levitation, experiences she perceived as indicative of a unitive state with God. In 1559, she became convinced that Jesus Christ had appeared to her in bodily form, though invisibly. These visions lasted for more than two years. In other visions, an angel drove the fiery point of a golden lance repeatedly through her heart, causing her deep spiritual and bodily pain. As word spread of her extraordinary experiences, the eyes of the Inquisition turned to investigate. However, Teresa's scrutiny of her own states was at least as severe as theirs.

Over time, Teresa found herself increasingly at odds with the superficial spirituality prevalent in her convent. Her wish to take practical steps to protect and strengthen spiritual practice and prayer was supported by the Franciscan priest Pedro de Alcantara, who met her early in 1560 and became her spiritual adviser. She resolved to found a "reformed" Carmelite convent. In 1562 she founded the first convent of "discalced" (that is, unshod) Carmelites under a stricter reformed rule, and the following year she received papal sanction for her principles of absolute poverty and renunciation of ownership of property. For the next five years, she remained in seclusion, mostly engaged in prayer and writing. In 1567, she received approval from her Carmelite superior to establish further houses of the new order, including setting up houses for men who wished to adopt her reforms. She convinced two Carmelite friars, John of the Cross and Anthony of Jesús, to help in this cause.

In 1576, unreformed members of the Carmelite order began to persecute Teresa, her supporters, and her reforms. Her general chapter instructed her to go into "voluntary" retirement at one of her institutions, and she obeyed, choosing St. Joseph's at Toledo. Meanwhile, her friends and associates were subjected to further attacks. Several years later, her appeals to King Philip II of Spain secured relief, and as a result, in 1579 the cases before the Inquisition against her and her associates were dropped. This allowed the reform to resume.

Expanding the order required many visitations and long journeys across nearly all the provinces of Spain, and by the time of her death in 1582, she had added twenty more reformed convents. Meanwhile, John of the Cross promoted the inner life of the movement through his power as a teacher and preacher. When she died in 1582, her final words were,

"O my Lord and my Spouse, the hour that I have longed for has come. It is time to meet one another."

Juan de Yepes, the future John of the Cross (1542–1591), came from a very different background than Teresa's. He was born in the small town of Fontiveros, near Ávila. Though born into a *converso* family like Teresa, he was brought up in poverty by a widowed mother who, in 1551, moved to Medina del Campo to find work. In Medina, John worked at a hospital and received an early education from the Jesuits, a new organization recently founded by the Spaniard Ignatius of Loyola. In 1563, John entered the Carmelite order, and the following year he enrolled at prestigious Salamanca University, where he studied theology and philosophy.

Ordained a priest in 1567, John subsequently thought about joining the strict Carthusian order, which appealed to him because of its strict practice and its emphasis on silent contemplation. During a journey from Salamanca to Medina del Campo, he met Teresa of Ávila, who was in Medina to found the second of her new convents, based on the restoration of the Carmelite order. Teresa urged John to delay entry into the Carthusian order and to join her in her endeavors to reform their order. John agreed, and in 1572 he arrived in Ávila, at Teresa's invitation. John became the spiritual director and confessor of Teresa and the other 130 nuns there, as well as of laypeople in the city. Sometime between 1574 and 1577, while praying in a loft overlooking the sanctuary in the monastery in Ávila, John had a vision of the crucified Christ, which led him to create a drawing of Christ crucified "from above." In 1951, this same drawing inspired the artist Salvador Dali's surrealist painting "Christ of Saint John of the Cross."

The years 1575 to 1577 saw an increase in tensions among Spanish Carmelite friars over the reforms of Teresa and John. On December 2, 1577, a group of Carmelites opposed to reform broke into John's dwelling in Ávila and took him prisoner. He was taken to a Carmelite monastery in Toledo, at that time the order's leading monastery in Castile, and accused him of disobeying the ordinances of the order. Sentenced to imprisonment, he was isolated in a small cell measuring ten feet by six feet, with no change of clothing and only a penitential diet of water, bread, and scraps of fish. While there, he was frequently scourged by the friars. This failed to break his spirit, and it was there that he wrote some of his greatest poetry, on paper passed to him by the friar who guarded his cell. He managed to escape eight months later and after being nursed back to health by Teresa's nuns, he continued with the reforms. There, in the face of opposition from other Carmelites, he decided to request from the pope their formal separation from the rest of the Carmelite order. In 1580, Pope Gregory XIII signed a decree that authorized the separation of the old and the newly reformed "Discalced" Carmelites. Subsequently, John held important offices in the new order. In 1591, in an isolated monastery in Andalusía, he fell ill and died soon thereafter.

The writings of the two mystics, while agreeing in fundamental belief, are as sharply contrasted as their family backgrounds. A poet of the highest order, John was also a consummate theologian, whose prose treatises (*The Ascent of Mount Carmel*, *The Dark Night*, *The Spiritual Canticle*, and *The Living Flame of Love*) are characterized by scholarly objectivity and precision, though, like his poetry, are shot through with a consuming love of God and a deep pastoral concern for his readers. Teresa, on the other hand, lacking formal theological training, always wrote from her own personal experience, though never lacking in charm or verve. Unfortunately, her disregard for clarity often gave rise to serious problems of interpretation, a problem evident in the best known of her works, her *Life*. Her *Way of Perfection*, however, is simpler and more accessible, as is her *The Mansions of the Interior Castle*, the work containing her definitive teaching and the book you are encouraged to read as you study this chapter. Nevertheless, one can never fully understand the works of either Teresa or John in isolation from those of the other.

It is impossible here to do more than suggest the outlines of Teresa's mystical writings. She added little that was new, but with a pungent literary style brought together many aspects of the Catholic mystical tradition. This may be illustrated by her analogy of the soul as a garden to be watered—by drawing water laboriously from the well by hand; getting it more easily and abundantly by a water wheel; having the ground saturated by a stream or brook; or seeing the Lord water it by showers of rain. These processes correspond to four degrees of mental prayer: a difficult beginning as the soul applies itself with effort to meditation; the prayer of Quiet, as the soul is led into peace by the Lord's presence; the Repose of the soul, in which union begins but the soul is still active; and the consummation of Union in which all the powers of the soul are absorbed in God with great joy.

The books *The Mansions of the Interior Castle* and the *Way of Perfection*, taken collectively, are practical blueprints for "seekers" who want to experience prayer as mystical union with God. Whether through fear of the Spanish Inquisition, investigating whether to call her experiences heretical or not, or through her humility ("I am not meant for writing; I have neither the health nor the wits for it"), Teresa may never have composed *The Interior Castle*. However, Teresa was finally convinced to write her book after she received a vision from God. According to Teresa, she had a vision of a most beautiful crystal globe, made in the shape of a castle, and containing seven mansions. In the seventh and innermost mansion was God, the King of Glory. The nearer one got to the center, the stronger was the splendor; outside the palace, everything was foul, dark, and infested with venomous creatures.

The Interior Castle is divided into seven mansions (also called dwelling places), each level describing a step to get closer to God. The first three groups of dwelling places speak of what is achievable through human efforts and the ordinary help of grace. The remaining four groups deal with the passive, or mystical, elements of the spiritual life. The gate of entry is prayer. Prayer is a door that opens up into the mystery of God and at the same time becomes a means of communing with God.

The first mansion begins with a person's state of grace, but the soul is surrounded by sin and only starting to seek God's grace through humility. This mansion corresponds to Teresa's first way of obtaining water, that of drawing the water up from a well by using a bucket, which entails a great deal of human effort. In the second mansion, called the Mansion of the Practice of Prayer, the soul seeks to advance through the castle by daily thoughts of God, humble recognition of God's work in the soul, and daily prayer. These people have experienced some growth from the first mansion, yet they are in a tug-of-war with earthly pleasures. The third mansion, called the Mansion of Exemplary Life, is characterized by divine grace and a love for God that is so great that the soul has an aversion to sin and a desire to do works of charitable service for the ultimate glory of God.

The fourth through seventh mansions comprise mystical or contemplative prayer. In the fourth mansion persons experience greater detachment and interior freedom. They lose cravings for earthly things and desire greater suffering on account of love for God. At this level of prayer, images, concepts, ideas, and visions are unnecessary and nonexistent. The fourth mansion corresponds to Teresa's second way of obtaining water, that is, by cranking a water wheel and having the water run through an aqueduct, which involves less exertion and produces more water. Here the spiritual life does not consist in thinking, but in loving much; here we are commanded to do whatever may excite us most to love. The fifth mansion is that of incipient Union, for in it the soul prepares itself to receive gifts from God. Here people are completely forgetful of self, excessively desire solitude, and painfully desire to die a thousand deaths for God's glory. The fifth mansion corresponds to Teresa's third way of obtaining water, namely, by having water run into the garden by a river or stream. This mansion is possibly the highest level to which people living in the world—that is, participating in families and in secular vocations—can aspire.

If the fifth mansion can be compared to a betrothal, the sixth mansion can be compared to love-sickness. The soul spends increasing amounts of time torn between favors from God and from outside afflictions. The sixth mansion corresponds to Teresa's fourth way of obtaining water, that is, by a gentle but abundant rainfall in which the soul does not have to work at all. In the seventh mansion, the soul achieves clarity in prayer and spiritual marriage with God. In the seventh mansion, transformation is complete, and no higher state can be reached, for here the King dwells. In describing the mansions of our interior castle, Teresa depended on the biblical Song of Songs, of which the Cistercian monk Bernard of Clairvaux had made such extensive use in the twelfth century.

The Interior Castle, like many of Teresa's other books, was written in a simplistic way, providing guidance on prayer for the sisters in her order. Despite having been written during a time of hardship and resistance, it was Teresa's answer to the Protestant Reformation, for it was an attempt to reform her church by reforming religious people within it. While providing hope and encouragement to pious Catholics in the sixteenth century, its purpose is relevant to Protestants as well as Catholics, for values such as self-knowledge and humility and desires like seeking intimacy with Christ are timeless.

Fundamental to the outlook of both mystics is their understanding that the human being is essentially a unity, a single entity in which body and soul are inextricably interdependent. Surprisingly, their writings provide less specific guidance on methods of prayer than on the Christian way of life in general. They show us a wide variety of approaches to prayer, and warn us against those that are bound to prove sterile, but our authors firmly decline to formulate any structured methods. The one incontrovertible rule is this: "Never neglect to pray." Ultimately, Christians are to pray as they can, but, as Teresa notes, "the important thing is not to think much but to love much" (*Interior Castle* 4.1.7).

DARK NIGHT OF THE SOUL

"Dark Night" is a poem written by John of the Cross. The poem, eight stanzas of five lines each, narrates the journey of the soul to mystical union with God. The time and place of the poem's composition are not certain, though it is possible that the poem was written while John was imprisoned in Toledo. While the author did not give the poem a title, he wrote two book-length commentaries on it: *Ascent of Mount Carmel* and *Dark Night*. For our study, try locating a copy of the poem, which is recommended reading for this chapter, rather than John's extended commentary in *Ascent* and *Dark Night*.[4]

The "dark night of the soul" does not refer to the difficulties of life in general, although the phrase has been taken to refer to such trials. Rather, the "nights" that the soul experiences are the two necessary purgations on the path to divine union: the first purgation is of the sensory or sensitive part of the soul, the second of the spiritual part. Such purgations comprise the first of the three stages of the mystical journey, followed by those of illumination and then union.

There are several steps in this "night," which are related in successive stanzas of the poem. The thesis of the poem is the joyful experience of being guided to God, in which the only light in this dark night is that which burns in the soul, which John describes as a guide more certain than the midday sun. The *Ascent of Mount Carmel* is divided into three books that reflect the two phases of the dark night. *Dark Night* further describes the ten steps on the ladder of mystical love described earlier. John's treatises, both left incomplete, are commentaries on the poem, explaining its meaning line by line. In the latter book, John's premise is that there are two "dark nights" or times of spiritual bleakness that a person must travel through in order to come to a mature and perfect union with God. The first, the dark night of the senses, is when God works in the beginner's soul to purge the desire for sensual pleasures and helps the soul to recognize and enjoy spiritual pleasures. During such "nights," the soul reaps additional benefits such as humility, delight in peace, and a deeper reverence for God. The first dark night, when it achieves full purgation of sense, brings the soul from the life of sense into that of the spirit, that is, from meditation to contemplation. Thus, the soul is not deprived of the things of God, though at first it may appear as such, but rather the things

---

4. John of the Cross's poem "Dark Night" appears in its entirety in Kavanaugh, *John of the Cross*, 55–57.

of God are apprehended more purely by simple contemplation. At this point, the novice might redouble personal efforts to experience a pleasurable meditation, thereby running the risk of becoming discouraged altogether. John encourages those in the dark night to take heart, for God never abandons those who truly seek him with a pure heart, nor will God fail to provide them the means to continue on this path.

The second, the dark night of the spirit, is when God works to bring the human spirit into perfect union and love with God. According to John, it is essential for the soul to have passed successfully through the first dark night before it enters the second dark night. However, this second night does not immediately follow the completion of the first night, but a long period of time elapses, during which the soul practices the state achieved. The second dark night may be described as an ascent to God in the ten steps of the ladder of love. This dark night is an inflowing of God into the soul, which purges it from its ignorance and imperfection, and which is called infused contemplation, for during this time God secretly teaches the soul and instructs it in perfection of love without the soul doing anything, or understanding what is taking place. It is during these times of spiritual darkness that God refines and perfects a human's soul, making it more conformable to God's nature.

In modern teaching on spirituality, the term "dark night" is often misused to refer to any sort of spiritual aridity, crisis of faith, or spiritual backsliding, but these are not what John had in mind. As we have seen throughout, John's the dark nights presume a strong, explicit faith. The darkness comes not from theological doubt, but rather from the deprivation of pleasant consolations, first sensual, then spiritual. While it might seem strange to refer to such supreme blessing as darkness, John explains the paradox with the analogy of how we are blinded by bright light. Similarly, the human soul is not capable of receiving the brightness of divine wisdom. It is only its impurity that causes it to see the infusion of God as an affliction. As a good instructor knows, teaching something above the understanding of a student can actually cause greater confusion at first rather than enlightenment. Thus, the belief that one has been cast away by God in moments of darkness need not be attributable to disbelief, but rather to an acute awareness of one's impurity in the presence of divine imperfection. In fact, John uses extremely strong language to describe the purgation of the spirit, seeing it as nothing less than the death of the temporary self in order that it might be resurrected in union with God.

The root of the matter, as John explains, is detachment from the things of this world, for only through voluntary privation of those things on which we rely for our comfort, our self-esteem, and our personal security, can we have a relationship with God. In this lies the interpretation of the much-misunderstood phrase "the dark night" in his writings. In truth, one is ultimately secure only in the darkness, as John so confidently affirms. The words "night" and "darkness" in his works thus come to include "privation" in all its forms, privation not only of satisfactions that are sinful by nature, but of any satisfactions other than that perfect loving relationship with God that both Teresa and John speaks of as union with God. Hence, John's doctrine of "nada, nada, nada" (nothing, nothing, nothing) is a doctrine neither of *nirvana* nor of extinction of human personality. On the contrary, embedded with his wise and sympathetic guidance for safe passage through the nights of privation, his doctrine has in view the one totally positive human aim of all, true self-fulfillment in accordance with the all-loving purpose of the Creator.

Properly speaking, the "dark night of the soul" in John of the Cross is a generic term denoting the whole discipline of privation that starts from the very beginning of the spiritual life, when the Christian first becomes seriously committed, and continues throughout his or her life. It has two distinguishable aspects: the active night of voluntary self-discipline, and the passive night into which God leads the believer, whether directly or through external circumstances. Each of these aspects has two phases, one that affects our senses (including our imagination), and a second that affects our spirit, with its three "faculties" of understanding, memory, and will. What must be stressed is that the passive contemplation characteristic of this "night" has little in common with the kinds of prayer most commonly spoken of as "contemplation," be they the techniques of Yoga, Zen, Transcendental Meditation, or even the different type of contemplation envisaged in the *Spiritual Exercises* of Ignatius Loyola. The distinction is crucial, for entry into the passive night of the senses necessitates a radical change in the Christian's mode of prayer. As Teresa and John both recognized, the stages of passive contemplation are both bewildering and distressing to those to whom God grants this prayer. While God leads seekers to Godself by an infinite variety of paths, the assistance of a qualified spiritual director or "soul friend" is often indispensable. As Teresa stated, practitioners cannot safely dispense with human assistance in this vitally important matter, and, given the choice, we should seek the guidance of a learned director. Significantly, it was the academic theologian,

John of the Cross, who reminds us that no one is saved by intellectual prowess, for, in the final analysis, the subject of our final examination will be love.

QUESTIONS FOR DISCUSSION AND REFLECTION

In addition to the questions listed at the end of the preface, answer the following questions, writing your answers in a journal. If you are in a group study, be prepared to share your answers with those in the group.

1. After reading this chapter, how would you define mysticism? In your estimation, what qualities—psychological, emotional, and spiritual—characterize people with a mystical spirituality?
2. After reading this chapter, what qualities characterize people living according to second half of life spiritual principles from those living according to first half of life spiritual principles?
3. After reading this chapter, what did you learn about prayer and its role in Christian spirituality?
4. After reading this chapter, how would you answer the question, "Can we 'know' God in this mortal life?"
5. Explain and assess Denys the Areopagite's three ways of knowing God.
6. After reading this chapter, explain what Denys meant when he claimed that "the most divine knowledge of God is through unknowing."
7. Explain the difference between apophatic and kataphatic spirituality. Do you prefer apophatic or kataphatic approaches to worship? Explain your answer.
8. In your own words, explain and assess the different understanding of prayer espoused by Spong, Dostoevsky, and the Spanish mystics Teresa and John.
9. In your estimation, did the formative experiences of Teresa and John contribute to their mystical spirituality, or did they choose this form of spirituality for temperamental reasons? Explain your answer.

10. After reading this chapter, what do you consider to be Teresa's greatest contribution to spirituality?

11. After reading this chapter, what do you consider to be John's greatest contribution to spirituality?

12. Explain and assess the meaning of John of the Cross's experience and explanation of "the dark night." Have you had experiences similar to John's "dark night of the soul"? If so, how would you describe them?

Chapter 7

Blaise Pascal's *Pensées* and George Fox's *Journal*

As we have seen thus far in our study, the canon of classic Christian literature includes works of theological, historical, and spiritual significance. Above all, this material provides guidance for the Christian life and its spiritual journey. Central to such literature is a body of spiritual writings known as devotional literature, which includes books of prayers, diaries, letters, and journals. The list of such works is long, beginning with the biblical psalms, the deeply personal prophetic writings, poetic and proverbial material known as wisdom literature, and most of the books in the New Testament.

Building on the biblical paradigm, later Christians produced classic devotional literature written by mystics such as the *Confessions* of Augustine, the *Revelations of Divine Love* by Julian of Norwich, and *The Imitation of Christ* by Thomas à Kempis, as well as treatises by Meister Eckhart, anonymous works such as *The Cloud of Unknowing* and the *Theologia Germanica*, and the writings of the Spanish mystics Teresa of Ávila and John of the Cross.

During the post-Reformation and modern periods, the list of personal and devotional writings includes Pascal's *Pensées*, Brother Lawrence's *The Practice of the Presence of God*, the journals of George Fox, Charles Wesley, John Woolman, and David Brainerd, and books by Søren Kierkegaard, Hudson Taylor, Henry Drummond, John Henry Newman, Frank Laubach, Dietrich Bonhoeffer, A. W. Tozer, Dag Hammarskjöld, Thomas Merton, Annie Dillard, Kathleen Norris, and Richard Rohr. Of the many daily devotional readings, among the best are L. B. Cowan's

Streams in the Desert and Oswald Chambers's *My Utmost for His Highest*, and booklets such as *The Upper Room* and *Our Daily Bread*. This chapter continues our study of mystical spirituality by examining the contributions of two original spiritual thinkers, the "intellectual" mysticism of the Roman Catholic scientist Blaise Pascal and the "social mysticism" of early Protestant sectarian mystic George Fox.

BLAISE PASCAL: LIFE AND WORK

To his contemporaries, Blaise Pascal (1623–1662) was known as an eminent mathematician and scientist, and for his work on probability theory, his experiments with the vacuum and atmospheric pressure, and the invention of a calculating machine that antedated the invention of the calculator in the twentieth century. Like his contemporary René Descartes, Pascal was also a philosopher as well as a pioneer in the natural and applied sciences. His two most famous works, the *Lettres Provinciales* (Provincial Letters) and the *Pensées* (Reflections), the latter left unfinished, provided him with the reputation of a brilliant and witty prose writer.

A lifelong resident of France, Pascal was three years old when his mother died, and thereafter he was raised and educated by his father. He had two sisters, Jacqueline and Gilberte. In the winter of 1646, Pascal's aged father fell and broke his hip, which, given the state of medicine in the seventeenth century, could have proved fatal. The city of Rouen was home then not only to the Pascal family but also to two of the finest doctors in France, Deslandes and de la Bouteillerie, and the elder Pascal would not allow anyone other than these doctors attend him. As it happened, both doctors were followers of Jean Guillebert, proponent of a splinter group from Roman Catholicism known as Jansenism, a controversial sect making surprising inroads into the French Catholic community at that time. A rigorous and extreme form of Augustinianism, Jansenism emphasized original sin, human depravity, the necessity of divine grace, and predestination. Jansenism was opposed by many within the Catholic hierarchy, especially the Jesuits, who saw it as a disguised form of sectarian Protestantism.

Blaise became friends with his father's doctors, and after their successful treatment of his father, borrowed from them works by Jansenist authors. In this period, Pascal experienced a sort of "first conversion" and began to write on theological subjects in the course of the following year. However, he fell away from this initial religious engagement and experienced a few years of what some biographers have called his "worldly period." His father died in 1651 and left his inheritance to Blaise and his sister Jacqueline, for whom Blaise acted as conservator. Shortly thereafter, Jacqueline announced that she wished to join the Jansenist convent of Port-Royal.

Suddenly there was war in the Pascal household. Blaise pleaded with Jacqueline not to leave, but she was adamant. By the end of October 1651, a truce was reached between brother and sister. In return for a healthy annual stipend, Jacqueline signed over her part of the inheritance to her brother. Gilberte had already been given her inheritance in the form of a dowry. In January 1653, Jacqueline left for Port-Royal, and in June, Blaise formally signed over the whole of his sister's inheritance to Port-Royal. With two-thirds of his father's estate now gone, the twenty-nine-year-old Pascal became consigned to genteel poverty.

For a while, Pascal pursued the life of a bachelor. During visits to his sister at Port-Royal in 1654, he displayed contempt for affairs of the world but was not drawn to God. However, on the night of November 23, 1654, Pascal had an intense religious experience and immediately wrote a brief note to himself that began: "Fire! God of Abraham, God of Isaac, God of Jacob, not of the philosophers and the scholars. Certainty, certainty, feeling, joy, peace. God of Jesus Christ . . . May I never be separated from Him." He seems to have carefully sewn this document into his coat and always transferred it when he changed clothes. At the time of his death, a servant noticed a curious bulge in the great scientist's jacket. Opening the lining, he found the folded parchment written in Pascal's hand. These words are now known as the *Memorial*. His belief and religious commitment revitalized, Pascal visited the older of two convents at Port-Royal for a two-week retreat in January 1655, and for the next four years, he regularly traveled between Port-Royal and Paris. It was at this point immediately after his conversion when he began writing his first major literary work on religion, the *Provincial Letters*. Pascal wrote this series of eighteen letters under the pseudonym Louis de Montalte in defense of the Jansenist views of Antoine Arnauld, a friend of Pascal from Port-Royal who in 1656 was condemned by the theological faculty at the Sorbonne in Paris for views that were claimed to be heretical.

Beginning an ascetic lifestyle, the phase of life at this time described by T. S. Eliot as "a man of the world among ascetics, and an ascetic among men of the world," Pascal's lifestyle derived from his belief that it was natural and necessary for a person to suffer. In 1659, Pascal fell seriously ill. During his last years, he frequently rejected the services of his doctors, viewing sickness to be the nature state of the Christian. Throughout his life, he was in frail health, and he died quite young, not yet forty years of age.

PENSÉES: PASCAL'S WAGER

The *Pensées*, Pascal's most influential theological work, is not only a philosophical and theological masterpiece, but a landmark in French prose. Hailed by Will Durant as "the most eloquent book in French prose" and praised by others as the finest pages in the French language, *Pensées* is the name given posthumously to fragments that Pascal had been preparing as an apology for Christianity. Unfortunately, they were left unfinished, mainly in two bundles, one classified and the other unclassified. The envisioned work is often referred to as the *Apology for the Christian Religion*, although Pascal never used that title. Although the *Pensées* appear to consist of ideas and jottings, it is believed that prior to his death Pascal had planned the order of the book. He had begun the task of cutting and pasting his notes into a coherent form, but death prevented him from his goal. His task incomplete, subsequent editors have proposed their own order.

In the *Pensées*, Pascal gave close attention to what philosophers and theologians call the faith-reason problem. This was one of the significant problems of his time, made more acute and urgent by the accelerated tempo of scientific discovery as well as by the emergence of new options in religion. Pascal believed that in science, methods of exact observation and controlled experimentation should be the only court of appeal. In other words, scientific questions must have scientific answers, not metaphysical or theological ones. By the same token, in dealing with questions of Christian truth, one has every right to appeal to established tradition and the testimony of its authoritative witnesses. The point is that Pascal would not accept either dogmatism in science or rationalism in religion. The two realms of truth must be kept separate. He wished to rid faith of superstition as well as purge science of pseudo-theological assumptions. What he envisioned is a commonsense, clear-cut division of labor that freed each sphere from encroachment or interference by the other.

Although Pascal did not deal with all the issues in the faith-reason problem, he professed to be fully orthodox with reference to his theology. Hence, when he speaks in the *Pensées* of his conversion, it is a from a theological perspective, and thus a conversion to "the God of Abraham, Isaac, and Jacob [and] not [to] the God of the philosophers and the *savants*."

The central point of the *Pensées* is the person of Jesus, the Redeemer who heals humanity's corrupt nature. Building on Augustinian and Jansenist theology, Pascal simply assumes a deep gulf between humanity's corrupt nature and the redeeming power of Christ. Likewise, he also assumes Augustine's doctrines of election and predestination, arguing that only the elect can come to God: "You would not seek me if you did not possess me." Using traditional biblical and theological scholarship, he further argues in favor of the unique validity of Christianity—particularly in Catholic dogma and practice—over all other religions.

In his *Pensées*, Pascal mentions three qualities of the Christian religion that make it superior to all other religions. First, Christianity is defensible, which he demonstrates throughout his "apology." Next, Christianity is venerable and hence attractive, desirable, and worthy of respect. Lastlly, Christianity is true, because it is both appealing and satisfying to the mind. In all respects, Christianity addresses the plight of all humans, who desire the good, the true, and the stable but are unable on their own to attain them, for humanity's natural state is one of uncertainty. The frustrating gap in our human minds and lives between what is and what ought to be (and, it seems, what can never be), is, for Pascal, a consequence of original sin. His remedy lies solely in conversion, whereby humans return to their original relationship with God, a path accessibly only through Jesus Christ. The preparation required for this return to God calls for a drastic reorientation of our mind and will, which occurs only by God's initiative and action. Using his calculus of probabilities, Pascal believes he can demonstrate that a disposition to believe is not contrary to reason. To accomplish this, he introduced his famous wager.

In his writings, Pascal divided people into three categories of faith, (1) those who serve God, having found him; (2) those who are busy seeking God, yet have not found him; and (3) those who live without either seeking or finding God. The first, Pascal noted, are reasonable and happy; the last are foolish and unhappy, and those in between are unhappy but reasonable.

The *Pensées*, constructed as a dialogue with skeptical unbelievers, is an argument Pascal intended for the cultivated agnostic of his day, primarily skeptics of his second category. One of Pascal's main strategies was to use contradictory philosophies in order to bring unbelievers to such despair and confusion that they would embrace God. In his dialogue, Pascal argues that a rational person should live as though God exists, and seek to believe in God. If God does not exist, such a person will have only a finite loss (for example, giving up certain luxuries and pleasures), whereas if God does exist, a person stands to receive infinite gains (as represented by eternity in heaven) and avoid infinite loss (as represented by eternity in hell). Hence, Pascal introduced the first step toward belief in God in terms of a wager, a sort of heads or tails approach; if you choose God and win, you gain everything, and if you lose you lose nothing but a finite lifestyle.[1]

Brushing aside the rational, scholastic proofs for God's existence, Pascal acknowledges that reason alone can neither prove nor disprove the existence of God. Rather, we should follow our heart, for "the heart has reasons that reason cannot know." According to this conception, faith and reason belong to different orders, but they need not be opposed to one another. In his view, Christian faith is not a leap *within* the order of the intellect—a leap that violates the essence of that order—but a leap *from* the order of the intellect to the order of the heart. Using the concept of mathematical infinity (which we intuit apart from sight or reason), we are able to accept the possibility of a hidden God. Using scientific and mathematical reasoning, Pascal transferred a mathematical argument into a metaphysical one.

For Pascal, there are three things to consider: what is to be risked, what may be won, and what the odds are. Each of us has one life to wager, infinite or eternal life to gain, and the odds are even. The wager uses the following logic:

- God is, or God is not. Reason cannot decide between the two alternatives
- A game of probability is played, where heads or tails will turn up
- Players must wager

---

1. Readers are encouraged to read the segment of Pascal's *Pensées* entitled "Of the Necessity of the Wager," particularly §233, available online through Project Gutenburg.

- In waging that God is, we must estimate the chances, weighing the gain and the loss; if we gain, we gain all; if we lose, we lose nothing

- Let us wager, then, without hesitation, that God exists. There is here an infinity of an infinitely happy life to gain, a chance of gain against a finite number of chances of loss, and what you stake is finite. So there are finite risks at stake to lose, but infinite ones to gain

- Nevertheless, some cannot believe; these should endeavor to convince themselves.

Pascal then cites a number of distinct areas of uncertainty in human life on which we gamble daily, affirming belief in life in all cases. Such areas include uncertainty in human purpose; in reason; in science; in religion; and even in skepticism (for it is not certain that everything is uncertain). Indeed, uncertainty exists in all things. Nature offers nothing that is not subject to doubt and insecurity. For Pascal, humans are finite beings trapped within an incomprehensible infinity, briefly thrust into being from non-being, with no explanation of why, what, or how.

Given that reason alone cannot determine whether God exists, Pascal concludes that this question functions as a coin toss. However, even if we do not know the outcome of this coin toss, we must base our actions on some expectation about the consequence. We must decide whether to live as though God exists or as though God does not exist, even though we may be mistaken in either case. In Pascal's assessment, participation in this wager is not optional. Merely by existing in a state of uncertainty, humans are forced to choose between the available courses of action for practical purposes.

While many traditional Christians find Pascal's wager persuasive, many others, believers and nonbelievers alike, do not. Criticism of Pascal's wager began in his own day, and came from atheists, who questioned the "benefits" of a deity whose "realm" is beyond reason, taking issue with the wager's deistic and agnostic language. The wager is commonly criticized with counterarguments such as (1) the failure to prove the existence of God; (2) the argument from inconsistent revelations; and (3) the argument from inauthentic belief. For example, the mathematician Pierre Simon de Laplace ridiculed the use of probability in theology, arguing that the hope of profit—equal to the product of the value of the testimonies (infinitely small) and the value of the happiness they promise (which is significant but finite)—must necessarily be infinitely small.

1. *The failure to prove the existence of God.* Voltaire, a prominent French writer of the Enlightenment a generation after Pascal, incorrectly rejected the wager in failing to prove the existence of God. Pascal, however, had never advanced the wager as a proof of God's existence but rather as a pragmatic decision that is "impossible to avoid." Nevertheless, Voltaire's criticism was accurate on several counts. Pascal had argued that abstaining from making a wager is not an option, and here Pascal was wrong, for many people, particularly nowadays, placing their faith in science or in their own odds to survive, live as if there is no God, giving God's existence little or no thought. In this regard, Voltaire's critique concerned not so much the nature of the Pacalian wager as proof of God's existence, but rather the fact that Pascal, as a Jansenist, believed that only a small, and already predestined, portion of humanity would eventually be saved by God. Here, too, Voltaire was right. Pascal actually agreed with this, for although he argued as an Augustinian that all people must choose to believe, he acknowledged that some are predestined not to believe.

As Pascal scholars note, Pascal was not always consistent, for his logic, like that of all thinkers, was based on unprovable hypotheses and assumptions that were themselves often contradictory or, at best, partial and incomplete. On crucial points, humans often disagree with one another, for as fallible creatures, our logic and reason are flawed and not always consistent. For this reason, the pages of the *Pensées* are filled with antitheses and paradoxes that testify to a restless, analogical technique of using and defining terms. This disconcerts many readers, an effect, no doubt, that Pascal intended.

2. *The argument from inconsistent revelations.* Some Pascal scholars disagree with Pascal's wager on the basis of "inconsistent revelations," by which they mean that Pascal's wager can lead, not to the choice of the Trinitarian Christian God, but rather to a high probability of belief in some other god (for example, Muslims and Jews would believe in Allah or in Yahweh, but certainly not in worshiping Jesus as God), possibly even reverting to the polytheistic deities of paganism.

Another version of this objection argues that for every religion that promulgates commandments based on revelation, there exists another religion that has rules of the opposite kind, meaning they cancel each other out. Others contend that because there are an infinite number of mutually exclusive religions, the probability of any one of them being true is zero; therefore, the expected value of following any particular religion is zero. To his credit, Pascal considers some objections in the notes compiled into the *Pensées*, only to dismiss them as obviously wrong and disingenuous. In his writings, Pascal notes that unbelievers who rest content with the many-religions objection are left with a fatal neutrality. If they truly wished to know the truth, they would be persuaded to examine "in detail" whether Christianity is like any other religion, something their skepticism prevents them from doing. If the subject were merely philosophical in nature, their objection might be valid, but not in religion, "where everything is at stake."

3. *The argument from inauthentic belief.* Some critics, such as Richard Dawkins, contest Pascal's wager by maintaining that accepting such a wager suggests that those who cannot believe must feign belief in order to gain eternal reward. Dawkins argues that this would be dishonest and immoral, and that, in addition, it would be absurd to think that God, being just and omniscient, would not see through this deceptive strategy on the part of the "believer," thereby nullifying the benefits of the wager. Pascal, however, far from suggesting that God can be deceived by outward show, states that God does not regard such deception at all, for "God looks only at what is inward." A traditional theist, Pascal notes that Christian salvation requires "faith," not simply in the sense of belief, but also of trust and obedience. In supporting the Jansenist school of thought, Pascal favored an understanding of salvation that was close to Protestantism in emphasizing faith over works. For Pascal, "saving" faith in God requires more than logical assent, so accepting the wager could only be a first step.

In his study of Pascal, Hugh Davidson draws on multiple passages and fragments of the *Pensées* to propose that Pascal had a series of states in mind in his wager regarding conversion from atheism to theism: (1) the original disposition or point of departure of the unbeliever; (2) the nature of doubt itself; (3) the nature of the search for truth; (4) the consideration of proposed solutions; (5) the nature of decision-making; (6) the acquisition of a moral habit or disposition; (7) the state of grace that prompts religious belief; and (8) the certainty that results from the state of grace.[2] In the *Pensées*, Pascal associates truth with the heart rather than with the head, for it is by intuition and not by reason that God can be known. Such knowledge of God is based on what Pascal called the "order of charity" or the "order of the heart."

---

2. Davidson, *Blaise Pascal*, 90.

In our study of the *Pensées*, we have examined only one aspect of this extraordinary work. From these fragments, we should not think we can develop a theology that is complete. Perhaps that is a good thing, for the *Pensées* and, more particularly, the apologetic texts embedded in them, are not like the parts of a jigsaw puzzle where a finished picture is cut arbitrarily into many pieces that with patience must be reassembled. Rather, the pieces are more like the *tesserae* of a mosaic, each of which maintains its identity, its contours, and its rough edges as it is joined to the whole.

In my estimation, Pascal's worldview, like that of postmodern thinkers, is such that only fragments can do justice to it. Like an impressionist artist, what Pascal left us is a blurred image, a book of sketches that have all the fascination and ambiguity of unfinished brushwork. The tentative order of the *Pensées*, though important, count perhaps far less than the impressionistic unity that shines through their multiplicity. As Pascal once wrote, "You must have an idea in the back of your mind and judge everything by that." For Pascal, that one idea can only be the image of God that Jesus exhibited and that the Bible calls "love," infinite love. This sounds so simple, and so it is; truth can be that simple and yet that profound. Thankfully, Pascal understood the divine and the human conditions so deeply yet so clearly that Christians in our own time can still gain perspective from him for their own spiritual pilgrimage.

GEORGE FOX AND QUAKER SPIRITUALITY

Modernity arose, in part, from the Protestant Reformation, which dissolved the unity of medieval Catholicism and resulted in competing churches or denominations. This movement fostered secularism, especially as national churches became less acceptable. As sectarian groups developed, they ran into opposition from the national church in their region, often suffering persecution as a result. In turn, groups like the Baptists and Quakers became critical of the established churches, and for good reason, since the ruling churches often used the existing governments to suppress their rivals. So modernity tended to push against national or established churches, against conformity with authorities external to the individual, favoring secularized government, one with decreasing responsibility for the religious welfare of its people.

As Western society and politics became more secularized and fragmented, modernity provided an environment more suitable to low rather than high churches, favoring theologies of the Spirit and experience over theologies of word and sacrament. High churches were more hierarchical and institutionalized, affirming distinctions between laity and clergy, while enforcing doctrinal orthodoxy. Low churches, like Baptists and Quakers, moved in the opposite direction, toward anticlericalism, though there was always the temptation toward holiness, purity, and withdrawal from social influences. In many ways, these groups represented the future of modernity, arguing for a form of individualism known as immediacy, a phenomenon called "inner light" by Quakers and "soul competency" by Baptists, thereby opposing institutional mediation between the individual soul and God.

Most Protestants were not that radical, but as modernity unfolded, they too tended to oppose institutional mediation. Thus, modernity favored a turn toward experience, toward the inner self, a view that says, "I can find God on my own, with little or no help from clergy or the church." This turn away from sacraments toward the Holy Spirit characterizes many Protestants, certainly those opting for the "gathered church" and away from highly ritualistic forms of worship.

The seemingly endless debate on dogma, and the intolerance of nonconformist Christians that arose in England and on the Continent in the sixteenth and seventeenth centuries, led many Christians to seek refuge in inner piety. One such figure was George Fox (1624–1691), born of humble origin in a small English village. There is no record of any formal schooling, but he had a serious, religious disposition from childhood. As he grew up, relatives thought he would enter the priesthood, but instead he became apprenticed to a local shoemaker and grazier. This suited Fox's contemplative temperament, and he became well known for his diligence among the wool traders who had dealings with his master. An obsession of his was the pursuit of "simplicity" in life—humility and the abandonment of luxury. The short time he spent as a shepherd was important to the formation of this view.

At the age of nineteen, he became acquainted with people who were "professors" (that is, followers of the standard Church of England), but he soon became disgusted by the licentiousness around him, particularly the excessive consumption of alcohol. At this point he began a life of wandering, seeking divine illumination. However, the English Civil War had begun, and troops were stationed in many towns through which he passed. At times he sought the company of clergy, but found little comfort from them as they seemed unable to help with the matters troubling him. On one occasion, a clergyman advised him to take tobacco and singing, but this left him highly dissatisfied. Fox became fascinated by the Bible, which he studied assiduously. He hope to find among the "English Dissenters" a spiritual understanding absent from the established church, but he fell out with one group, for example, because he maintained that women had souls. He began referring to the churches of his day as "steeple-houses," and he was seldom welcomed there. Instead, he spoke to small groups and then, as they grew, to larger assemblies of those who came to hear him.

His study of the Christian scriptures and his attendance of varied religious meetings led to the conviction that all religious sects were in error, and that public worship was an abomination. Church buildings, clergy, hymns, sermons, sacraments, creeds, liturgies—all seemed to him hindrances to life in the Spirit. Against all of these, Fox placed the "inner light," a pathway common to all human beings, no matter their race, faith, or creed. True Christianity is not a matter of conforming to a set of doctrines or performing rituals led by a professional priest. Rather true believers are illumined by an inner light.

In religious gatherings across England, Fox declared he had been ordered by the Spirit to announce his spiritual version of Christianity. For disturbing the proceedings, he was repeatedly beaten, thrown out of meetings, and cast into jail. His followers grew rapidly, calling themselves "Friends," but others begin calling them Quakers, for their religious enthusiasm. Espousing their belief in equality, they spoke out against war, violence, slavery, paying tithes, and swearing by oath. Conflict with civil authority was inevitable. Fox was imprisoned countless times on charges such as blasphemy, civil disobedience, traveling without a pass, participating in unauthorized worship, refusing to take hats off in court or bow to those who considered themselves socially superior, refusing to take up arms, and refusal to swear oaths. The latter meant that Quakers could be prosecuted under laws compelling subjects to pledge allegiance; it also made testifying in court problematic. In prison Fox continued writing and preaching, feeling that imprisonment brought him into contact with people who needed his help. In his *Journal* he indicates that he spoke boldly to people such as magistrates, citing scripture to prove his points.

The 1650s, when the Friends were at their most confrontational, was one of the most creative periods of their history. Under the

Commonwealth, Fox had hoped that the movement would become the major church in England. Disagreements, persecution, and increasing social turmoil, however, left Fox deeply troubled. In 1659, he sent Parliament his most politically radical pamphlet, but the year was so chaotic that his points were never considered.

The period from 1649 to 1660, known officially as "The Protectorate" or "The Commonwealth" but unofficially as the Interregnum (meaning gap between kings), left England without a monarch. After years of civil war,[3] Cromwell disbanded the Rump Parliament and took over the country. He chose to be "Lord Protector" rather than king, because he did not think the country needed another king. Cromwell was a Puritan, and during the Interregnum, he imposed a very strict form of Christianity upon the country. He ruled the country until his death in 1658, when he was succeeded by his son, Richard. However, after seven months, Richard was removed from office, and in 1659, the British army re-installed the Rump Parliament, which was soon forcibly disbanded. However, the new Long Parliament was soon elected, and it decided to restore the monarchy with Charles II as the king. This event is known as the English Restoration. However, kings would never be as powerful as they had been before the Civil War.

During the Commonwealth, Parliament grew suspicious of monarchist plots and fearful that groups traveling with Fox aimed to overthrow the government; by this time, his meetings were regularly attracting crowds of over a thousand. On several occasions, he was brought before Oliver Cromwell, with whom he established a frank and cordial relationship. On one occasion, Cromwell invited Fox to visit him again in his house, "for if thou and I were but an hour of a day together, we should be nearer one to the other." This episode, recounted in Fox's *Journal*, was later recalled as an example of "speaking truth to power," a preaching technique by which subsequent Quakers hoped to influence the powerful.

With the restoration of the monarchy, Fox's dream of establishing the Friends as the dominant religion seemed at an end. He was again accused of conspiracy, this time against Charles II, and of fanaticism—a charge Fox resented. During his imprisonment, Fox wrote to the king offering advice on governance: Charles should refrain from war and

---

3. From 1639 to 1653, there was fighting in England, Scotland, and Ireland, three separate countries that were ruled by the same king. In England, the civil war lasted from 1641 to 1651. Some historians view the English Civil War as one continuous war, while others view it as three separate wars.

domestic religious persecution, and should discourage oath-taking and other such requirements. At least on one point, Charles listened to Fox, for the seven hundred Quakers who had been imprisoned under Richard Cromwell were released.

In 1669, Fox married Margaret Fell, a woman of high social position and one of his early converts. She was ten years his senior and had eight children by her first husband, Thomas Fell, a judge and an influential legal figure in England. Margaret was very active in the movement, and had campaigned for equality and the acceptance of women as preachers. As there were no priests at Quaker weddings to perform the ceremony, the union had taken the form of a civil marriage approved by witnesses at a meeting. Ten days after the marriage, Margaret returned to her home at Swarthmoor Hall to continue her work there, while George went back to London. Their shared religious work was at the heart of their life together, and they later collaborated on much of the administration the Society required.

By 1671, Fox resolved to visit the Caribbean and North America, where he remained for two years, preaching, teaching, and gaining many converts. In 1677 he visited Friends in the Netherlands and in Germany, and on returning to England, he continued his activities, despite worsening health, writing to leaders in Poland, Denmark, Germany and elsewhere about his beliefs and their treatment of Quakers. In his final years, under King James II, his presentations to Parliament resulted in the pardon of religious dissenters jailed for failure to attend the established church, leading to the release of about fifteen hundred Friends. Though the Quakers lost influence after the Glorious Revolution of 1688, which deposed James II, the Act of Toleration of 1689 put an end to the uniformity laws under which Quakers had been persecuted, permitting them to assemble freely. By the time of Fox's death in 1690, his followers were counted by the tens of thousands.

George Fox performed hundreds of healings throughout his preaching ministry, the records of which were collected in a notable but now lost book entitled *Book of Miracles*. Another of his writings, his *Journal*, was first published in 1694, after editing by Thomas Ellwood, a friend and associate of John Milton, with a preface by William Penn. Like most similar works of its time, the journal was not written contemporaneously to the events it describes, but rather compiled many years later, much of it dictated. Parts of the journal were not written by Fox, but were constructed by editors from diverse sources and written as if by him. The *Journal*, intended to be inspirational, excludes references to internal dissent within the movement, and the contributions of others to the development of Quakerism are largely lacking. However, as a religious autobiography, now considered a devotional classic, it has been compared to such works as Augustine's *Confessions*, John Bunyan's *Grace Abounding to the Chief of Sinners*, and John Henry Newman's *Apologia pro Vita Sua*.

While an intensely personal work, its dramatic power only succeeds in appealing to readers after substantial editing. Historians have used it as a primary source because of its wealth of detail on ordinary life in the seventeenth century, and the many towns and villages that Fox visited. In addition to Fox's *Journal*, hundreds of his letters—mostly intended for wide circulation, along with a few private communications—have also been published. Written from the 1650s onwards, they give enormous insight into the detail of Fox's beliefs and show his determination to spread them.

As is well known, the influence of Fox's *Journal* within the Quaker movement was immense, due to its extensive circulation. At his death, Fox left instructions that the *Journal* be printed at the expense of his estate, and that free copies be sent to every organized community of Friends in the world. In addition, each copy was to be made available for members of the meeting to borrow in turn.

The Religious Society of Friends, as Quakers called themselves, was inspired by the notion of radical immediacy, a concept based on the belief that revelation is not limited to the past but is ongoing, and that truth is known experientially, affirmed by the heart rather than by the head. Immediacy is a modern notion, which arises when one disagrees or finds irrelevant national churches, established churches, and governments that enforce religion through persecution. Citizens of modern nations find the notion of forced worship repugnant, not only for being undemocratic but because it actually suppresses religion.

According to the Quakers, there is only one requirement in religion, namely, one's relation with God. The central Quaker conviction, articulated by Fox and other early Quaker leaders, is that the same Holy Spirit that inspired the Bible also speaks today within the human heart. For that reason, Quaker meetings have no liturgy or clergy but only members of the congregation speaking as they are moved by the Spirit. When they speak, their words have the same authority as scripture. For Quakers, the scriptures are a declaration of the fountain, not the fountain itself. The Fountain is the Holy Spirit; the scriptures are merely an expression of that fountain, as is the testimony of a good Quaker at a Quaker meeting. The scriptures are secondary, always subordinate to the Spirit. This is radical immediacy. The Holy Spirit is the inner light in one's heart, and that is all one needs. Believers don't even need the Bible. They do, however, need to meet together, but they don't need a liturgy, the sacraments, or any external forms, because those who have the Spirit already possess the means they need for the spiritual life. Unlike most Christian sectarians, who practice the ordinances of baptism and the Lord's Supper, Quakers find them unnecessary.

Quakers believe that the inner light of divine revelation is available to all; every human has the Holy Spirit. For this reason, everyone is equal. Like Arminians, Quakers believe that Christ died for every human being, even those who have never heard of Christ. Because Quakers are radical egalitarians, they are resolute pacifists. From the beginning, they refused to take their hats off for anyone, since they recognized no one as their superior. Like Baptists, Quakers became consistent advocates of religious liberty for all.

In America, the most famous Quaker exemplar is John Woolman (1700–1772), known for campaigning against slavery, but the best known Quaker is William Penn, after whom the state of Pennsylvania is named. In 1681 Penn received a charter to found a colony in North America in which there was complete religious freedom. Other British colonies were in existence in the New World by then, but with the exception of Rhode Island, all were marked by religious intolerance. Despite his land grant, Penn was convinced that the Indians, and not the crown, were the legitimate owners of the land. And he hoped to establish such cordial relations with them that the settlers would have no need to defend themselves. The capital of this "holy experiment" was called Philadelphia—the city of "fraternal love." Under the leadership of Penn, the first governor of the colony, relations with the Indians were excellent, and for a long time his dream of a peaceful settlement was a reality. In the seventeenth century, if you were a Roman Catholic in the American colonies, the only place you could celebrate the Mass freely in the British world was in Pennsylvania, because as a Quaker colony, it advocated freedom of worship for all.[4]

---

4. In England, it was not until the "Glorious Revolution" that accompanied the accession of William and Mary that full religious tolerance for Quakers and all other dissenting groups was made into law. In 1688, the Catholic monarch James II was deposed and replaced by his daughter Mary II and her husband William of Orange, James's Dutch nephew. William and Mary ruled together for five years. The Act of

In his 1903 address at the Wesley Bicentennial Celebration in Boston, the American historian Edward Everett Hale called George Fox, John Wesley, and John Henry Newman the three most influential Englishmen of the past three centuries. While the issue is debatable, there is no question that Fox should be numbered among the prophets of the Christian era, possible as the first true prophet of the English Reformation. He was certainly a visionary, even a pioneer in social activism. His actions were based on the belief that to be human means to have a "seed of God" within. It is this experience of human-divine contact that places Fox among the mystics. However, here we must not overlook differences in types of mysticism. Unlike the Spanish mystics Teresa of Ávila and John of the Cross, who painfully strived to find God through a path of negation, George Fox belongs among the positive mystics, who, like Brother Lawrence or Thomas à Kempis, sought to realize the presence of God in everyday life. Such mystics recognize that God transcends all finite experiences, but the reality of finite human experience, as Fox's friend Isaac Penington noted, is that any mortal can "become an organ of the life and power of God," and "propagate God's life in the world." In this regard, Fox's great mystical insight was his discovery that God is near, and not beyond the reach of the ladder God has given us. A social reformer and a religious organizer like Francis of Assisi, Fox attempted the difficult task of bringing religion from heaven to earth.

It should not be forgotten, however, that Gorge Fox emerged at a "dawning" time in English religious history, for few periods are more significant in the life history of England than that commonly called the Commonwealth period. For a century, the burning questions had been religious. The Church of England at that time was the result of compromise. It had inherited much medieval thought, and had absorbed much medieval tradition. A spirit of fresh reform was awakening, which could not be set aside and would not be silenced. The old idea of an authoritative church was outgrown, and yet no religious system had come into place that provided for a free personal approach to God.

The long struggle for religious reform in England followed two lines of development. There was, on the one hand, a well-defined movement toward Calvinism, as well as a somewhat chaotic search for freer religious life—a movement towards Arminianism and Independency. George Fox

---

Toleration of 1689 became part of the Bill of Rights that confirmed the primacy of parliament over the British crown. After Mary's death in 1694, William ruled England, Ireland, and Scotland until his death in 1702.

came to his spiritual crisis under Calvinist theology, but at the same time, Arminian theology was gaining ascendency with the masses. Fox came directly into contact with at least four of the leading sectarian movements at that time, and there can be no question that they exerted an influence upon him both positively and negatively.

The first "sect" in importance, and the first to touch the life of Gorge Fox, was the Baptist. They already had a long history, reaching back on the continent to the time of Luther, and their entire career had been marked by persecution and suffering. As "independents," they believed that church and state should be separate, and that each local church should have its own independent life. Another group, the "Seekers," were widely scattered throughout England during the Commonwealth. They saw nowhere an adequate embodiment of the true church on earth, and that there had been none since the time of the apostles. They did not celebrate any sacraments, for they believed the apostolic authority was no longer present on earth. The Seekers felt the days of apostasy would soon end, and that the Spirit would make new revelations.

A third "sect" was the "Ranters," who believed that God was in all things, and that every person is a manifestation of God. They were above all authority, for as they had God within them, they were freed from all law. A fourth movement was the "Fifth-monarchists," who concluded that the last of the four world monarchies—the Assyrian, Persian, Greek, and Roman—had come to an end, and that the Fifth universal monarchy—Christ's—was about to be set up.

Many of these Independents became Friends, for there was hardly a belief in the Quaker message that had not been held by one of the many sects of the time. However, though England had been facing religious problems of a most complex sort since the time of the Reformation, it had produced no religious genius. George Fox filled that role, for it can be argued that the progress of religious thought and practice during the past several centuries has been toward the beliefs he made central to his message. In founding a Society, as he called it, he evidently hoped it would become universal. As he envisioned it, every individual was a vital, organic part of the whole; free, but possessed of a freedom exercised with a view to the interests and edification of the whole. His vision, modeled on the conception of Paul's universal church, clearly reflected the church as the "Body of Christ," unified not from without, but by the living presence of the one Spirit of God.

QUESTIONS FOR DISCUSSION AND REFLECTION

In addition to the questions listed at the end of the preface, answer the following questions, writing your answers in a journal. If you are in a group study, be prepared to share your answers with those in the group.

1. In your estimation, should Pascal be considered a mystic? If so, how might his frail health have contributed to his spirituality?

2. Explain and assess the merits of Pascal's contributions to "the faith-reason problem." Assess his distinction between science and religion, particularly his view that these two realms must be kept separate.

3. Explain and assess Pascal's belief in the superiority of Christianity—particularly Catholic dogma and practice—over all other religions.

4. Explain and assess the influence of Augustinian theology (via Jansenism) on Pascal's theology and spirituality.

5. Explain Pascal's wager, and assess its value and usefulness for Christian theology.

6. Assess the value and usefulness of Pascal's wager for Christian spirituality.

7. Explain and assess the contributions of the Baptists to Christian spirituality.

8. Identify the formative experiences of George Fox that contributed to his distinct sectarian spirituality.

9. Explain and assess George Fox's understanding of the meaning of the "inner light" within human beings, and the role of this "radical immediacy" in the sacred and secular lives of Quakers.

10. Explain the influence of Fox's *Journal* in the growth and expansion of the Quaker movement.

11. Explain and assess the contributions of the Quakers to Christian spirituality.

12. Explain the difference between the mysticism of George For and that of the Spanish mystics Teresa of Ávila and John of the Cross.

Chapter 8

John Milton's *Paradise Lost* and William Blake's *The Marriage of Heaven and Hell*

IN THIS CHAPTER WE find two artistic geniuses discussing similar topics, all related to the problem of good and evil, yet arriving at different conclusions. The reasons for their methodologies and conclusions are complicated, but they can be reduced to two opposing perspectives or worldviews: dualism and nondualism.

In *Paradise Lost*, John Milton's vision is dualistic, for he views good and evil as antithetical, distinguished by clear boundaries and unchanging identities. Like Blake, Milton was willing to admit that ambiguity exists, for he would have agreed with Blake that good and evil spring from the same root. Unlike Manichean dualism, which posits an eternal conflict between two antithetical kingdoms, Milton's dualism was Augustininan in the sense that evil emerges out of good, as a privation or absence of good caused by cosmic rebellion and hence temporal rather than eternal in nature.

Unlike Blake, Milton never claimed that good and evil are rendered indistinguishable, even if they have a common source. They are often hard to distinguish, but it is human duty to do so. Milton's writings display forms of dualism that are clearly thought out and rather sophisticated, but in *Paradise Lost*, readers have a sense at once of completeness, actuality, and of limitation. The boundaries between good and evil are set, and this is as Milton would have wished.

William Blake's vision, to the contrary, requires that the concepts of good and evil be depolarized and unified, for according to his perspective of the cosmos, the material world and physical desire are equally part of the divine order and hence, a marriage of heaven and hell. This is not to say there is no good and evil, better or worse, but only that, if we are to affirm unity, or even to grasp the idea of unity, we must trace life's polarities to their common source. With Milton and Blake, we can explore the depths and heights of biblical myth, and feel that we have seen and known the span of human experience. When engaging with great art, we cannot pretend that understanding is anything but hard and rare, but as the seventeenth century Dutch philosopher Baruch Spinoza noted, "all noble things are as difficult as they are rare."

JOHN MILTON: LIFE AND WORK

John Milton (1608–1674) was born in London, the son of composer John Milton and his wife Sarah Jeffrey. The senior John Milton had moved to London from Oxfordshire around 1583, after being disinherited by his devout Catholic father for embracing Protestantism. As a prosperous musician, Milton's father provided his son with a private tutor, after which Milton attended St. Paul's School, where he studied classical languages. He graduated from Cambridge University intending to become an Anglican priest, but he decided to further his education, experimenting with poetry. Upon receiving his M.A, he undertook an extended period of self-directed private study, including ancient and modern theology, philosophy, history, politics, literature, and science, all in preparation for a prospective poetical career.

In 1638, Milton embarked on an extended "grand tour" of France and Italy, meeting famous theorists and intellectuals, including the astronomer Galileo, then under house arrest. He returned to England in 1639, in response to reports of civil war in his homeland. On returning to England, Milton began to write prose tracts against episcopacy, in the service of the Puritan and Parliamentary cause. Supported by his father's investments, he became a private schoolmaster for a time, educating his nephews and other children of the upper classes. This experience led him to write his short tract *Of Education* in 1644, urging a reform of the national universities.

In 1642, he met and married Mary Powell; he was thirty-three and she seventeen. The marriage got off to a poor start as Mary did not adapt to Milton's austere lifestyle or get along with his relatives. Milton found her intellectually unsatisfying and disliked the royalist views she had absorbed from her family. Mary soon returned home to her parents and did not come back until 1645, partly because of the outbreak of the Civil War. In the meantime, Milton published a series of pamphlets arguing for the legality and morality of divorce beyond grounds of adultery. The hostile response he received over these writings spurred Milton to write *Areopagitica*, his celebrated support of free speech. In this work, he aligned himself with the parliamentary cause.

The trial and execution of Charles I drew Milton back into the fray of English political and religious debate. Two weeks after the execution, Milton published a pamphlet on *The Tenure of Kings and Magistrates*, in which he argued that monarchy holds power by virtue of a contract with the people. If monarchy fails in its stewardship—and Milton suggests that Charles had done so—it should be called to account by its subjects. As well as justification for regicide, the document involved a lengthy attack upon the Presbyterian party of the Commons, whom he treats as hypocrites. The Cromwellian, republican commonwealth, the shadowy precursor to modern democracy, was imminent, and Milton was soon drawn into contemporary politics. In 1649, he was appointed Secretary of Foreign Tongues to the newly organized Council of State, the republican cabinet, for it was known that Milton's skill as a rhetorician, along with his sympathetic affiliations, would be on enormous benefit in the Council's early dealings with the rest of Europe. As chief propagandist in defense of the republican principles represented by the Commonwealth, he published *Eikonoklastes*, a defense of regicide in response to the *Eikon Basilike*, a best-seller attributed to Charles I that portrayed the king as an innocent Christian martyr. In 1652, Milton's publication of his defense of the English people quickly made him a European reputation, and a second defense, published in 1654, won him the praise of Oliver Cromwell, now Lord Protector.

Milton held the position of Secretary for Foreign Tongues until 1660, although by 1652, after years of poor eyesight, he had become totally blind, most of his work now being done by his deputies. The cause of his blindness seems to have been retinal detachment or possibly glaucoma. His blindness forced him to dictate his verse and prose to scribes, including the poet Andrew Marvell. By this time, Milton was becoming, in the public consciousness and professionally, the official spokesman for the fledgling Cromwellian state. Nevertheless, Cromwell's death in 1658 caused the English Republic to collapse into feuding military and political factions. Meanwhile, Milton stubbornly clung to the beliefs that had originally inspired him to write for the Commonwealth, including attacking the concept of a state-dominated church as well as denouncing corrupt practices in church governance. As the Republic disintegrated, Milton continued writing proposals to retain a non-monarchical government, against the wishes of Parliament, the military, and the general populace. Sometime in the mid-1650s, when his work for the government was becoming less burdensome, Milton began to assemble his *The Christian Doctrine*, a long-forgotten document that was discovered in manuscript form in the Public Record Office in 1823. Even after it went into print in 1825, some doubted its authenticity.

Upon the Restoration in 1660, Milton, fearing for his life, was forced into hiding, while a warrant was issued for his arrest and his writings were burnt. He emerged after a general pardon was issued. He spent the remaining decade of his life living quietly in London, publishing several minor prose works and the first edition of his magnum opus, *Paradise Lost*, in 1667. Milton followed up that publication with its sequel *Paradise Regained*, which was published alongside the tragedy *Samson Agonistes* in 1671. Both of these works also reflect Milton's post-Restoration political situation. Just prior to his death in 1674, Milton supervised a second edition of *Paradise Lost*, as well as a collection of poems and letters.

MILTON'S *PARADISE LOST*

According to biographer John Aubrey, Milton began *Paradise Lost* about 1658 and finished about 1663. However, he almost certainly wrote parts earlier, its roots lying in Milton's youth. Prior to England's Civil War, Milton had considered writing an epic poem to encompass "all space and time." This epic was not initially intended as a biblical epic, but probably about heroic kings and queens going back to legendary Saxon or British rulers such as the legendary King Arthur.

Milton's epic poem, written in blank verse, likely originated as a reflection on his personal despair at the failure of the republican cause, while affirming ultimate optimism in human potential. Dispensing with the epic tradition established by the *Odyssey* and the *Aeneid*, written in the form of twelve books or as a multiple of twelve, Milton published the first edition of *Paradise Lost* in ten books to demonstrate his independence from tradition. However, the second edition was arranged into twelve books, thereby conforming to the epic pattern.

Following the traditional epic pattern, Milton begins the action of *Paradise Lost* in *media res* (in the midst of things), at a dramatically advanced point in the action and at the furthest possible point from the presence of God—in Hell—and then works back simultaneously to the beginning and forward to the end. The total action is cyclical in shape, as that is the nature of the mythological quest theme—loss (departure), illumination, and return.[1] The cycle that forms the background action of *Paradise Lost* is the cycle of the Bible, beginning and ending in God's eternal presence. The foreground action deals with the conspiracy of Satan and the fall of Adam and Eve, and the two speeches of the archangels Raphael and Michael deal with the rest of the cycle.

Raphael begins with what is chronologically the first event in the poem, the presentation of Christ to the angels, and brings the action down to the point where the poem begins. After Adam's fall, Michael picks up the story and summarizes the biblical narrative through to the Last Judgment, which brings us back to the point where God is all in all.

Milton's epic has two narrative arcs, one about Satan (Lucifer), and the other about Adam and Eve. The poem begins after Satan and the other fallen angels have been defeated and banished to Hell, where they are found chained to a lake of fire. They free themselves and fly to land, where they construct Pandemonium, their capital city in Hell. Inside Pandemonium, the rebel angels, who are now devils, debate whether they should begin another war with God. Beelzebub suggests that they attempt to corrupt God's beloved new creation, humankind. Satan agrees, and volunteers to go himself. As he prepares to leave Hell, he is met by his children Sin and Death, who follow him and build a bridge between Hell and Earth. After an arduous traversal of the Chaos outside Hell, Satan, disguised as a cherub to get past the Archangel Uriel, enters God's new material world and then the Garden of Eden.

---

1. Following the mythological quest pattern, the *Odyssey* begins with Odysseus at the furthest point from home, on the island of Calypso, subjected to the temptations of his wife Penelope's only formidable rival. The action of the *Aeneid* similarly begins with Aeneas's shipwreck on the shores of Carthage, the hereditary enemy of Rome and the site of the citadel of Juno, Aeneas's implacable enemy.

At several points in the poem, an Angelic War over Heaven is recounted from different perspectives. Satan's rebellion follows the epic convention of large-scale warfare. The battles between the faithful angels and Satanic forces take place over three days. At the final battle, the Son of God single-handedly defeats the entire legion of angelic rebels and banishes them from Heaven. Following this purge, God creates the World, culminating in his creation of Adam and Eve. In Heaven, God tells the angels of Satan's intentions, and the Son volunteers to make the sacrifice for humankind. While God provides Adam and Eve complete freedom and power to rule over creation, he gives them one explicit command: not to eat from the Tree of the Knowledge of Good and Evil, on penalty of death.

Meanwhile, Adam and Eve tend the Garden, carefully obeying God's command not to eat from the Tree of Knowledge. Worried about his creation, God sends Raphael to Earth to teach Adam and Eve of the dangers they face with Satan. Like his figure of Satan, Milton elevates the first human couple to the level of heroic figures. The story of Adam and Eve's temptation and fall is a fundamentally different kind of epic—a domestic one. Adam and Eve are presented as having a romantic and sexual relationship while still being without sin. They have passions and distinct personalities. Satan, disguised in the form of a serpent, successfully tempts Eve to eat from the Tree by preying on her vanity and tricking her with rhetoric. Adam, learning that Eve has sinned, knowingly commits the same sin. He declares to Eve that since she was made from his flesh, they are bound to one another—if she dies, he must also die. In this manner, Milton portrays Adam as a heroic figure, but also as a greater sinner than Eve, as he is aware that what he is doing is wrong.

After eating the fruit, Adam and Eve have lustful sex. At first, Adam is convinced that Eve was right in thinking that eating the fruit would be beneficial. However, they soon fall asleep and have terrible nightmares, and after they awake, they experience guilt and shame for the first time. Realizing that they have committed a terrible act against God, they engage in mutual recrimination.

Meanwhile, Satan returns triumphantly to Hell, amid the praise of his fellow fallen angels. He tells them how their scheme worked and humankind has fallen, giving the fallen angels complete dominion over Paradise. As he finishes his speech, however, the fallen angels around him become hideous snakes, and soon Satan turns into a snake, deprived of limbs and unable to talk. Thus, they share the same punishment, as they shared the same guilt.

Eve appeals to Adam for reconciliation of their actions. Her action enables them to approach God, and pray for forgiveness. God hears their prayers, and sends the Archangel Michael down to Earth. When Michael arrives, he tells Adam and Eve that they must leave Paradise. In a vision shown to him by Michael, Adam witnesses events that will happen to humankind, culminating in the Great Flood. Adam is upset by this vision of the future, so Michael also tells him about the triumph of Moses and the Israelites, and then humankind's potential redemption from original sin through Jesus Christ (whom Michael calls "King Messiah"). Adam and Eve are cast out of Eden, and Michael says that Adam may find "a paradise within thee, happier far" (12.587). They leave Paradise hand in hand, accepting their fate but acknowledging both the necessity of obedience to God's will and also the importance of their own free will in moral decision-making. Adam and Eve now have a more distant relationship with God, who is omnipresent but invisible (unlike the tangible Father in the Garden of Eden).

The literary scholar Northrop Frye suggests in his *Return to Eden* that readers should examine *Paradise Lost*'s formal symmetry by visualizing the dial of a clock,[2] with the presence of God at the top, with the figure 12. Moving clockwise, the numbers on the dial represent the following events:

1. First epiphany of Christ: the generation of the Son from the Father.
2. Second epiphany of Christ: the triumph in heaven after a three-day conflict.
3. Establishment of the natural order in the creation.
4. Establishment of the human order: creation of Adam and Eve.
5. Epiphany of Satan, generating Sin and Death.
6. Fall of the human order.
7. Fall of the natural order: triumph of Sin and Death.
8. Re-establishment of the natural order at the end of the Great Flood.
9. Re-establishment of the human order with the giving of the Law.
10. Third epiphany of Christ: the incarnation of the Word as Gospel.

2. Frye, *Return of Eden*, 18–20.

11. Fourth epiphany of Christ: the Apocalypse or Last Judgment.

12. The eternal Kingdom, when God is "all in all."

The final point in the vast cycle is the same point as the beginning, yet not the same point, because the ending is the starting point renewed and transformed by the heroic quest of Christ. Thus there can be only one cycle, not an endless series of them.

Traditionally, for both medieval and Renaissance poets—and actually for most poets until Newton's age—there are four levels of existence (notice the hierarchical and dualistic nature of this way of thinking): the divine, the angelic, the human, and the demonic order, corresponding loosely to the four orders of existence. There is, in the first place, the order of grace or heaven, the place of the presence of God. Below this is the human order, the way in which God intended humans to live, the order represented by the Garden of Eden in the Bible and by the legend of the Golden Age in classic literature and philosophy. This order, though in the psalmist's phrase "a little lower than God (than the angels)" (see Ps 8:5), is not, at least in Milton, qualitatively different from the angelic order. Below this is the physical world of animals and plants, into which humans are born, though technically they do not belong. Below the physical world is the world of sin, corruption, and death, a level that is not actually part of nature, in the sense that it was never intended to be there, although it now permeates the physical world and causes everything alive in it to die. As this sequence indicates, prior to the rise of the modern age most Christians adopted the primitive belief that there is no such thing as natural death, meaning that death was ultimately seen to be the result of a personal and malignant agency.

According to this perspective, all humans since Adam are born into the third level of existence. They do not belong there, and at birth are faced with a moral choice, whether to rise above it to their proper home, or whether to sink below it into the state of sin, a degradation animals cannot reach. If we keep this choice in mind, we can understand Milton's conception of the aim of education (stated in his pamphlet *On Education*) as being to repair the loss of our first parents by regaining their knowledge of God. According to Milton's Calvinist theology, the entire order of nature is fallen. The abolition of the Garden of Eden in the Great Flood[3] symbolizes the fact that the two levels of nature—the heavenly

---

3. For Milton, the most important event of the Flood was the washing away of Eden. If Eden disappeared as an outward environment, it was revived as an inner state

and the earthly—both once part of the order of nature, cannot both exist in space, but must succeed one another in time, and that the upper level of human nature can be experienced only as an inner state of mind, not as an outward or external environment.

Those who get far enough into *Paradise Lost* see that Milton has turned its universe inside out, with God sitting within the human soul and Satan on a remote periphery plotting against human freedom. In dealing with Satan, however, Milton moves with supreme confidence, because Satan is his poetic creature. From this perspective, perhaps, we can see what Blake meant when he said that Milton was a true poet and of the devil's (that is, the revolutionary) party.

Blake's comment raises the question of the hero in *Paradise Lost*. Satan, formerly called Lucifer, is the first major character introduced in the poem. He was once the most beautiful of angels, but has become a tragic figure who famously declares, "Better to reign in hell than serve in heaven" (1:263). In *Paradise Lost*, Satan is not only charismatic and powerful, but he gets all of the best lines. Although he is cunning and deceptive, and able to rally the fallen angels after their agonizing defeat in the Angelic War, he is more of an antagonist than a protagonist, an inferior being aspiring to be like God.

In order to understand Milton's view of heroic action, we must go back to his conception of an act. In his unfinished manifesto, *The Christian Doctrine*, where Milton lays out many of his theological views, he states clearly what he means by an act. An act is the expression of the energy of a free and conscious being. For Milton, all acts are good. Consequently, there is no such thing, strictly speaking, as an evil act. Evil or sin implies deficiency as well as the loss or lack of the power to act. What happened when Adam and Eve ate the forbidden fruit was not, then, an act, but the surrendering of the power to act. Humans are free to lose their freedom, and when they do, their freedom ends.

For example, when a person stands at the edge of a precipice, if he or she jumps, it appears to be an act, but it is actually the giving up of the possibility of action, a surrender to the law of gravitation that takes over that person's will. In this surrendering of the power to act lies the key to Milton's conception of the behavior of Adam and Eve. Their act of disobedience was not actually an "act," but a pseudo-act, for it was really

---

of mind, the "Paradise within Thee, happier far" that Michael promises Adam. While it is no good looking for Paradise anywhere on earth, there is a Garden inside our spirit, guarded by angels still, yet a place that the Word of God within us can open.

a refusal to "act," an irregularity or deviation that went against their God-given goodness and freedom. In temptation, a person is being persuaded to do something that looks like an act, but that is actually the loss of the power to act. Consequently, abstaining from such pseudo-activity is often a sign that one possesses a genuine power of action and hence, that one is truly free.

According to Milton's own definition of an act, it is only the divine that can act freely, and in *Paradise Lost*, the quality of the divine act reveals itself as an act of creation, which becomes an act of re-creation after Adam and Eve's expulsion from the Garden. Satan, as Milton notes, cannot create; he can only rebel and destroy. Like evil, which masquerades as good, Satan is only a parody of divine action, antiheroic rather than heroic. The true hero of *Paradise Lost* is Christ, who creates the world and then recreates or restores humanity. As the agent or acting principle of the Father, Christ is ultimately the sole actor in Milton's poem.

Of course, there are angels and archangels in *Paradise Lost*, but the angelic order is there to provide models for human action. They have superior intellectual and physical powers, but in *Paradise Lost* they are moral models only, solely a community of service and obedience to God's will. In terms of the theme of heroism, there is the angel Abdiel, who remains faithful to God in the midst of the revolted angels. As his speech to Satan at the time of the war in heaven indicates, he models the pattern of genuine heroism that later is exhibited in the life of Christ, a pattern found also in the stories of Enoch and Noah and followed by the prophets and apostles. As for Adam and Eve, theologically and conceptually, there is no sin they did not commit when they ate of the forbidden fruit. In this regard, then, the course of human history is more demonic than heroic, and that makes *Paradise Lost* a profoundly unheroic poem.

Despite Milton's portrayal of Satan as a congenial and attractive figure, Satan is a rebel, and into Satan Milton put all the horrors and distress with which he viewed the radical revolutionaries of his time, whose unstable theories and loyalties made them enemies of the republican principles represented in England during the Commonwealth period. Even though some have found Milton's Satan irresistibly attractive, Milton was not a Satanist. The demonic action in *Paradise Lost* ends with a metamorphosis, in which devils are changed into serpents. Satan also has taken the form of a serpent, and even in Hell he cannot rid himself of it. Indeed, the demons, in looking at Satan, become serpents as well, a reminder of the remark about idols in Psalm 115:8, "Those who make them are like them; so are all who trust in them."

The first words of *Paradise Lost* state that the poem's main theme will be "man's first disobedience." Milton then narrates the story of Adam and Eve's disobedience, explaining how and why it happened, and placing the story within the larger context of Satan's rebellion and Jesus' resurrection. In essence, *Paradise Lost* presents two paths that people can take after disobedience: the downward spiral of increasing sin and degradation, represented by Satan, and the road to redemption, represented by Adam and Eve. Satan's decision to continue to disobey God after his fall into Hell ensures that God will not forgive him. Adam and Eve, on the other hand, decide to repent for their sins and seek forgiveness. This path is obviously the correct one to take; as books 11 and 12 demonstrate, obedience to God, even after repeated falls, can lead to humankind's salvation.

In addition to obedience and disobedience and their consequences, *Paradise Lost* is also about hierarchy. The layout of the universe—with Heaven above, Hell below, and Earth in the middle—presents the universe as a hierarchy based on proximity to God and God's grace. This spatial hierarchy leads to a social hierarchy of angels, humans, animals, and devils. The Son is closest to God; archangels and cherubs come next, with Satan and the other fallen angels following last. Since hierarchy represents God's will, to question this hierarchy is to question God. Likewise, humanity's disobedience is a corruption of God's hierarchy. Before the fall, Adam and Even treat visiting angels with proper respect in acknowledgment of their closeness to God, while Eve embraces the subservient role allotted to her in marriage. When Eve persuades Adam to let her work alone, she challenges him as her superior, and he yields to her, his inferior. Again, as Adam eats from the fruit, he knowingly defies God by following his inner instinct instead of God and his own reason. As Adam's visions in books 11 and 12 demonstrate, with the Son's sacrifice, this hierarchy will once again be restored.

In a Catholic poet such as Dante, the separation of eternal and temporal worlds is something that humans overcome through a process of purgation and sacramental discipline. In Milton, the place of sacrament and purgation is taken by *agon*, by the temptation, task, or contest that is the theme of his major poems. In works such as *Comus*, *Paradise Regained*, and *Samson Agonistes*, victory over temptation flows from a source that is both identical with and yet different from the victor. All victors, the Lady in *Comus*, Christ in *Paradise Regained*, and Samson in

Samson Agonistes, adhere steadily to the divine vision, and as they do, the demonic world becomes increasingly evil. The theme of externalizing the demonic and internalizing the divine flows through Milton's writings. Thus, in *Paradise Lost*, Paradise is internalized, transformed from an external place to an inner state of mind.

Applying the principle of internalizing and spiritual discernment to our reading of *Paradise Lost*, we find in this poem a supreme sovereign who seems arbitrary and inscrutable. There is nothing to be done with this God than obey his will. For Milton, the heaven of *Paradise Lost* can only be set up on earth within one's mind. Hence, the free person's mind is a dictatorship of God, obeyed by the will without argument. Society goes wrong, however, when it takes conceptions of divine rule as social models. Hence, absolute monarchs and their minions on earth always go wrong, for when the inner sovereignty of God is externalized, it follows models of Hell, not of Heaven. Such projections will eventually disappear, even in Heaven, when God becomes "all in all."

Unlike earthly monarchies, which cannot rule on behalf of God, divine sovereignty has its earthly model in the minds and hearts of individuals such as the biblical Enoch, Noah, and Samson, who refuse to compromise with evil, who refuse to admit the arguments evil advances in favor of compromise, and who, faced with the supreme test, can produce out of some unknown depth the ability to suffer and die. For Milton, such individuals suffer alone. The lonely fight in the life of Christ becomes the theme of *Paradise Regained*, a poem that dramatizes the third and fourth epiphanies, in which Christ confronts Satan. *Paradise Regained* refers back to the original war in heaven as recounted in *Paradise Lost*, and forward to the final binding of Satan prophesied in Revelation 20:2. The defeat of Satan as tempter also fulfils the prophecy in Genesis that the seed of Adam would strike the serpent's head (Gen 3:15), as well as Paul's prophecy in Romans 16:20.

In his day, Milton hoped for a revolutionary hero. When he first seriously considered possible epic subjects, he thought of the legendary King Arthur as his archetypal hero, but this project never came to fruition. There is such a human figure in Milton—not Adam in *Paradise Lost*, but the biblical Samson, whom he transforms from an overgrown juvenile delinquent into a figure of great dignity and power in *Samson Agonistes*. Adam, surely, is what leaders were intended to be—peaceful patriarchs. Samson, however, is what the ascendancy of Nimrod and the

Philistines had forced human leaders to become: powerful, ruthless, and tragic.

In a revolutionary situation, Milton had a good deal of respect for the political wisdom that recognizes prudence, which makes the best of the confused mixture of good and evil that comprise human life. When Milton speaks of Lucifer before Adam, he is "the first prelate angel," but as Milton notes in the opening books of *Paradise Lost*, Hell is the model for perverted orders of society, whether in state or church. In his writings, Milton does not object to monarchy *per se*, but only to monarchy as an occasion for idolatry, for the tendency for a king to acquire the same kind of "false glitter" that Satan has in Hell is endemic to monarchy.

Milton was willing to consider Oliver Cromwell as an emergency leader, like the judges of Israel to whom Samson belonged, but was determined to point out that peace is not merely the end of war, but a qualitatively different human condition from war, one that requires far more complex qualities than human commanders possess. The temporal authority represented by Nimrod in book 12 of *Paradise Lost* derives its structure from the demonic warrior aristocracy, and this authority, however inevitable, is still illegitimate. We seem to find in Milton, then, a revolutionary who became disillusioned with the failure of the English people to achieve a free commonwealth, and was finally compelled to find the true revolution within the individual.

WILLIAM BLAKE: LIFE AND WORK

England's world in the late eighteenth century was quite different from Milton's mid-seventeenth century world of civil war. Many of Milton's ideas were now obsolete, except for his defense of freedom of speech in *Aeropagitica*. Milton's most important legacy may not have been his political views, however, but the personal example of sincerity and self-sacrifice in a cause he deemed to be just. Editions of Milton's *Paradise Lost*, first published in 1667, reissued almost immediately, and the book never went out of print. As early as 1732, *Paradise Lost* appeared with full scholarly apparatus and explanatory notes befitting the book's status as a classic.

Another way to mark Milton's literary influence is to examine the biographical traditions, and the degree to which biographers succeeded in creating an enduring image of the writer. In part because of his extraordinary public career—twenty years in service of the Commonwealth—Milton very early attracted biographical defenders and detractors. In his 1794 *Life of Milton*, biographer William Hayley called Milton one of the "visionaries of public virtue." Milton was named by many eighteenth century biographers as a literary hero, as one who combined genius and learning, rationality and spirituality, and Christianity and classicism in a way no English writer had before. One of Hayley's early readers and friends was the English poet, printer, and printmaker William Blake (1757–1827), who represents in the most visible way the powerful impact Milton made on early Romantic imagination.

From 1801 to 1825, Blake produced some ninety illustrations of Milton's works, in addition to two sets of watercolors illustrating *Paradise Lost* and a set of designs for *Paradise Regained*. As many commentators have suggested, Blake's work does not simply illustrate Milton; it also interprets. During 1804 to 1808, Blake wrote a long poem entitled *Milton*, in which the older poet descends from heaven to inspire and redeem the world from Satan and eternal death. However, Blake's best-known response to Milton is one of his earliest remarks, the "Note" in *The Marriage of Heaven and Hell* that Milton was "of the Devil's party without knowing it." Unfortunately, few Miltonists have looked closely at what Blake actually meant.

Without question, the early Blake thought contemporary Christianity psychologically repressive and politically tyrannical, and he found Milton's God the Father to embody the worst aspects of the Old Testament heritage. Nevertheless, we cannot overlook the fact that *The Marriage of Heaven and Hell* is a deliberately provocative and satiric work, designed to unsettle the complacent. It is also important to remember that Blake never sustained one attitude or tone for very long. In *Marriage*, as in many of his other works, he can be both strident and mocking, playful and serious, continually veering from theme to theme as if he did not wish to settle upon any specific point.

William Blake was born in London, where he lived almost his entire life. Blake's father, a hosier, came to England from Ireland. Blake attended school only long enough to learn reading and writing, leaving at the age of ten, and was otherwise educated at home by his mother. As English Dissenters, the Blakes impressed upon young William the importance of the Bible, which remained a source of inspiration throughout his life. At an early age, Blake started engraving copies of drawings of Greek antiquities purchased for him by his father, a practice that was then preferred to actual drawing. When Blake was ten years old, his parents enrolled him in drawing classes, and shortly thereafter, at the age of fourteen, he became apprenticed to engraver James Basire for a term of seven years. At the end of that term, he became a professional engraver. Nevertheless, soon thereafter he enrolled at the Royal Academy, where he rebelled against the style of fashionable painters such as the Flemish artist Peter Paul Rubens, championed by the school's president, Joshua Reynolds. Over time, Blake came to detest Reynolds's attitude toward art, especially his pursuit of "general truth" and "general beauty." As Blake wrote in marginalia of his personal copy of Reynolds's *Discourses*, "To Generalize is to be an Idiot; To Particularize is the Alone Distinction of Merit."

In 1782, Blake married Catherine Boucher, an illiterate woman five years his junior. Later, in addition to teaching her to read and write, Blake trained her as an engraver. Throughout his life she proved a valuable aid, helping to print and color his relief etchings (which he called "illuminated works" and used to accompany his books, pamphlets, and poems) and bolstering his spirits on numerous occasions. In 1784, shortly after his father's death, Blake and former fellow apprentice James Parker opened a print shop. Over time, they worked with radical publisher Joseph Johnson, whose home was a meeting-place for leading English intellectual dissidents such as Joseph Priestley, early feminist Mary Wollstonecraft, and English revolutionary Thomas Paine.

In 1804, Blake began to write and illustrate *Jerusalem* (1804–1829), his most ambitious work. At the age of sixty-five, he began work on illustrations for the book of Job. In later life he sold a great number of his works, particularly his Bible illustrations, to Thomas Butts, a friend and patron. In 1826 he received a commission for Dante's *Divine Comedy*, an enterprise cut short by Blake's death in 1827, leaving only a handful of watercolors completed.

During his life, Blake was not active in any established political party. His poetry consistently embodies an attitude of rebellion against the abuse of class power. Opposed to senseless wars, slavery, and the blighting effects of the Industrial Revolution, Blake championed "free love." Because his later poetry contained a private mythology with complex symbolism, his late work has been less published than his earlier more accessible work. His earlier work is primarily rebellious and satirical in nature, qualities evident in his protest against dogmatic religion notable in *The Marriage of Heaven and Hell* (1790–1793), in which the figure represented by Satan is virtually a hero rebelling against an authoritarian deity.

Largely unappreciated during his life, Blake is now considered a seminal figure in the history of the poetry and visual art of the Romantic Age. Known primarily as a painter and printmaker, Blake's visual artistry led twenty-first-century critic Jonathan Jones to proclaim him "far and away the greatest artist Britain has ever produced." As an artist, Blake championed imagination as the most important element of human existence, viewing human imagination as "the body of God." During the Modernist period, his work influenced a wide set of writers and artists, including the poet William Butler Yeats, who edited an edition of Blake's collected works in 1893. British surrealist art in particular drew on Blake's conceptions, and his poetry came into use by British classical composers such as Benjamin Britten and Ralph Vaughan Williams.

After World War II, Blake's role in popular culture came to the fore in a variety of areas such as popular music, film, and the graphic novel, leading Edward Larrissy to assert that "Blake is the Romantic writer who has exerted the most powerful influence on the twentieth century." Blake also had an enormous influence on the beat poets of the 1950s and the counterculture of the 1960s, being cited by such seminal figures as Allen Ginsberg and Aldous Huxley, and songwriters Bob Dylan, Jim Morrison, and Van Morrison.

A committed Christian who was hostile to the Church of England and indeed, to almost all forms of organized religion, Blake was influenced by the ideals and ambitions of the French and American revolutions. Initially influenced also by the grand and mystical cosmic conception of Emanuel Swedenborg, a contemporary Swedish philosopher and theologian, he later rebelled against Swedenborg's conventional moral strictures and his Manichean view of good and evil. Scholars such as Diana Hume George have claimed that Blake can be seen as a precursor to the ideas of Sigmund Freud, while June Singer has argued that Blake's thoughts on human nature anticipate and parallel the thinking of the Swiss psychiatrist Carl Jung.

Although Blake's attacks on conventional religion were shocking at the time, his rejection of religiosity was not a rejection of religion. In *The Everlasting Gospel*, Blake presents Jesus as a supremely creative being, above dogma, logic, and even morality. For Blake, Jesus symbolizes the vital relationship and unity between divinity and humanity. In *A Vision of the Last Judgment*, Blake notes that one of his major objections to orthodox Christianity is that he believes it encourages the suppression of natural desires and discourages earthly joy. Blake abhorred self-denial, which he associated with religious repression and particularly sexual repression. For Blake, the body is not distinct from the soul, but rather an extension of the soul. Thus, the emphasis orthodox Christianity places upon the denial of bodily urges is a dualistic error born of misapprehension of the relationship between body and soul. Likewise, he saw the concept of "sin" as a trap to bind human desires, and believed that restraint in obedience to a moral code imposed from the outside was against the spirit of life. Blake also rejected the doctrine of God as sovereign Lord separate from and superior to humankind. This is seen clearly in his words about Jesus Christ, "He is the only God . . . and so am I, and so are you." A telling phrase in *The Marriage of Heaven and Hell* is that "all deities reside in the human breast."

Blake held a complex relationship with religion, particularly in his claims to have seen visions of God and of angels throughout his life. Clearly, religious concepts and imagery figure centrally in his works, and he believed he was personally instructed and encouraged by archangels to create his artistic works. Despite seeing angels and God, Blake also claimed to have seen Satan. Aware of Blake's visions, William Wordsworth commented, "There was no doubt that this poor man was mad, but there is something in the madness of this man which interests me more than the sanity of Lord Byron and Walter Scott." As with religion, Blake also held a complex relationship with Enlightenment philosophy. His championing of the imagination as the most important element of human existence ran contrary to Enlightenment ideals of rationalism and empiricism.

In originality, comprehensiveness of vision, and in his analysis of the religious dimensions of human experience, Blake's artistic achievement is matched in Western literature only by that of Dante and Milton. Religion was arguably the primary motive of his artistry, poetic and pictorial. However, to compare Blake's art with the work of other poets and painters soon makes clear that his own vision and artistry differed strikingly from what is commonly understood to be the purpose of religious art. Although one catches glimpses of personal piety in his letters, Blake's illuminated verse is primarily social in its concern, focusing on the psychic and historic origins of religious faith and on religion's influence on human behavior. Blake was convinced that religion profoundly affects every aspect of human life, and that its influence has generally been more negative than positive. He detected flawed religious thinking at the root of most of the social disorders afflicting England in his time, and found that even the highest virtues associated with religion, such as mercy, empathy, peace, and love, were routinely misconceived or manipulated for destructive ends.

His poetry, then, is a form of protest, a sustained denunciation of the cruelties perpetrated in the name of God by those who claim to be doing God's will. In a time of intense political agitation, he came to believe that a radical transformation of the nation's religious consciousness was the first prerequisite to serious political or economic reform. In his estimation, state religion was a tool, if not an embodiment, of Antichrist. His writings generally support his view that true reformation required a mental apocalypse more unsettling than any revolution envisioned by the political and religious radicals of his day. Against the pretense of organized religion, Blake proclaimed what he understood to be the true religion of Jesus,, the distinguishing qualities of which were a radical demand for social justice, the cultivation of mutual love and forgiveness, and the fostering of creative freedom in religion, morality, and the arts. The difficult mission that Blake understood was to combat the deformed Christianity that had become the national religion of Britain, to take religion back from the priests who had subordinated it to the political, economic, and cultural agenda of the ruling classes, and to make it a truly revolutionary force in society. And he undertook to accomplish all this through the media of poetic and pictorial art.

Blake was convinced that Milton's *Paradise Lost* contributed substantially to the religious ideology that dominated life in Britain by its reinforcement of belief in a distant, judgmental God who took pleasure in crushing rebellion against authority and who required the future death of his only Son before he could bring himself to pardon the sin of Adam and Eve. Blake had always understood religion and poetry to be intimately connected. In *The Marriage of Heaven and Hell* he argued that religion originated in poetry and that priests had abstracted theological systems from poetic tales. In his poem *Milton*, Blake went further to suggest that religion exists on earth as the fallen form of the eternal art of poetry. To repair the damage done by the fall of humanity, then, would entail transforming religion back into poetry. Blake's strategy resembled what twentieth-century theologians would call demythologization—the practice of detaching the Christian faith from the mythical world picture of the first century so that it could be reimagined in more modern terms.

BLAKE'S *THE MARRIAGE OF HEAVEN AND HELL*

Considered as William Blake's most inspired and original work, *The Marriage of Heaven and Hell* is both a humorous satire on religion and morality and a work that concisely expresses Blake's essential wisdom and philosophy, much of it revealed in seventy aphorisms he calls his "Proverbs of Hell." Like most of his books, this work was published as printed sheets from etched plates containing prose, poetry, and illustrations. The book consists of a series of texts written in imitation of biblical prophecy but expressing Blake's own intensely personal Romantic and revolutionary beliefs.

In *The Marriage of Heaven and Hell*, written between 1790 and 1793, Blake is responding to Swedenborg's work *Heaven and Hell*, published in Latin thirty-three years earlier. Swedenborg had essentially adopted the classic dualistic Christian view of the afterlife, where the virtuous are sent to paradise in Heaven and the evildoers are sent to burn in Hell. Blake, being a Romantic and a rebel, largely rejected this simplistic view of the universe, using *Marriage* as his response.

The book is written in prose, except for the opening "Argument" and the "Song of Liberty." The first section, called "The Argument," introduces a character named Rintrah, a "just man" who is raging against the "Vale of Death." The poem concludes with an announcement that a new heaven is beginning. Then Blake explains that without "contraries" (that is, without polarities), there is no progression: "Attraction and Repulsion, Reason and Energy, Love and Hate, are necessary to Human existence. From these Contraries spring what the religious call Good & Evil. Good is the passive that obeys Reason. Evil is the active springing from Energy. Good is Heaven. Evil is Hell." Rather than being opposites, good and evil (heaven and hell) belong together, for together they represent moral and physical harmony, unity, and spiritual wholeness. Blake's theory of contraries stemmed from the belief that each person reflects the contrary nature of God, and that progress in life is impossible without contraries. Unlike Milton and Dante, Blake's concept of Hell begins not as a place of punishment, but as a source of unrepressed energy, opposed to the authoritarian and regulated perception of Heaven.

The next section is "The Voice of the Devil," which contains a list of "errors" that the speaker blames on the Bible and other "sacred codes." Essential to Blake's thinking in this section is the notion that the body and soul are not opposites, but are actually one. The next section is entitled "A Memorable Fancy." It is basically a travelogue of the speaker's trip to Hell, which leads to the next section, the "Proverbs of Hell," which include sayings that are pro-desire, pro-temptation, pro-creativity, and anti-repression.

Blake follows this section with four segments each entitled "A Memorable Fancy." In the first, the speaker has dinner with the biblical prophets Isaiah and Ezekiel. He interviews them, asking how they knew that God was speaking to them. They respond by telling him that the origin of religion is poetry. In another segment, the speaker distinguishes between people called the Prolific and those called the Devouring. The Prolific are creative folks who gain energy from following temptation, while the Devouring are tame, obedient, and oppressed. In the third segment, the speaker is visited by an angel and in the final segment, by a devil talking to an angel. We are told that this angel is Elijah. "A Song of Liberty" tells us about the politics of Blake's time, including the revolutions in France and America, and the final section, "Chorus," calls for an end to religious repression, ending with the famous line, "For every thing that lives is Holy."

In *The Marriage of Heaven and Hell*, Blake turns convention on its head. The main theme seems to be that light and dark, good and evil, angels and demons, form an interdependent circle, and that one cannot exist without the other. The creative force in humanity, and in the universe as a whole, is something called the Energies, which were traditionally thought to be evil but should be viewed as a great force for good. What Blake is saying here, through the voice of the Devil, is that the bodily part of existence (that is, the senses), should not be suppressed, because they are a creative energy.

Throughout the work, Blake adopts a mystical approach to spirituality and religion, affirming a direct relationship between the individual and God while denying structural religious convention. In *Marriage*, Blake contends that Angels and Demons are essentially two sides of the same archetypal coin. Demons represent the Feminine, Liberal, and Creative Energies from which Genius flows, and Angels represent the Masculine, Conservative, and Controlling Energies that seek to constrain genius and put order to things. Blake realized that both forces are needed, although, as a Romantic, he obviously sympathized with the "Evil" demonic energy as being the source of rebellion and liberation, unlike the Angels, who seek to stifle creativity.

To Blake, the Angels are the Church, religious conservatives who wish to control, while the Demons are the classical liberals, the Romantics who seek to liberate humanity from social orders and false constructions. Blake ends his work with the story of how an Angel and a Demon are arguing about the nature of God, and how Christ was actually a rebel who bucked the religious conventions of his time: "Jesus was all virtue, and acted from impulse, not from rules." The Angel then embraces the Devil and becomes a Devil, one with whom Blake was apparently friends. In this marriage of heaven and hell, angels become devils, something Blake finds attractive, because in Blake's world, everything is Holy.

CONCLUSION

To describe the meaning of a work of art is impossible, since the meaning often eludes even its artist, author, or composer. Our first experience in reading a poem, an essay, or a novel, is often simplistic, possibly even erroneous. To read an epic poem such as *Paradise Lost*, not merely in its historical or literary context, but as a work of art, is to understand its underlying "mythic" nature. A myth seeks to depict and explain basic realities of human experience, and, in the end, the facts we call basic are few. Like Milton's poem, Blake's *Marriage of Heaven and Hell* is most truly mythological in its comprehensiveness, in the breadth of its themes, and in the relevance of its design to the fundamental issues of the spiritual life. Both works address the polarities of life, following the threefold pattern of the mythological adventure known as the human quest (departure, illumination, and return). The themes contained in this mythological adventure are perfectly congenial to Milton and Blake's genius. No theme or setting, other than the primeval conflict of good and evil, could have expressed so completely the vision that compelled their imagination.

QUESTIONS FOR DISCUSSION AND REFLECTION

In addition to the questions listed at the end of the preface, answer the following questions, writing your answers in a journal. If you are in a group study, be prepared to share your answers with those in the group.

1. Explain and assess the merit and usefulness of the concepts of dualism and nondualism for Christian theology and spirituality.

2. Explain and assess the distinction between dualism and nondualism for understanding moral good and evil.

3. Milton and Blake both deal with the problem of good and evil artistically rather than philosophically or conceptually. Explain the merit and usefulness of exploring moral and theological issues artistically rather than dogmatically.

4. Explain how Milton's involvement in local politics influenced his views on moral issues such as good and evil and theological issues such as heaven and hell.

5. In your estimation, is it useful or necessary for Christians to believe in Satan, demons, or angels as personal beings? Explain your answer.

6. From both spiritual and psychological perspectives, explain and assess the usefulness of the historicity of Adam and Eve's fall from grace and their expulsion from the Garden of Eden. In your estimation, did such an event occur historically, or is this more a mythological rendering of the spiritual struggles occurring in every person's life? Explain your answer.

7. In today's scientific age, is it possible for modern people to believe in hierarchical levels and orders of existence, as assumed by biblical and medieval Christians, or should we view these hierarchies through mythical, literary, and artistic eyes? Explain your answer.

8. Explain and assess Milton's understanding of *agon*, and the usefulness of this concept for Christian spirituality.

9. In your estimation, what was Milton's greatest contribution to Christian spirituality? Explain your answer.

10. Explain and assess Blake's conception of human imagination as "the body of God."

11. While Blake may have considered himself to be a committed Christian, describe some of his greatest objections to traditional Christianity. Contrast Blake's view of the biblical "fall" of humans from grace with Milton's view.

12. Contrast Blake's views of heaven and hell, angels and demons, and good and evil, with those of Milton.

13. In your estimation, what was Blake's greatest contribution to spirituality?

Chapter 9

Tozer's *Pursuit of God*, Drummond's *Greatest Thing in the World*, and Murray's *Humility*

CHAPTER 7 INTRODUCED THE topic of Christian devotional literature, listing some of its classic exponents and contributors. In this chapter and the next, we examine this topic through the lives and writing of six modern thinkers, each uniquely suited to guide us further along our spiritual path.

Since the emergence of human consciousness, one question underlies all theological discussion and continues to be the burning theological issue of the day: "Is there purpose to life?" The Westminster Shorter Catechism utilizes traditional language to frame the question as follows, "What is the chief end of man?" The answer is intriguing yet succinct: "The chief end of man is to glorify God and enjoy God forever." Building on this understanding of spirituality, in this chapter we focus on three facets of the Christian life: its supreme *goal*, its sublime *good*, and its superior *grace*.

LIFE'S SUPREME GOAL: A. W. TOZER'S *THE PURSUIT OF GOD*

Aiden Wilson Tozer (1897–1963), longtime American pastor, author, magazine editor, and spiritual guide to thousands of believers, is best remembered for his inspirational classic *The Pursuit of God*, which made him a household name among evangelical Christians. Born and raised in a small farming community in western Pennsylvania, Tozer experienced a life-changing conversion to Christianity as a teenager while working for The Goodyear Tire and Rubber Company in Akron, Ohio. There, at the age of seventeen, he overheard a street preacher declare, "If you don't know how to be saved, just call on God, saying 'Lord, be merciful to me a sinner.'" Convicted, Tozer returned home and heeded the preacher's advice.

In 1919, five years after his conversion and without formal education in homiletics or Christian theology, Tozer accepted an offer to serve as a church pastor. That began forty-four years of ministry with the Christian and Missionary Alliance (C&MA) denomination. Beginning at a storefront church in West Virginia and continuing in churches in Toledo, Ohio and Indianapolis, Indiana, he later served thirty years as pastor of Southside Alliance Church in Chicago, ending his career as pastor of an Alliance church in Toronto, Canada.

Considered a spirit-filled, modern-day prophet by his followers, in 1931 Tozer began writing regular columns for the C&MA denominational magazine *Alliance Weekly* (now *Alliance Life*), serving as the magazine's editor from 1950 until his death in 1963. In the 1940s, he wrote biographies of A. B. Simpson and Robert A. Jeffrey, but it was his publication in 1948 of *The Pursuit of God* that widened his audience. In addition to the twelve books he published in his lifetime, over forty other books have been compiled from his magazine features, editorials, and transcribed sermons.

Living a simple lifestyle based on prayer and compassion, Tozer never owned a car, and even after becoming a well-known author, he gave away much of his royalties to people in need. His bestselling *The Pursuit of God* has been called "one of the all-time most inspirational books" by a panel of Christian magazine writers, and in the year 2000, the book was named to *Christianity Today*'s list of one hundred "Books of the Century."

Focusing on spirituality, Tozer notes that modern-day Christians live overly compromised lives, their goals, thoughts, and desires consumed with "worldly" (temporal and often frivolous) concerns. In *The Pursuit of God*, Tozer calls for a lifelong pursuit of God. With deep conviction and flowing prose, he urges believers to replace materialistic goals and issues with spiritual ones, and to live lives of peace and quiet in order to know God's presence. For Tozer, to know God is to pursue God, and in that pursuit, to be drawn to deeper and higher spirituality. One reader, impressed by Tozer's depth, sincerity, and straightforward style, called

Tozer "a theologian for the masses," singling out Tozer's point in chapter 3 about the veil that separates us from God as convincingly explaining the human predicament.

Tozer divides *The Pursuit of God* into ten chapters, summarized in the following chapter headings:

1. *Following Hard after God*. Tozer begins chapter 1 by speaking of "prevenient grace," noting that the impulse to pursue God originates not with us, but with God. As Jesus states in John 1:44, "No one can come to me unless drawn by the Father who sent me." As modern science has lost God among the wonders of nature, so modern believers seem to forget that God is personal, and as such, that we humans can experience a relationship with the eternal God just as one might with other persons. Having been made in God's image enables us to know God. However, as occasional glimpses and casual chitchat with others do not lead to meaningful relationships with them, the same hold true for God. To know God requires prolonged time interacting with God, primarily through prayer, silence, and compassionate service to those in need. To experience intimacy with God means we do not settle for occasional spiritual highs or too-easily satisfied experiences, for "to have found God and still to pursue Him is the soul's paradox of love."[1] "That I may know him" (Phil 3:10) was the goal of Paul's heart; this goal, the mainspring of his life, for which he sacrificed everything, must be our goal as well.

2. *The Blessedness of Possessing Nothing*. According to Tozer, "the way to deeper knowledge of God is through the lonely valleys of soul poverty and abnegation of all things."[2] The blessed are they who have repudiated every external thing and have rooted from their hearts all sense of possessing. These are the "poor in spirit." They are blessed because they are no longer slaves to the tyranny of things. In Genesis 22 we find a dramatic picture of the surrendered life in God's ultimate testing of Abraham. God never intended to allow Abraham to sacrifice his son, but in order to save Abraham and Isaac from self-centered lives, God showed Abraham the meaning of a surrendered life. From then on, Abraham would have all things necessary for success, yet possessing nothing. If we would know God in increasing intimacy, we too must go the way of renunciation.

3. *Removing the Veil*. Citing the Westminster Shorter Catechism, Tozer notes that "God formed us for his pleasure.... He meant us to see

---

1. Tozer, *Pursuit of God*, 15.
2. Tozer, *Pursuit of God*, 23.

Him and live with Him and draw our life from His smile."[3] However, our sin caused us to rebel, and the whole work of God in redemption is to undo sin's tragic effects and bring us back into fellowship with him. Our return to God is well illustrated in the configuration of the Jerusalem temple (based on the wilderness tabernacle), comprising three chambers: the outer court, where blood sacrifices were performed; "the holy place," centered on the golden candelabra and the table of showbread; and the innermost chamber, "the Holy of Holies," where God's presence dwelt. A veil covered the entrance to this chamber, and only the High Priest could enter, once a year, with blood offered for the sins of the people. According to the New Testament, it was this veil that was torn in two when Jesus died on the cross (Matt 27:51), opening the way for every believer to come into the divine Presence. The reason many believers consent to live outside the Holy of Holies and never enter to look upon God is the veil of our fleshly nature (what modern mystics call our False Self) living within us, uncrucified and unrepudiated. The False Self is the veil that prevents our entry into God's Presence. To enter, we must set aside the "self-sins," the veil woven from self-righteousness, self-pity, self-confidence, self-sufficiency, self-admiration, self-love, and self-promotion. Let us beware of accomplishing this through our own effort. To rend this veil, God must do everything for us. Our part is to yield and trust. The veil's removal requires suffering, persecution, even death, for without crucifixion, there can be no resurrection.

4. *Apprehending God*. The Bible assumes that women and men can know God with the same degree of immediacy as they known other humans. The terms used in scripture to express the knowledge of God—taste, smell, hear, feel, and see—are the same as those used to express knowledge of our physical world: What all this means is that we have in our spirit organs by means of which we can know God as certainly as we know material things through our five senses. Just as we apprehend the physical world by exercising the faculties we possess for that purpose, so we possess spiritual faculties by means of which we can know God and the spiritual world. To enter this realm means we must both obey the Spirit's urges and begin using the gifts we have been given. This process begins with faith, by which we mean trusting in the promises of God: "O *taste* and *see* that the Lord is good," says the psalmist (Ps 34:8), and "Blessed are the pure in heart," says the gospel writer, "for they shall *see*

---

3. Tozer, *Pursuit of God*, 34.

God" (Matt 5:8). A spiritual realm lies all about us, "enclosing us, embracing us, altogether within reach of our inner selves, waiting for us to recognize it."[4] God is in our midst, waiting our response to his Presence. At the root of the Christian life lies faith in the invisible. While faith is necessary, faith creates nothing; it simply acknowledges that which is always and already there. If we truly want to know and obey God, we must be "other-wordly," for as we focus upon God, the things of the Spirit will take shape before our inner eyes, and we will begin to *taste* and *hear* and inwardly *feel* the God, whose Presence is the glory and wonder of our lives.

5. *The Universal Presence.* God is everywhere present at every moment. Thus, there is no place where God is not. This approach should not be viewed as pantheism, which declares God and nature to be one and the same, but rather as panentheism, meaning God is immanent within all things yet transcendent and greater than all things. Why do some persons find or experience God in ways others do not? The difference is what Tozer calls "spiritual receptivity." The great saints of the past (and present) differ from the average person in that when they felt the inward longing, they responded. They are like the psalmist, whose heart declares, "Come, seek his face," and whose will responds, "Your face, Lord, do I seek" (Ps 27:8). According to Tozer, modern spirituality has reversed the biblical path, making religious truth conform to our experience and squeezing God into our timeframe, rather than giving God sovereignty and preeminence in our lives. "We will know (God) in increasing degree as our receptivity becomes more perfect by faith and love and practice."[5]

6. *The Speaking Voice.* God is by nature continuously speaking. God has never been silent: "The voice of God is the most powerful force in nature, indeed the only force in nature, for all energy is here only because the power-filled Word is being spoken."[6] Furthermore, God speaks through Christ, the living Word of God, and through scripture, God's mediated Word. Ancient Hebrews called this universal voice of God "Wisdom," and it is our spiritual response for which the Wisdom of God is pleading. To people caught up in the bluster and noise of life, possibly the most important verse in the Bible is when God says, "Be still, and know that I am God!" (Ps 46:10).

---

4. Tozer, *Pursuit of God*, 52.
5. Tozer, *Pursuit of God*, 71.
6. Tozer, *Pursuit of God*, 74.

7. *The Gaze of the Soul.* Apart from a brief fourteen-word definition of "faith" in Hebrews 11:1, the Bible primarily shows "faith" in action. According to John 3:14–16, "looking" and "believing" are synonymous terms. In Numbers 21, after a time of rebellion led to a plague of serpents, a serpent of brass was set as a standard, that if a serpent bit any person, when that person looked to the bronze serpent, he lived (Numb 11:9). When we cultivate the gaze of our soul upon the living God, we stop seeing ourselves and our concerns and find the object of our soul's true and deepest longing: the Triune God becomes our dwelling place, and we will have found life's *summum bonum.*

8. *Restoring the Creator-creature Relation.* Because all relationships must start somewhere, our relationship with God starts with accepting God as he is, without trying to make God into our image. When we encounter the God whose name is "I Am Who I Am" (Exod 3:14), and as we get to know him as he is, we will find God to be the source of unspeakable joy. God created human beings for his pleasure, and when we decide to exalt God over all other loyalties, goals, and desires, we learn the meaning of John 14:23, "Those who love me will keep my word, and my Father will love them, and we will come to them and make our home with them." If sin violates the Creator-creature relation, salvation becomes "the restoration of a right relation between (humans) and (their) Creator, a bringing back to normal the Creator-creature relation."[7] When we place God first in our lives, God promises to honor us (John 12:26). To exalt God above all things in our life is to experience spiritual victory, for when we exalt God, we gain the key that unlocks the door to great treasures of grace.

9. *Meekness and Rest.* Among the secular world's values, we find nothing approaching the virtues in Jesus' famous Sermon on the Mount. Instead of poverty of spirit, we find pride; instead of mourning, we find pleasure seeking; instead of meekness, we find arrogance; instead of mercy, we find vengeance; instead of purity of heart, we find corruption; instead of peacemaking, we find quarreling and resentment; and instead of rejoicing in mistreatment, we find retaliation. Jesus told his followers, "Come to me, all you that are weary and are carrying heavy burdens, and I will give you rest. . . . For my yoke is easy, and my burden is light" (Matt 11:28, 30). What is our burden? Much of it is pride, arrogance, vengeance, and other worldly values. However, people trusting in God need not bear such a burden. Meek persons care not at all who is greater that

---

7. Tozer, *Pursuit of God*, 99–100.

they, for they long ago decided that the esteem of the world is not worth the effort. Paradoxically, human beings are nothing in themselves, but in God, they are everything. Furthermore, the rest that Jesus promised is simply release from our burden. Rest, then, is not something we do, but is rather what comes to us when we cease to carry our burden alone. Meek persons are yoked with God, and therein is their rest. Jesus calls us to rest, and meekness is his method. The meek person is not a weak, inferior being, but rather is like an energetic colt under restraint. While meek persons know they are weak and helpless in God's sight, they know at the same time that in the sight of God they are of infinite value and importance, for they are made in God's image and bear the divine status as children of God.

10. *The Sacrament of Living.* Tozer, it turns out, is a nondualist, for as he states, Christians should not separate life into "spiritual" and "secular," since for them, all life is "spiritual." Paul, an early follower of Jesus, likewise took up Jesus' call to liberty by indicating that all food is clean, every day is holy, all places are sacred, and every act is acceptable to God. Such essential nondualist spirituality continued in the early church until Christianity lost its connection with its Jewish roots and became a primarily Gentile and Roman phenomenon. At that point, the church came again to observe special days, and holy seasons and times. As differences between people were emphasized, sacraments were introduced, growing from two until with the triumph of Romanism they were fixed at seven. In speaking of the sacramental quality of every-day living, Tozer made clear he was not advocating a cookie-cutter approach to spirituality, or implying that all acts are of equal importance. As followers of Jesus, our task is to focus on our motives. If our motivation is rooted in the primacy of God, then all our actions will be good and acceptable to God. For such a person, living will be sacramental and the whole world will be a sanctuary. And if all life is viewed as spiritual, then for us there is only one command; not a negative one, as in the Garden or at Mount Sinai ("you shall not'; see Gen 2:17, Exod 20:1–17), but a positive one: Love!

LIFE'S SUPREME GOOD: HENRY DRUMMOND'S *THE GREATEST THING IN THE WORLD*

Unlike many of the writers whose works we are examining, Henry Drummond (1851–1897) was neither a poet nor a theologian, nor did he assume a clerical role. Nevertheless, few people exercised more religious influence in their own generation than Drummond, particularly on people in late adolescence or early adulthood.

Born in Stirling, Scotland, the son of a business entrepreneur, Drummond was educated at Edinburgh University, where he displayed a strong inclination for physical and mathematical science. Nevertheless, the religious element was a powerful part of his nature, and he prepared for ministry in the Free Church of Scotland. At this time he became deeply interested in the evangelizing ministry of Dwight L. Moody, remaining active in the movement for two years.

In 1877, he became a lecturer on natural science in the Free Church College in Glasgow, which enabled him to combine all the pursuits for which he felt a calling. An advocate of theistic evolution, which combined belief in divine creation with biological evolution, his studies resulted in his writing *Natural Law in the Spiritual World*, finding continuity and compatibility between the physical and spiritual realms. In 1880, he traveled to southcentral Africa to conduct a geological survey for the African Lakes Company. The following year, upon his return to Scotland, he found himself to be rather famous. Large numbers of serious readers, including both religious and scientific specialists, discovered in *Natural Law* the common ground they needed. The universality of support for this work seemed to prove the reasonableness of its thesis.

Drummond continued to be actively interested in missionary work, which led to travels in Australia, where he participated in religious and scientific endeavors, and to Boston, where he delivered the 1893 Lowell Lectures, which appeared in 1894 under the title of *The Ascent of Man*. His underlying interest in this work was to ratify altruism, as evident in the care and compassion of animals for each other, important in undergirding the evolutionary concept of the survival of the fittest, thereby combining religious and scientific principles. A lifelong bachelor, Drummond succumbed to bone cancer in 1897, dying at the age of forty-four.

First preached to a group of fellow missionaries in 1884, *The Greatest Thing in the World* is an exposition of 1 Corinthians 13, one of the best loved passages in the Bible. In his book, Drummond explains the importance of love and why it can be called the greatest thing in the world. Parishioners are often told that the greatest thing in life is faith. However, Paul would not have agreed, and neither should we. For Paul, as for other authors of the New Testament, love is the fulfilment of the law of God (see Rom 13:10). Such a statement, uttered in a first-century

Jewish context, would have been found faulty, for in those days, Jews were expected to keep the commandments in obedience to God's will. However, if we examine any of the Ten Commandments, we find that none could be fulfilled without love. If we loved God, for example, we would honor our parents. Likewise, if we loved God, we would not kill, steal, bear false witness against our neighbors, or covet what belonged to others. And Paul is not alone in singling love as the *summum bonum*, for the author of 1 Peter also declares that love for others should be our first priority (see 1 Peter 4:8), as does the author of 1 John, who declares, "God is love" (1 John 4:16).

Drummond divides his study of love as the supreme good into three parts: (1) love contrasted; (2) love analyzed; and (3) love defended. In 1 Corinthians 13, Paul begins by contrasting love with other things that people in those days praised. First, he contrast love with eloquence, then with prophecy, with mysteries, with faith, and even with deeds of charity. The reason love is greater, we learn, is that the whole is greater than the parts. Love is greater than faith, because the end is greater than the means. If the purpose of connecting with God is our ultimate goal, and if God is love, then love is greater than faith. Love is also greater than charity because charity is only a portion of love. Love, Paul continues, is greater than sacrifice and martyrdom, for nothing is more important to witnessing and evangelism than love. If we sacrifice all we have for the cause of Christ, even to the point of sacrificing our very life, and have not love, such actions are meaningless. As a person who considered himself a missionary, Drummond knew that the ultimate form of communication is not words, but character. In evangelism, love is the universal language, the most important ingredient in the spiritual life.

After contrasting love with things we value and cherish (1 Cor 13:1–3), Paul, in four short verses, provides an amazing analysis of what this supreme good consists (1 Cor 13:4–7). Like a beam of light, when passed through a crystal prism, comes out on the other side as multiple colors, so Paul speaks of the spectrum of love, which consists of nine specific virtues or ingredients: patience, kindness, generosity, humility, courtesy, unselfishness, good temper, guilelessness, and sincerity. Love, composed of numerous ingredients, cannot be reduced to an emotion or a feeling, for in the end, love is a way of life, a way of life lived in awareness of the Presence of God. When we realize that spirituality is a life stance, a way of living fully in the moment, then we understand why many mystics have called love "the sacrament of the present moment." When we become aware that we are made in the image of God, we enhance the flow of the stream of divine love flowing through us, and we realize that the task of spirituality is not to be a better person, to be more loving, or to try harder, but simply to keep choosing to abide in God's divine love. Where God is, love is, and those who dwell in love dwell in God. When Paul speaks in verse 6 of love as rejoicing in the truth, we must keep in mind that "truth" is not ultimately to be equated with beliefs or doctrines, but rather is a reference to what is Real; in that respect, truth is a Person, the eternal Person, none other than the One we call God.

Having analyzed love, the task of spirituality is to have these qualities fitted into our characters. That is the supreme work to which believers are called—to learn love. What is life, if not a laboratory for learning love? The world in which we live is not a playground, but a schoolroom, and life is not a vacation, but an education. And the one eternal lesson for us all is how better we can love. What makes a good artist, a musician, an athlete, a linguist, or a teacher? Practice! What makes a person good? Practice; nothing else. As Johann von Goethe noted, "Talent develops in solitude; character in the stream of life." Spiritual talent develops itself in solitude—in the discipline of prayer, meditation, and faith—but character grows in the Potter's workshop, where we learn to love. There is no mystery about love. Understood biblically, love is not a command, but a response. Those who are "in Christ" know that to love God is to love others, for in loving God, we become like God, following the primary principle of spirituality: "We love, because (God) first loved us (1 John 4:19).

Having defined love, Paul closes his great love chapter by defending love. Why is love the supreme good? Simply put, love is our supreme possession because it lasts. "Love," Paul declares, endures ("never ends; never fails"). Paul then names qualities that people thought were going to last, and shows that by comparison with love, they are all fleeting and temporary. As for prophecies, languages, and knowledge, they shall vanish or cease. As in every branch of religion, so also in science, all theories, beliefs, and teachings are partial or passing truths: "Now we know in part; now we see in a mirror, dimly" (1 Cor 13:12). In his defense of love, Paul did not mention money, fortune, or fame, but rather he selected out the great things of his time, and brushed them aside. They were great things, but not supreme things. Knowing that human being are prone to give themselves to many things, Paul emphasizes that they should be held in proportion and moderation. However, only one thing is eternal.

To love abundantly is to live abundantly. Hence, eternity is inextricably bound up with love.

In Matthew 25: 31–46, where the Judgment Day is depicted in the imagery of One seated upon a throne dividing the sheep from the goats, the test of our character is not, "How have I believed?" but "How have I loved?" The test of spirituality, the final exam of religion, is not piety or religiosity, then, but love, since, according to 1 John 5:7, "everyone who loves is born of God and knows God. "

LIFE'S SUPERIOR GRACE: ANDREW MURRAY'S *HUMILITY*

Born in South Africa to Scottish Dutch Reformed Church missionary parents, at the age of ten Andrew Murray (1828-1917) was sent to Scotland for his education, together with his older brother, John. In Scotland, the brothers lived with their uncle, a devout Christian minister. Under their uncle's influence and guidance, both boys eventually pursued the ministry as their vocation. While at the University of Aberdeen, Murray was influenced by Scottish revivalists Murray McCheyne, Horatius Bonar, and William Burns. Completing his master's degree in 1845, Murray studied theology at the University of Utrecht, in Holland, where he experienced an intense spiritual conversion and participated in Het Réveil, a religious revival movement opposed to the rationalism then in vogue in the Netherlands.

In 1848, at the age of twenty, Murray was ordained by the Dutch Reformed Church, after which he returned to South Africa to serve a congregation in the frontier town of Bloemfontein. While sparsely populated, his parish covered several thousand square miles. In spite of his youth, Murray soon won the hearts of the Dutch colonists. In 1855, he met and married Emma Rutherford, the daughter of parishioners. A devout and gregarious woman, she was accomplished in music, literature, and the arts. Her temperament and religious fervor made her well suited to the ministries of hospitality and pastoral care that she assumed, in addition to her role as mother of eight children.

In 1860, the family moved to Worcester to take a new congregation. A revival occurred in that church, which later came to be known as the Great Revival of 1860. Respect for Murray continued to grow in his denomination, and in 1864, he became joint pastor of a large Dutch

Reformed church in Cape Town. In addition to his pastoral work, Murray became involved in social work among the poor, establishing schools, and serving on international church councils.

In time, Murray's exhausting schedule exacerbated his already weakened health, and he was offered a call to a much smaller congregation, which he accepted. From his small parsonage in Wellington, Murray's ministry spread around the world through his writings. His thoughts and ideas concerning the spiritual life, church renewal, and revival flowed freely, producing many books that were eventually translated into several languages. A bibliography compiled by D. S. B. Joubert estimates that Murray published some 50 books and 200 tracts, many of them authored in both Dutch and English, including *The Deeper Christian Life*, *Abide in Christ*, *The Prayer Life*, *The Spiritual Life*, *With Christ in the School of Prayer*, and *Humility*. Through his writings, Murray became a leader of the Keswick movement, and his theology of faith healing and belief in the continuation of the apostolic gifts made him a significant forerunner of the modern Pentecostal movement. In 1906, Murray retired from the pastorate, while continuing to write, speak, and travel until his death in 1917, at the age of eighty-eight.

Murray wrote to interpret the Bible in such a way that Christians were free to believe and experience the grace of God. He believed that God had done everything necessary for people to live productive and meaningful lives that participated in the life of God. The obstacles to such lives included half-hearted surrender to God, a lack of confidence in the anointing of the Spirit, and skepticism about the power of prayer. One of his most popular books, *With Christ in the School of Prayer*, takes New Testament teachings about prayer and illumines them in thirty-one lessons designed to help readers move past shallow, ineffectual prayer into a fuller understanding of the work God has called them to do. According to Murray, the church does not realize that "God rules the world by the prayers of his saints, that prayer is the power by which Satan is conquered, and that by prayer the church on earth has disposal of the powers of the heavenly world."

Murray strove to align his spiritual insights with his Reformed theology, but he was accused by critics of teaching free will and that God wills the redemption of all. Murray's teaching on free will and divine election seems to describe the paradox Paul had in mind in Philippians 2:12, where Paul exhorts his followers to "work out your own salvation with fear and trembling," disclosing in verse 13 that "it is God who is working in you, enabling you to will and to work for his good pleasure." Thus understood, the Christian life is a two-way street, for believers are to do their best while allowing God to do the rest. In actuality, God's activity is all encompassing, for as the Bible attests, God's grace in our lives begins before our birth, carrying us through our lives and into eternity.

In *Humility*, Murray considers humility as primarily a vertical issue, the major indicator of one's relationship with God. Real humility, he argues, requires a complete surrender of one's self to God. In this short book, he talks about the relationships between humility and holiness, sin, faith, death to self, happiness, and exaltation. He also provides wonderful examples about how Jesus displayed humility, as well as examples of humility or lack of humility in his disciples. Murray also includes important lessons about being humble before God, but most importantly, about being humble in our everyday life among others. Such living, which Murray calls "dying to self," is not our doing, but rather God's work. If we would enter into full fellowship with Christ in his death, and know the full deliverance from our egocentric self, we must humble ourselves. This is our one duty, to place ourselves before God in our utter helplessness, consenting heartily to the fact of our inability to slay our False Self or resurrect our True Self. Sink into your own nothingness, he advises, and in the spirit of meekness, patience, and trust, surrender to God. Accept every humiliation, and look upon those who try or vex you as a means of grace to humble you.

According to Murray, humility cannot be discussed in isolation, but must be viewed in reference to three aspects of our lives before God: our status (1) as creatures, (2) as sinners, and (3) as saints. The first is modeled by Jesus; the second indicates our need to return to our rightful place as creatures; and the third speaks of the mystery of grace, which teaches that as fallen creatures lose themselves in God's redeeming grace, humility marks the consummation of our spiritual journey in eternal blessedness. Indicating that much religious teaching focuses on the second aspect—that is, on attaining humility in our sinful state—Murray notes that his emphasis is on the first aspect, on the humility that becomes us as creatures.

If Jesus is to be our example, and if meekness and lowliness of heart are to be the distinguishing features of discipleship, as they characterized Jesus, then we need to find this "common ground in which we stand with

Him, and in which our likeness to Him is to be attained."[8] If humility is to be our joy, we must see it apart from sin, in its very beauty and blessedness. As the early church taught in the christological hymn found in Philippians 2:6–11, there is exaltation and blessedness in imitating Jesus, "who, though he was in the form of God, did not regard equality with God as something to be exploited, but emptied (humbled) himself, taking the form of a slave (servant) . . . and became obedient to the point of death." If as Jesus taught his disciples, they must become servants of others (Mark 9:35), such humility must go far deeper than contrition, but rather be accepted as participation in the life of Jesus, for in becoming servants we discover our true nobility and origin as beings created in the image of God.

Humility, as Murray describes it, is not a state of self-deprecation. Understood rather as the state of full dependence on God, it becomes the highest virtue of God's creatures. Pride, likewise, should not be understood dualistically—that is, as the polarity of humility—but rather as the loss or absence of our original goodness. "Hence it follows that nothing can be our redemption except the restoration of the lost humility, the original and only relation of the creature to its God. And thus Jesus came to bring humility back to earth, to make us partakers of it, and by it to save us . . . [Hence, Christ's] humility is our salvation (and) his salvation is our humility."[9] Humility, misunderstood as something that we bring to God, is not what saves us, for we are not saved by effort but by grace. However, this humility is not something that comes of itself. Rather, we must desire it, pray for it, and practice it when it comes.

Having clarified what Murray means by humility, namely, that it is a state of entire dependence on God, we must clarify what we mean by salvation, for the word "salvation" is complex and multilayered, both in scripture and in the Christian tradition. It can range in meaning from "general health and well-being" and "material and political protection and preservation in the present" to "eternal blessedness." Broadly speaking, we might say that salvation is the overarching theme of the entire Bible. The biblical writers speak of salvation as a reality that is both individual and communal, objective and subjective, physical and spiritual, historical and eternal. Since the biblical writers view salvation as a historical reality, the temporal dimensions of past, present, and future

---

8. Murray, *Humility*, 8.
9. Murray, *Humility*, 13–14.

further intensify and deepen the concept. Hence, salvation is both a process and a reality. Further, as understood theologically, salvation involves the paradox of human freedom and divine election. Despite the complexity of these dimensions, the Bible regularly speaks about salvation in the context of relationship—between humans, between humans and nature, and between humans and God.

In general, Old Testament writers see salvation as a reality more physical than spiritual. Salvation from sin, though not a dominant concern, is by no means absent, especially in the prophets. Ezekiel, for example, combines national restoration with personal righteousness. In Ezekiel 36:22–32, salvation involves the gift of a new heart of flesh and a new spirit, which will finally empower God's people to keep the commandments. Here we also learn that salvation is ultimately not for the sake of Israel, but for God's glory.

In the New Testament, salvation is clearly a process, for it is viewed as both an accomplished fact and yet as something still anticipated, a process begun in the past, ongoing in the present, and fulfilled in the future. The New Testament continues the Old Testament affirmation that salvation belongs to God alone, but with greater specificity. Now, it is God's presence in and through Jesus that proves decisive. In Jesus' teaching, salvation is linked to the advance of God's kingdom. By using God's kingdom as a circumlocution for salvation, Jesus deepens the Old Testament conviction that salvation belongs to God, for the kingdom of God, as theologians now understand it, is not a place as much as a perspective—God's perspective.

Humility, often associated by legalistic Christians with perfection, actually has little to do with effort. Christians often believe that only perfect things are loveable in God's sight, yet the gospels declare clearly that God loves imperfect things, which means everything. Only God can lay claim to perfection; the rest of us are imperfect, loved unconditionally as we are. The good news of the gospel is that we are already saved—accepted by God just as we are. Thus, there is nothing we must do to be saved, except accept and live in God's grace. The gospel is not a call to live perfectly, but to trust perfectly. Thus, those who spend their lives trying to ascend the spiritual ladder of perfection miss Christ, who comes down the ladder of incarnation to abide with us.

As Murray makes clear, "no tree can grow except on the root from which it sprang."[10] As pride comes from Satan's pride, so believers must walk "rooted in Christ." The life of God, which entered human nature through the incarnate Christ, is the root from which we come and through which we grow spiritually. Thus, the power that worked in Christ's life and resurrection is the same that works daily in us. Our one need is to study, learn, and trust the life that has been revealed in Christ and is now ours to claim, waiting for our consent to process and master our whole being. And what is that power but heavenly humility! Therefore, because Christ humbled himself . . . God also highly exalted him" (Phil 2:8–9). However, Christ's exaltation, his sitting on the throne, is nothing but humility, for the highest glory of the creature is in being only a vessel, to receive, enjoy, and show forth the glory of God. Is not this the "chief end of man," as the Westminster Shorter Catechism affirms?

If Christ is the root of the tree, his nature "must be seen in every branch and leaf and fruit."[11] If humility be the secret of Christ's atoning work, then the health and strength of our spiritual life depends upon our making this grace paramount in all we think, say, and do. Though humility is a grace, underserved and unearned, it requires our simple consent as creatures to allow God be "all in all."

In his life of absolute submission and dependence upon the Father's will, Christ found a life of perfect peace and joy. And because Jesus thus humbled himself before God, he found it possible to humble himself before others as well, and to be servant of all. His humility was simply to surrender himself to God, no matter the consequences, and it is in this childlike frame of mind and heart that the redemption of Christ has its virtue and efficacy, a redemption rooted in love of God and of others as of oneself.

Murray's book has been called "the best work on humility ever written." This praise is not due to deep insight or lofty rhetoric, but rather to the book's essential truth. If the greatest teaching books are the simplest ones, Murray's book is both simple and powerful, for Murray does not waste words but clearly and convincingly presents his thesis that humility is the essential characteristic of the Christian life, and that pride stands as the one defiant obstacle to everything God desires to do in us and through us. If we would be like Christ, there is one thing we must do

---

10. Murray, *Humility*, 19.
11. Murray, *Humility*, 23.

daily, and that is to humble ourselves. God stands near to the humble, yet distant to the proud. According to Murray, humility is the attribute that Christians need most yet least desire. Humility, called the "forgotten" virtue, enables us to be most like Christ. True humility involves dying to self and letting Christ live in us. A common misconception of "death to self" is that it annuls our personality. However, the opposite is true. Murray states that the "death-life" enables us to be our True Self because as ego diminishes, we become more like Christ, his image restored in us.

QUESTIONS FOR DISCUSSION AND REFLECTION

In addition to the questions listed at the end of the preface, answer the following questions, writing your answers in a journal. If you are in a group study, be prepared to share your answers with those in the group.

1. Do you agree with Tozer that life's supreme goal is "the pursuit of God"? Explain your answer.

2. Explain and assess the necessity of a personal God in Tozer's spirituality.

3. Explain and assess the merits or usefulness of Tozer's image of the veil that separates human beings from God. Does Tozer's use of the veil require a literal reading of the biblical story of Adam and Eve's fall from grace, or does his image also hold value for nonliteralists? Explain your answer.

4. In your estimation, was Tozer a panentheist or simply a traditional theist emphasizing God's immanence? Explain your answer.

5. In your estimation, was Tozer a dualist or a nondualist regarding the secular and sacred realms of life? Explain your answer.

6. In your estimation, what was Tozer's greatest contribution to Christian spirituality? Explain your answer.

7. Drummond's *Greatest Thing* is an exposition of 1 Corinthians 13. In your estimation, why is this passage considered one of the most inspirational in the Bible?

8. Do you agree with Murray's assessment regarding the power and purpose of corporate prayer? Explain your answer.

9. Explain and assess the meaning and usefulness of Murray's statement, "Christ's humility is our salvation, and his salvation is our humility."

10. After reading this chapter, what did you learn about humility?

11. Explain and assess the merit of the author's statement, "The good news of the gospel is that (humans) are already saved . . . Thus, there is nothing we must do to be saved, except accept and live in God's grace."

Chapter 10

Nouwen's *Reaching Out*, Conway's *Acres of Diamonds*, and McLaren's *Generous Orthodoxy*

HAVING EXAMINED THE LIVES and devotional works of A. W. Tozer, Henry Drummond, and Andrew Murray in chapter 9, this chapter examines the lives and writings of Henri Nouwen, Russell Conwell, and Brian McLaren.

HENRI NOUWEN'S *REACHING OUT*

The renowned professor, theologian, and Dutch Catholic priest Henri Nouwen (1932–1996) was born in Nijkerk, the Netherlands. His father was a tax lawyer and his mother worked as a bookkeeper for her family's business. Nouwen's uncle Toon Ramselaar was a Catholic priest in the Archdiocese of Utrecht. Nouwen attended the Jesuit Aloysius College in The Hague prior to his years at the seminary in Rijsenburg studying philosophy and theology in preparation for the priesthood.

Ordained a Catholic priest in 1957, Nouwen requested permission to further his education by studying psychology at the Catholic University of Nijmegen. His wish to study clinical psychology was motivated by his need to explore the human side of faith, as well as to learn more about himself and the people he counseled. For his thesis, Nouwen focused on Anton Boisen, an American minister credited with founding the clinical pastoral education movement. Completing his studies in 1964, Nouwen studied for two years as a Fellow in the Religion and Psychiatry Program at the Menninger Clinic in Topeka, Kansas, where he was influenced by psychologist Gordon Allport. During this period, Nouwen began to engage with social events in the United States, including the civil rights movement.

From 1966 to 1968, he was a visiting professor at the University of Notre Dame, and from 1971 to 1981 he was a professor of pastoral theology at Yale Divinity School, where he began to establish a broad readership of his articles and other publications. In addition to his teaching responsibilities, Nouwen traveled extensively leading retreats and preaching. He appealed to diverse audiences, including Anglicans and evangelicals because of his Jesus-centered spirituality. While a professor at Yale, Nouwen spent extended periods at the Abbey of the Genesee, writing about his experiences there. Though he concluded he was not well suited for the Trappist life, the Abbey served as his home base for a year after he resigned from Yale. Following a six-month trip to Bolivia and Peru, he taught at the Harvard Divinity School from 1983 to 1985, after which he spent nine months with the L'Arche community in France. In 1986 he moved to L'Arche Daybreak near Toronto, Canada, where he spent the last ten years of his life. While at Daybreak, Nouwen was paired with Adam Arnett, a core member of the community with profound developmental disabilities. Nouwen wrote about his relationship with Arnett in a book entitled *Adam: God's Beloved*.

Throughout his life, Nouwen struggled with his sexuality, alluding to his loneliness, self-doubts, and depression in his book *The Return of the Prodigal Son*. Only toward the end of his life was he able to make peace with his sexual orientation. He died from a sudden heart attack in 1996, while traveling to Russia to participate in a Dutch documentary about his book *The Return of the Prodigal Son*. During his lifetime, he published 39 books and authored hundreds of articles. His best-known books include *The Wounded Healer*, a bestseller among Catholic and mainline Protestant clergy, *In the Name of Jesus*, *The Life of the Beloved*, and *The Way of the Heart*, together with such popular titles as *The Return of the Prodigal Son* and *Reaching Out*. He recounts his struggles reconciling his depression with his Christian faith in the *Inner Voice of Love*, based on his diary from 1987 to 1988.

In *Reaching Out*, described by Nouwen as a book "closer to me than anything I have written," the author articulates his personal thoughts and feelings about being a Christian. Autobiographical in nature, its message stems from his personal struggles. This book is written, not to offer answers or solutions, but in the conviction that the quest for an authentic Christian spirituality is painful and difficult, yet worth the effort and pain, since it is through conflict and struggle that we find hope, courage, and confidence. Nouwen views the spiritual quest as frightful yet exhilarating, for it is the great experience of being alone, both alone in the world and alone before God.

Reaching Out, as the book's subtitle suggests, involves us in the three movements of the spiritual life: an inner movement, an outer movement, and an upward movement. The first movement is a reaching out with courageous honesty to our innermost self; the second movement a reaching out with relentless care to our fellow human beings; and the third movement a reaching out with increasing prayer to God. In this progression, readers of *Rebuilding the Temple* will discern a modern understanding of the medieval ascent to God, which consists of the three successive stages known as purgation, illumination, and unity.

Nouwen describes the spiritual life as a tension between three polarities. The first polarity deals with our relation to ourselves, and it features the polarity from loneliness to solitude. The second polarity forms the basis of our relationship to others, and it features the polarity between hostility and hospitality. The third polarity, the final and most important, structures our relationship with God and features the polarity between illusion and prayer, that is, between separation and unity. The more we come to the painful confession of our loneliness, hostilities, and illusion, the more we embrace solitude, hospitality, and prayer as spiritual resources in our life.

To live spiritually means not only facing honestly and courageously our broken and sinful condition, but also finding in the midst of these tensions and polarities elements that give shape to the newness waiting to emerge. It need hardly be stressed that the three movements of the spiritual life are not clearly distinct or separated from one another, for certain themes recur in the different phases in various tonalities and often flow into one another as do the different movements of a symphony. However, the distinctions remain as reminders of the need to reach out to our innermost self, to our fellow human beings, and to God.

According to Nouwen, the inner movement (from loneliness to solitude) involves letting go of expectations from others, and being willing to be alone. Once we find contentment there, we can act in accordance with our deep desires, rather than reactively and impulsively. In his opening chapters, Nouwen suggests that the solution to loneliness is not "human togetherness," but rather finding free and friendly places where one can explore the solution of solitude, promoting solidarity with pain instead of judging and interpreting it. The solitude that is beneficial comes not from withdrawal but through "the solitude of heart," which does not depend on isolation from others. Those who develop this solitude of heart are no longer pulled apart by the divergent stimuli of the surrounding world, but are able to perceive and understand this world from a quiet inner center.

When we learn to convert our loneliness into deep solitude, we create that precious space where we can listen to our own inner voices. Such solitude, which Nouwen calls "receptive solitude," not only deepens our affection for others, but also creates "holy ground," the place where real community becomes possible. Once we have tasted this solitude, a new life becomes possible, in which we can become detached from false ties and attached to God and each other in surprisingly new ways. The movement from loneliness to solitude, therefore, is not a movement of growing withdrawal, but rather a movement toward deeper engagement in the burning issues of our time.

The outer movement (from hostility to hospitality) follows from the inner movement. If we can avoid being desperate and impulsive, we can focus on other people, and create free, receptive space for them to grow. Nouwen introduces a form of hospitality that is paradoxically full of emptiness, which creates the safety necessary for spiritual growth. In other words, by removing personal agendas and the need to fix and control others, an environment of discovery provides the hospitality necessary for others to find God.

Next, Nouwen applies hospitality to specific relationships including parents and children, teachers and students, and healers and patients. Hospitality need not be limited to its literal sense of receiving strangers in one's house—though that should not be neglected—but as a fundamental attitude toward other human beings. Comparing hospitality to parenting, hospitality at home means not clinging or controlling, but enabling development and departure. Nouwen adds that churches should not be places of coercion and conformity, but of feeding. Pastors and religious teachers should be less people with answers and more people who are able to listen. Creating space for others to be known and affirmed is the goal of hospitality. One cannot force others to make themselves known. However, an invitation can be given and space created for others to thrive.

Nouwen suggests that poverty is necessary for hospitality. Not material poverty necessarily, but rather two forms of poverty that hosts must embrace: poverty of mind and poverty of heart. Poverty of mind is the willingness to believe that one does not know everything; it is the willful posture of one who wants to learn. Poverty of heart is an openness to receive the emotions and experiences of others. It is the assumption that one's own emotional and experiential reservoir is insufficient and can be expanded by learning from others. Poverty of the mind and heart empowers listening and serving by eliminating the need to protect through defending and blaming.

The third movement (from illusion to prayer) concerns one's relationship to God. Solitude and hospitality can only bear lasting fruit when they are embedded in a broader, deeper, and higher reality from which they receive their vitality. The illusion is that of immortality, which comes to mean that the things we own, the people we know, the plans we have, become immortalized. Intimacy with and dependence on temporal things can lead to depression and despair when temporality is masked with immortality. When we anchor our lives in temporal people and things such as experiences, jobs, institutions, and the like, these can be misunderstood as having eternal significance and hence as being immortal.

Nouwen suggests that there are two visible symptoms of such a view: sentimentality and violence. Sentimentality occurs when we "load our fellow human beings with immortal expectations." On the other hand, violence takes place when we treat people, property and institutions as things to be conquered and not as gifts to be received. If we can view the transitory things of this world as gifts from God rather than as idols to worship, adore, and protect, then we will be able to anchor our lives in God, the source of all intimacy and immortality. When we unmask our illusions of immortality and fully accept death as our human destiny, then we can reach out beyond the limits of our existence to the God out of whose immortality we are born. When we move from illusion to prayer, we move from the human shelter to the house of God.

In the chapter, "The Prayer of the Heart," Nouwen introduces three rules of prayer that include a contemplative way of reading scripture, silent listening to the voice of God, and a trusting obedience to a spiritual guide. Without the Bible, without silent time, and without someone to direct us, finding our own way to God is very hard and practically impossible. The movement from illusion to prayer requires a gradual detachment from all false ties, and an increasing surrender to the One from whom all good things come. While we typically view prayer as a private, individualistic, and nearly secret affair, because it is so personal and because it arises from the center of our life, it must be shared with others. The community of faith is the climate and source of all prayer. Unity with God does not occur in isolation from others. Nor does it occur fully in the present. The church—the community of the faithful—is a community guided by prayer. Prayer as a hopeful and joyful waiting for God is a superhuman task unless we realize that we do not have to wait alone. The community of faith, however, offers the protective boundaries within which individuals can listen to their deepest longings, not to indulge in morbid introspection, but to find the common God to which they point.

It is important to remember that the Christian community is a waiting community, meaning that it is a community that not only creates a sense of belonging, but also a sense of estrangement. This awareness requires a constant criticism of those who make the community into a safe shelter or a cozy clique. The basis of Christian community is not programming, participation, or even outreach. While these are important, they are preliminary. The church's calling is to be a "pilgrim church," always moving forward. The temptation to settle in a comfortable oasis must be resisted, both individually and congregationally.

Communal and individual prayer belong together as two sides of a coin. Without community, individual prayer easily degenerates into egocentric and eccentric behavior, but without individual prayer, the prayer life of a community can easily become a meaningless routine. When we reach out to God individually as well as communally, constantly casting off the illusions that keep us captive, we can enter into intimate union with our Lord while still awaiting the day of final consummation.

RUSSELL CONWELL'S *ACRES OF DIAMONDS*

Some years ago, I wished to write a book about the lives and legacies of inspirational twentieth-century Christians. The list included such figures as Albert Schweitzer, Frank Laubach, Dietrich Bonhoeffer, American presidents Franklin D. Roosevelt and John F. Kennedy, Martin Luther King, Jr., Pope John Paul II, Billy Graham, Mother Teresa, and Russell Conwell. Unfortunately, that project was left unfinished, but on this occasion, I wish to include one member from that list, perhaps the least known of that group, but certainly one worthy of study.

A Baptist minister, Russell Conwell (1843–1925) was also known for his philanthropic work. He is best remembered as the founder and first president of Temple University and as the pastor of the Baptist Temple, both in Philadelphia, and for his inspirational lecture, "Acres of Diamonds." Born of poor parents in a small cottage in South Worthington, Massachusetts, Conwell overcame great odds to become one of the most remarkable individuals of his time. A great visionary, he pursued his dreams with relentless vigor. In his biography of Conwell, Robert Shackleton notes that at every stage in his life, no matter the situation, he was able to turn dust into diamonds: As a farmer's boy, he was the leader of the boys of the rocky region that was his home; as a schoolteacher, he won devotion; as a newspaper correspondent, he gained fame; as a soldier in the Civil War, he rose to important rank; as a lawyer, he developed a large practice; as an author, he wrote books that reached millions. He left the law for the ministry and became the active head of a great church that he raised from nothing. As a philanthropist, he also founded Samaritan Hospital, open to patients of any race or creed, where the poor were never refused admission. In addition to the Samaritan, Conwell acquired a second hospital, the Garretson, and promptly expanded its usefulness.

At the height of his career, he was the most popular lecturer in the world, speaking annually to hundreds of thousands of people, most of them paying to hear him deliver his famous talk, "Acres of Diamonds," which he delivered over five thousand times to an estimated eight million hearers. Remarkably, the entirety of the proceeds from his lectures went to further the education of needy students. According to Conwell, the lecture was designed to help young people, regardless of sex, race, or creed, who sought to pursue a career "of usefulness and honor." Remembering his poverty as a student at Yale University, he determined to do whatever he could to make the way easier at college for deserving students, asking them to continue his legacy by "paying it forward."

The son of Massachusetts farmers, whose home was a station on the Underground Railway, Conwell left home to attend a college preparatory school and then, after graduation, proceeded to Yale. In 1862, before graduating from Yale, he enlisted in the Union Army during the American Civil War. Serving the war effort in North Carolina, Conwell soon gained a reputation for self-sacrifice. During one encounter, he returned to the battlefield to retrieve the bodies of two deceased soldiers. Later, during the same campaign, he was shot in the shoulder when he purposefully drew enemy fire upon his position in order to gain a tactical advantage on his adversaries. In 1864, during the battle of Kennesaw Mountain, now Lieutenant-Colonel Conwell's arm and shoulder were broken during battle from an exploding artillery shell. While recovering from this injury, Conwell converted to Christianity in large part due to the heroism exhibited by his loyal private assistant, John Ring, who, during an attack on his position by Confederate soldiers, dashed back to Conwell's tent to retrieve Conwell's prized sword, a gift from the men of his company. Dodging enemy fire, Ring dashed across a burning bridge with the sword, suffering burns and wounds from which he would not recover.

When Conwell stood beside the body of John Ring, a youngster of strong Christian convictions who died selflessly out of love and devotion, Conwell resolved to live from that moment on not only for himself, but also for John Ring. On account of Ring's devotion and giving of his life, Conwell became a Christian, resolving from that moment on to work sixteen hours every day—"eight for John Ring's work and eight hours for my own."

After the Civil War, Conwell studied law and began working as an attorney, journalist, and lecturer, first in Minneapolis, then in Boston. During this period he published some ten books, including campaign biographies of Ulysses S. Grant, Rutherford B. Hayes, and James A. Garfield. While a lawyer in Boston, he was approached by a woman seeking his advice on how to dispose of a small church in Lexington. Conwell went to look at the site, and agreed that the structure was probably beyond repair. However, at a meeting with members of the congregation, he suggested that they all come back the following day and proceed to prepare the building for worship the next Sunday. When Conwell showed up the next day with a few tools, no one else showed up. Examining the structure once again, he saw that repair was out of the question, and that only a new building would do. Taking an axe, he began to tear the building down. In a short while, a local resident, not a member of the church, came by and asked Conwell what he was doing, to which Conwell replied, "I'm tearing down this old building in preparation for a new church."

Noting that the congregants were physically and financially unable to erect a new structure, the man watched Conwell work for a while and then said, "Well, you can put me down for one hundred dollars for the new building. Come up to my livery-stable and get it this evening."

Soon another man came along and questioned the idea of a new church, but when Conwell told him of the livery-stable man contributing one hundred dollars, he said, "You will never get the money from that sort of man. He's not even a church man! However, if he does give you the money, come to me and I'll give you another hundred." As it turned out, both men paid their money, and when the church people saw what had happened, they provided the work and money for the new church. However, they needed a pastor, and it was there in Lexington in 1879 that Conwell decided to give up his law practice and become a minister.

When they offered him a salary of six hundred dollars, Conwell agreed to come, but only if they would double his salary as soon as he doubled the church membership. In less than a year, the congregation double in size, and Conwell's salary was doubled accordingly. Soon, a struggling church in Philadelphia heard about the Lexington church and a church leader was sent to Lexington to offer Conwell a job. He agreed to go at a salary of eight hundred dollars, but with the same stipulation as he gave to the parishioners in Lexington, and before long the struggling Philadelphia congregation occupied a new church building that at that time seated more people than any other Protestant church in America.

When Conway began his ministry in Philadelphia, the congregation was small both in membership and in the size of its building. However, worship under Conway's leadership quickly became so popular that church services and Sunday-school services were crowded to the point that there was no room to accommodate all who came. On one occasion, a small girl named Hattie May Wyatt was turned away from the Sunday-school building because there was no room. While she was crying, a tall, dark-haired man stopped to ask her why she was crying, and on hearing her story, lifted her to his shoulder and carried her inside, assuring her that one day they would have a room big enough for all who wished to come. The tall stranger was none other than Conwell.

A few weeks later, Hattie was suddenly taken ill and died, and at the funeral, her father told Conwell that the young girl had been saving money to help build a bigger church and gave him her little purse, containing fifty-seven cents. At a meeting of the church trustees, Conwell told of this gift of fifty-seven cents—the first gift toward the proposed building fund of the new church. In a few days, one of the trustees proposed the idea to buy a lot on Broad Street, and Conwell went to see the owner, telling him the story of the little girl. The owner, who was not a churchgoer, listened attentively to the tale and agreed to sell the house and land for ten thousand dollars, taking a down payment of fifty-seven cents and letting the entire balance stand on a 5 percent mortgage. In that house, the first classes of Temple College, later Temple University, were held. The house was later sold to allow Temple College to move and the Temple Baptist Church to grow.

One evening, after a worship service, a young man of the congregation come to Conwell with a request. Supporting himself and his mother financially, he had no funds to study to become a minister. Would Conwell be able to help him achieve his goal? Conwell replied that he would begin teaching him, and soon six friends were added to the group. By the third evening, the number of students had increased to forty, and a room was provided, then a small house, and eventually a second house. From that start, Temple University was begun, its aim being to provide an education to all who had the ambition and determination but were unable to pay through the usual channels. Within thirty years, the group of seven pupils had grown to nearly one hundred thousand students, all in the lifetime of the founder. Early on, Conwell determined that classes would be held at times best suited to the convenience of the students. If any ten students joined in a request for any hour from nine in the morning to ten at night, a class was arranged for them. Furthermore, if students could do four years' work in two or three years, they were encouraged to do so. Obviously, Temple University was a place for committed workers, not a place of ease or leisure. Temple University, to quote its own words, is "An institution for strong men and women who can labor with both mind and body."

The original inspiration for "Acres of Diamonds," Conwell's most famous talk, occurred in 1869, when Conwell was traveling along the Tigris River in present-day Iraq, using a guide hired in Baghdad. From this river guide he heard the story of Ali Hafed, who lived on the banks of the Indus River in a lovely farm with orchards and gardens. He was "wealthy" because he was contented. One day a priest visited Ali Hafed and told him about diamonds, and how if he had a few diamonds, he could have not just one farm, but many. The farmer listened, and he went to bed that night discontented because he feared he was poor.

Soon thereafter, Ali Hafed sold his farm, left his family, and went traveling in search of diamonds, across Persia, Palestine, and into Europe. A couple of years later, what money he had was gone, and his health failed him. Dejected, he cast himself into the sea. However, the man who had purchased Ali Hafed's farm had a very different story to tell. One day, while watering his animals in the stream that ran through the property, he noticed a glint in the watery sands. It was a diamond. Digging produced more diamonds; in fact, it was one of the richest diamond finds in history. Known as the mines of Golconda, they yielded not handfuls of diamonds, but acres of diamonds.

The point of the story is that we often dream of fortunes to be made elsewhere, when instead we ought to be open to the opportunities that are around us. Conwell illustrated his lecture with several other stories, including that of the discovery of gold in California in 1847. When the owner of a ranch in Northern California heard they had discovered gold in southern California, he sold his ranch to Colonel Sutter, never to return. Colonel Sutter put a mill upon a stream that ran through his ranch, and one day his young daughter brought some wet sand from the stream into their home and, sifting it through her fingers, saw the first shining scales of real gold to be discovered in California. The man who had owned that ranch wanted gold, and he could have found it on his property. Instead, he lost all he had searching for gold in all the wrong places. Another story concerns a farmer in Pennsylvania who sold his farm in Titusville and went to work collecting coal oil for his cousin in Canada. Soon after, the man who purchased the first man's farm found oil worth millions of dollars, right there in Titusville.

In his lecture, Conwell tells of the financier John Jacob Astor, who had to go into partnership in a millinery store because the owners could not keep up mortgage payments. In order to get this business up and running, Astor went to the park to watch the women strolling along, particularly the most confident and elegant, and taking careful note of the hats they wore. Back in the store, he had these hats copied exactly. The result was that the store never made a hat or bonnet that a woman didn't like, and business boomed. Leaving behind the failed idea that "we make hats and try to sell them," Astor came up with the prosperous idea, "what women want, we sell!" Meeting needs led to great success, all based on the principle on selling what people want. According to Conwell, people cannot succeed unless they have an interest in others and their needs. In Conwell's words, "you must make yourself necessary to the world." What all great salespeople have in common is that they become a "medium" for good, making the best goods and providing them to the largest number of customers.

In other words, if you wish to succeed at sales, whether of goods or ideas, start thinking about what you need. Chances are, if you need something, others will too. The woman who invented the snap button, first used in gloves, made her fortune this way. Conwell emphasized that open-mindedness to little things is what brings human success. The greatest minds think in simple terms, and the greatest people are always honest and straightforward.

While "Acres of Diamonds" was written and delivered long ago, Conwell was one of the original American motivational speakers and his talk still inspires. Its message can be reduced to several key points:

- Don't put yourself down, and don't belittle your environment. Don't compare yourself with others, but be open to the possibilities around you. There is no need to look beyond yourself and your immediate circumstances to find the seeds of your fortune.

- Look at the familiar in new ways. Conwell lists important inventions such as the cotton gin and the mowing machine, and notes that these were created by everyday people who found new approaches and new uses for commonplace objects.

- Learn what people want, and then provide it. Service is the key to success. If you want to sell things to others, find out what people really want, and make it available to them at a fair price.

- Knowledge is more important than capital. Lack of capital is a common excuse for not starting a business venture. Conwell provides examples of wealthy people who started with nothing but an idea.

Some people might read Conwell's lecture as an example of the "prosperity gospel" and put it down as leading to elitist attitudes, selfishness, and dishonesty. While selfish or greedy people might read "Acres of Diamonds" this way, this is clearly not what Conwell intended. In his estimation, the proper response must come from the heart. If individuals are resourceful and hard-working, and if their motivation is sincere, trusting, and benevolent, then they should work to be prosperous, for those who get the largest salary are then able to do the most good with what they have earned.

Having read Conway's "Acres" years ago and having reread it recently, his lecture has left me more hopeful and trusting, more compassionate about people in need, and more desirous to invest and believe in those around me. In other words, Conway's "Acres" has left me a better Christian and a better human. Conway's theme is simple: If you want to be successful—and you should—find a need and meet it. As you proceed, "do what you love, and love what you do!"

In like manner, John Wesley, the founder of Methodism, built on the biblical principle of stewardship, teaching Christians to "gain all you can; save all you can; give all you can." Wesley believed that when it comes to economics, Christians should be industrious and clever, working hard and long in order to gain all they can. Wesley followed his own advice, becoming one of the highest earning preachers of all times. Based on current dollar amounts, he earned the equivalent of $1.4 million in a single year. However, Wesley encouraged Christians to be thrifty and industrious, not in order to hoard their money, but in order to be generous. Wesley practiced what he preached. In the year he earned the equivalent of $1.4 million, he lived on 2 percent of his income and gave 98 percent of it away. During his lifetime, he earned the equivalent of $30 million, but when he died he left only a few miscellaneous coins and a couple of silver spoons. He had given away all the rest. What a way to die . . . and live!

BRIAN MCLAREN'S *A GENEROUS ORTHODOXY*

A former college English teacher and pastor, Brian McLaren (born 1956) is an author, speaker, and public theologian. In 1982, while he was teaching English, he helped form Cedar Ridge Community Church in Spencerville, Maryland. In 1986, he became the church's full-time pastor, which under his leadership quickly grew to include five hundred members. In 2006, he left this position to pursue writing and speaking full time. McLaren is a leading figure in the emerging church movement. He is also associated with postmodern Christianity and is a major figure in post-evangelical thought. In 2015, McLaren was recognized by *Time* magazine as one of the "25 Most Influential Evangelicals in America."

The author of some twenty books, including titles such as *The Great Spiritual Migration, Finding Faith, A New Kind of Christian, A New Kind of Christianity, A Generous Orthodoxy, Naked Spirituality, The Secret Message of Jesus, Everything Must Change,* and *Faith after Doubt*, McLaren is a leading figure in the Convergent Leadership Project as well as a core member of the teaching faculty at the Center for Action and Contemplation in Albuquerque, New Mexico.

A popular author and a progressive Christian, McLaren has come under significant criticism from Christian thinkers across the theological spectrum, not only for his interpretation of Christian beliefs and practices, but also for his self-proclaimed identity as an evangelical Christian.

Eschewing theological labels, McLaren seems content as a proponent of post-liberal, post-conservative, and post-protestant Christianity. Exactly what this means theologically is hard to say, for McLaren takes what he calls a "narrative approach" to theology, interpreting Christianity through the ongoing stories of people and communities rather than trying "to capture timeless truths in objective statements systematized in analytical outlines and recorded in books and institutionalized in schools and denominations."[1]

Thinking of religious or theological identity, I recall the concluding words in *Wading in Water*, my book on spirituality and the arts. There I told the story of former U.S. Vice President Mike Pence, who was greeted by a 2021 pro-Trump rally with hissing and booing for not having attempted to change, or at least to challenge, the results of the 2020 presidential election. Trying to speak over a disgruntled minority, who apparently defined him by partisan standards, Pence responded by baring his soul, informing the audience that he was a Christian, a conservative, and a Republican, in that order. While labeling others or oneself is not generally helpful, since self-awareness changes over time, sometimes situations require taking a stand. Mike Pence took a stand, and if I were forced to name my top three descriptors, they would be human (a global citizen), panentheist, and nondualist, in that order. What such terms mean, of course, changes frequently. If asked to define your current identity in three words, what would they be?

Moving beyond the theological division between the "left" and the "right," namely, between theological "liberals"—who construct theology upon the foundation of religious experience—and "conservatives"—who look to an error-free Bible as the foundation of their theology— in his 2004 work, *A Generous Orthodoxy*, McLaren seeks a way to move beyond the liberal/conservative impasse of modernity by describing an understanding of Christianity that contains elements of both liberal and conservative thought.[2] By looking at the best qualities of perspectives across the theological spectrum, McLaren can call himself simultaneously "liberal/conservative," "charismatic/contemplative," and "fundamentalist/Calvinist." He does so by envisioning an orthodoxy that focuses on Jesus, that is driven by love, and that is defined by missional intent (that is, by

---

1. McLaren, *Generous Orthodoxy*, 329.

2. The term "generous orthodoxy" was coined by Yale theologian Hans Frei, who once noted, "Generosity without orthodoxy is nothing, but orthodoxy without generosity is worse than nothing." Cited by McLaren, *Generous Orthodoxy*, 18.

the good news of the gospel, by which McLaren means good news for the whole world).

Rather than define "orthodoxy" as the hard mental work of holding in one's mind an increasing bank of complex opinions about many theological notions, McLaren associates "orthodoxy" (right thinking about the gospel) with "orthopraxy," (right practice of the gospel). Furthermore, by qualifying the term "orthodox" with the term "generous," McLaren is suggesting that orthodoxy should be identified with a consistent practice of humility, charity, courage, and diligence, qualities usually associated with orthopraxy.

Dividing his book into two parts, in the first four chapters (Part I) McLaren tells us that to be a Christian means trusting in Jesus Christ. Then in the remaining sixteen chapters (Part II), McLaren describes the progressive, inclusive, and multifaceted kind of Christian he has become. In chapter 1, he describes the seven Jesuses he has known in his lifetime, beginning with a picturebook Jesus of his childhood, then the Jesus of his conservative Protestant upbringing (the Jesus born to die), followed by a Pentecostal/ charismatic Jesus, and on through to a liberal Jesus (a Jesus concerned with social justice), an Anabaptist Jesus (a Jesus concerned with pacifism), and a Liberation Theology Jesus (a nonviolent Jesus concerned with the oppressed).

In chapter 2, McLaren speaks about the relationship between Jesus and God, distinguishing between "God A" (who stands for dominance, control, and submission), and "God B" (who stands for interdependence, relationship, and possibility). According to McLaren, Christians live in universe B, a dangerous yet wonderful place for a generous orthodoxy. In chapter 3, McLaren asks the intriguing question, "Would Jesus Be a Christian?" noting that the more he reads the New Testament, the more he thinks most of Christianity as practiced today has little to do with the historical Jesus.

In chapter 4, McLaren asks us to consider what we mean when we call Jesus "Savior." For too many Christians, salvation has become "saved from hell," but this is not what the Bible means by "saved." Rather, its meaning varies from passage to passage, but in general, "save" means "rescue" or "heal." In the Bible, sometimes God saves by judging, that is, by establishing justice in the world, followed by forgiving. Hence, salvation involves both justice and mercy. Finally, God saves by teaching or revealing. To say that Jesus is Savior is to say that in Jesus, God is intervening as Savior in all of these ways: judging, forgiving, and by showing how to set chain reactions of good in motion.

In Part II (chapters 5–20), McLaren addresses sixteen aspects vital to his faith, indicating why generous orthodoxy draws us toward a way of living that looks beyond the "us/them" paradigm to the ancient paradox of "we." In chapter 5, McLaren explains that he is a missional Christian. Rather than "us versus them" thinking, or in-grouping and out-grouping, McLaren opens up a third alternative beyond exclusive (we are in, you are out) and universalist religion (we are all in). Missional Christian faith asserts that Jesus did not come to make some people saved and others condemned, but that Jesus came to save the whole world. In chapter 6, McLaren explains that he is "evangelical" with a small "e," thus distinguishing himself from the "Religious Right" or from Fundamentalists with a "Big F." By adopting an evangelical identity, he goes beyond a belief system to an attitude toward God, our neighbor, and our mission that is passionate and daring and not sentimental or hotheaded.

In chapter 8, McLaren argues that he is both liberal (in the sense that he encourages free inquiry) and conservative (in the sense of valuing scripture and building on a foundation that is generously orthodox). Valuing the mystical/poetic path to truth, he argues for a belief system that is imaginative and expansive rather than literal and frozen. This mystical/poetic approach takes special pains to remember that the Bible contains precious little expository prose and no systematic theology, preferring story laced with parable, poem interwoven with vision, personal letter and public song, all thrown together in artistic passion. In chapter 10, McLaren calls himself a biblical Christian, meaning that his regard for scripture grows higher and deeper with time. Interestingly, when the Bible talks about itself, it doesn't use language such as authority, inerrancy, infallibility, or words like absolute and literal. Rather, the purpose of scripture is to equip us for good works, something it does primarily through story and by example.

In the remaining ten chapters, rather than establishing what is and is not "orthodox," McLaren walks through the many traditions of faith, bringing to the center a way of life that draws humans closer to Christ and to one another. In chapter 18, McLaren argues that Jesus didn't come to start another religion. He concludes in chapters 19 and 20 with an explanation as to why for him theology is fluid, progressive, and dynamic rather than static and unchanging. As an emergent Christian, he has in mind a small sapling growing up under a mature forest canopy. Whatever understanding of Jesus we claim, to be emergent means we cannot despise our roots or reject our past. We won't be better or worse than our forebears, just different, as we journey onward toward our final home in God. To be a Christian in a generous orthodox way is not to claim to have the truth captured in a book or as a trophy mounted on the wall. It is rather to be in a loving community seeking the truth, on the road to mission, and launched on the quest by Jesus, who guides us still. Generous Christians are not yet complete, and have not yet arrived. Rather, they are works in progress, still on the way. Forever seeking, they find enough to keep them going.

QUESTIONS FOR DISCUSSION AND REFLECTION

In addition to the questions listed at the end of the preface, answer the following questions, writing your answers in a journal. If you are in a group study, be prepared to share your answers with those in the group.

1. In preparing for ministry, Nouwen studied clinical psychology, in addition to theological and philosophical studies. Explain the significance of studying psychology on his self-understanding, his sexuality, his humanity, and on his writings and vocation as a priest.

2. After reading the segment on Nouwen's life, what did you learn about Christian spirituality?

3. After reading the segment on *Reaching Out*, explain and assess Nouwen's teaching regarding the distinction between loneliness and solitude.

4. After reading the segment on *Reaching Out*, explain and assess Nouwen's teaching regarding hospitality.

5. After reading the segment on *Reaching Out*, explain and assess Nouwen's teaching regarding prayer.

6. After reading the segment on Conwell's life, what did you learn about Christian spirituality?

7. In your estimation, what is the secret behind the success of Conwell's *Acres of Diamonds*? If you had to reduce the book's message to one point, what would it be?

8. In your estimation, was Conwell's lecture simply another example of the "prosperity gospel"? Explain your answer.

9. Explain and assess the merit of John Wesley's principle of stewardship.

10. Explain and assess the merit of the "narrative approach" to theology.

11. If you were asked to define your current identity in three words, what would they be?

12. Explain and assess the merit of defining oneself as nondualistically as McLaren does in *Generous Orthodoxy*. In terms of identity, is clarity better than ambiguity, and exclusivism better than inclusivism? Is McLaren's inclusivism simply too positive, generous, and accepting? Explain your answer.

Chapter 11

Matthew Fox's *Original Blessing* and Richard Rohr's *The Naked Now*

EVERY AGE HAS ITS VISIONARIES. In the Judeo-Christian tradition, some have been called seers, prophets, or mystics, and others saints. When they appeared, they were rarely popular, for their message was often critical, negative, or counter-cultural. Many were reviled, ostracized, or exiled, and some even killed for their beliefs or lifestyle. Always they have been courageous, and while some had influential followers in their day, over time, most came to be honored, revered, even canonized.

In our time, four have challenged the church from the margins, each attracting large audiences through their talks, sermons, and writings. In this chapter we examine the lives and works of Matthew Fox and Richard Rohr. Roman Catholics by training, the former a convert to the Episcopal Church following his expulsion from the Dominican Order, while the latter, regularly under attack, remained a Franciscan priest. The following chapter comments on progressive writings by the recently deceased Protestant thinkers John Shelby Spong and Marcus Borg.

Both Fox and Rohr are nondualists, and both emphasize religious orthopraxy (what we have been calling "spirituality") as the natural and proper expression of Christian orthodoxy. While both individuals are focused on what it means to be a Christian in today's world, in *Original Blessing* Fox looks to the past, particularly to the doctrine of creation, for an understanding of the meaning of Christ, sin and salvation. In *The Naked Now*, Rohr looks to the present for an understanding of Christian spirituality, focusing on ecology, compassion, and justice as key themes in the "alternative orthodoxy" of Franciscan spirituality, which he sees as a "third way" between traditional orthodoxy and heresy.

RECAPTURING THE SACRAMENTAL SENSE OF REALITY

The central defining characteristic of spirituality is an individual's sense of connection to a much greater whole. At its heart, spirituality involves an emotional experience of awe and reverence. As such, it is something that is highly desired, fervently sought, endlessly disagreed upon, and thoroughly fascinating.

The world we live in today is the world we know through scientific observation, a much different world from the classical world where Western civilization first emerged. At that time, there was greater continuity between religion, culture, and nature. Today, however, we are experiencing a discontinuity unequaled in its order of magnitude. That is why there is suspicion and misrepresentation among the religions of the present time and why we are experiencing new fundamentalisms: Islamic, Jewish, Christian, Buddhist, Hindu, and Shinto.

Fundamentalism is a defensive tactic. It is one reason why few of the religions of the world are dealing with the ecology issue on a widespread scale. They simply do not feel equipped to deal with this new challenge. By not accepting a responsibility for the fate of the earth, there is a failure of religious responsibility to the divine, as well as to the human. We seem not to realize that as the outer world becomes damaged, our sense of the divine is degraded correspondingly.

Why did our ancestors have such a wonderful idea of God? Because they lived in an awesome world. They wondered at the magnificence of whatever it was that brought the world into being. This led to a sense of adoration. This adoration, this gratitude, we call religion. But now, as the outer world is diminished, our inner world is drying up.

Religion involves the sense of God, of the human, of creation, and of revelation. All of these aspects belong together, and they cannot be treated separately. We would have no sense of the divine without creation. Speculatively, we could talk about God as being prior to or outside creation or independent of creation, but in actual fact there is no such being as God without creation.

It is no secret that our world is in a state of crisis. The prognosis is bleak and the conditions may be irreversible. The tip of the iceberg, evident to almost everyone nowadays, is the environmental fate of our entire planet. During the second half of the twentieth century we learned that deterioration in the quality of the air we breathe, the water we drink, and the soil in which we grow our crops seriously threatens our continued life and well-being on this earth.

In addition to environmental degradation and anticipated ecological factors such as unpredictable weather patterns, increasing number and severity of storms, and sea-level rise, we can add pandemics and the outbreak of new diseases, species extinction, malnutrition and widespread famine, terrorism, violence and crime, the breakdown of the family, increased addictive behavior, unemployment, corporate scandals, an increasing income gap between rich and poor, religious fanaticism and sectarian wars, and the list goes on and on.

The current crisis involves many factors: ecological, political, economic, sociological, and ethical. At its core, however, the problem is spiritual. The crisis of spirit, dubbed "the impoverishment of soul" by Matthew Fox, one of today's leading spiritual teachers, is particularly evident in our Western civilization today. It is characterized by imbalance, or more accurately, by dissociation between the spiritual and physical realms of life.

The current generation outpaces all others in history in terms of wealth, health, education, and convenience—yet it doesn't seem to be happier or more content than preceding generations. Perhaps, in our passion for acquiring things, we have actually lost something profound—something so valuable that we would never knowingly sell it or trade it away. Some may refer to values, standards, or patriotism, but what it comes down to is the loss of the sacred.

Rather than being rooted in a spiritual worldview and in principles espoused by the traditions of the world's great religions, particularly in their mystical approaches to reality, modern humans see the world through the lenses of crass materialism, scientism, and positivism. In his thoughtful volume, *Man and Nature: the Spiritual Crisis in Modern Man* (1997), Islamic scholar Seyyed Nasr takes the reader through history and explores the causes of the desacralization of nature in the West and the resultant ecological crisis we face today. He demonstrates how the West, by divorcing science from spirit, has wrecked havoc on our planet. He also argues that the Christian faith helped accelerate this process when it removed elements of its metaphysical doctrines that kept nature as a part of the divine.

Whether the current crisis is curable is debatable, but it will clearly require massive cultural reorientation. More importantly, it will require a transformation of the human spirit and a commitment of will. Only a relationship of genuine harmony with nature and a love of nature's God can transform humans from consumers to caretakers. When historians look back at the start of the twenty-first century, it is hoped that they might remember it most for two commitments: as a time when the peoples of the world made a profound commitment to one another and made an equal commitment to nature.

John F. Haught, professor of theology at Georgetown University, argues that when it is wholesome, religion maintains four components: sacramental, mystical, silent, and active. Each of these dimensions suggests a distinct "way" of being religious, he argues, "but religion is most healthy and alive when it blends all four ways harmoniously. And it begins to dissolve into something other than 'religion' whenever any of the four aspects is isolated from contact with its three partners. In the actual world of religious life, such sundering of one aspect from the others is not unusual. But when this splintering occurs, religion rapidly decays into magic, escapism or obsession with esoteric teachings, or into cynicism, iconoclasm or vacuous activism."[1] When, on the other hand, religion concretely preserves the four components in a balanced way, it will function in an ecologically supportive way.

What fascinates me most about these aspects is the sacramental dimension. Religion is sacramental in the sense that it can speak of unspeakable mystery only through the use of symbols, or what theology calls sacraments. A sacrament, in its broadest sense, includes any object, person or event through which religious consciousness is awakened to the presence of sacred mystery. Historically, most of religion's sacraments have been closely related to nature. For example, the luminosity of sunshine, dawn, and dusk; the experience of wind or breath; the purifying power of clean water; the fertility of soil and life—all of these natural phenomena, and many more, have been used by religions to symbolize the way in which ultimate mystery affects us.

Since nature provides many of the fundamental sacraments of human religion, it is easy to see how the conservation of nature is

---

1. Haught, *Promise of Nature*, 73–75.

indispensable for the survival of religion. If we lose the environment, we lose God as well. And it is equally true that when religion loses touch with its sacramental origins, it begins to grow indifferent to the natural world. A sacramental vision, Haught reminds us, makes nature, at least in a fragmentary way, transparent to divinity. In this sense it concedes to nature an inherent value without allowing it to become a substitute for God. According to this Christian perspective, nature is worth saving not because it is sacred, but because it is sacramental.

Of course, religion can exaggerate its sacramental side. It does so when it loses its association with mysticism, its essential polarity, as well as silence and action, another set of opposites that exists in a sort of tension with sacramentalism. When mysticism is lost, the sacrament becomes an end in itself, losing its symbolic value. But mysticism alone, if it diminishes the value of nature by looking exclusively beyond the natural order, can decay into sheer escapism. Occasionally it has even gone to the extreme of hating the earth and everything natural. Mysticism and sacramentalism are necessary, as are silence and action, but they need to be delicately balanced. Mysticism dissociated from a vigorous sacramentalism promotes the doctrine of "cosmic homelessness," whereas sacramentalism without the mystical aspect of religion collapses into idolatry or pure naturalism (the view that nature is all there is).

MATTHEW FOX'S *ORIGINAL BLESSING*

In his seminal work *Original Blessing*, Matthew Fox, one of today's leading spiritual teachers, calls for a paradigm shift in religious thinking about human origins and the nature and destiny of human beings, from the fall/redemption paradigm to creation spirituality. The author of thirty-six books, with sales in the millions worldwide, Fox is well known for having revived the tradition of "creation spirituality," and for being a compelling voice for ecological and socially progressive causes. His tenets of creation spirituality appear in books such as *Original Blessing*, *A Spirituality Named Compassion*, and *Creation Spirituality*. Fox's 1996 autobiography, *Confessions: The Making of a Post-Denominational Priest*, describes his life as a Dominican priest and his struggle with the Vatican over his understanding of Christianity.

Born in 1940 in Madison, Wisconsin, Timothy James Fox received the religious name "Matthew" when he entered the Roman Catholic

Dominican Order in 1960. He received master's degrees in both philosophy and theology from the Aquinas Institute of Philosophy and Theology, and later earned a Doctorate of Spiritual Theology from the Institut Catholique in Paris. After receiving his doctorate, Fox began teaching at various Catholic universities, including Loyola University in Chicago and Barat College of the Sacred Heart in Lake Forest, Illinois. In 1976, he moved to Mundelein College (now part of Loyola University) to start the Institute of Culture and Creation Spirituality (ICCS), a master's program in creation spirituality. In 1983, he moved ICCS to Oakland, California, and began teaching at Holy Names University, remaining there for twelve years.

In 1984, Cardinal Joseph Ratzinger (the future Pope Benedict XVI), then head of the Congregation for the Doctrine of the Faith, questioned Fox's teaching of the doctrine of original sin and asked the Dominican Order to investigate Fox's writings. When the review of his work concluded that it was not heretical, Ratzinger ordered a second review, which was never undertaken. As controversy continued, in 1988 Cardinal Ratzinger forbade Fox from teaching or lecturing for a year. After a sabbatical year, Fox resumed writing, reaching, and lecturing. In 1991, his Dominican superior ordered Fox to leave the ICCS and return to Chicago. Fox's refusal led to his expulsion from the Dominican Order for "disobedience," effectively ending his professional relationship with the Roman Catholic Church. Among the issues Ratzinger objected to were Fox's feminist theology; preferring the concept of original blessing over original sin; not condemning homosexual behavior; and teaching the four paths of creation spirituality—the Via Positiva, Via Negativa, Via Creativa, and Via Transformativa—instead of the Church's classical three paths of purgation, illumination, and union.

In 1994, following his expulsion, Fox was received into the Episcopal Church as a priest. In 1996, he founded the University of Creation Spirituality in Oakland (later renamed Wisdom University), offering master's degree programs in creation spirituality and related studies. His program received initial accreditation through an affiliation with New College of California before shifting in 1999 to affiliate with the Naropa Institute of Boulder, Colorado. Fox's "Cosmic Masses," which attempt to combine the religious ritual of the Eucharist with dance and multimedia material, have gained attention in the West, attracting many youth but appalling traditionalist believers. In 2005, following the election of Ratzinger as pope, Fox created 95 theses that he posted to the door of the

Wittenberg church where Martin Luther nailed the original 95 Theses in the sixteenth century, an act associated with the origins of the Protestant Reformation. In his theses, Fox called for a new reformation in Western Christianity, a call later supported in his book, *A New Reformation*.

In *Original Blessing*, Fox argues that the fall/redemption paradigm, based upon the doctrine of original sin, developed during medieval times and is essentially foreign to scripture. This paradigm, dualistic and patriarchal, considers all nature "fallen" and does not seek God in nature. The doctrine of original sin plays particular havoc on people whose self-trust and self-image are in jeopardy. Fox tells of a woman in her sixties who came to him at a conference and said, "I have always wondered what I was redeemed from. But I was afraid to ask."[2] Furthermore, original sin has become a veritable weapon in the hands of religious authorities bent on supremacy or on controlling others. Think of the haunting insecurity experienced by women who have been told to consider their sex as an original sin; or of Blacks in a white society who have been told to look at their blackness as an original sin; or of homosexuals or lesbians who have been told to view their sexuality as an original sin. Taught and proclaimed this way, the doctrine of original sin has itself contributed to sin. This tradition has not taught believers about creativity, justice-making, and social transformation, or about the God of play, pleasure, and delight. Unfortunately, this perspective has also proven unfriendly to artists, prophets, and even to science. Creation spirituality, on the other hand, begins with original blessing, embodying the biblical emphasis on the goodness of creation.

Whereas fall/redemption theology begins with original sin and ends with redemption. creation theology begins with original blessing and flows to all subsequent blessings, including those we share with our loved ones and those we affirm in creativity, compassion, birthing, and justice-making; all are prefigured in the grace of creation. Creation spirituality does not ignore sin, but views it differently. Boredom, depression, arrogance, violence, addictive behavior—these occur when we are cut off from the sense of grace and blessing. In this respect, original sin is not "original" or primary in time or in biblical theology but derived. Evil, in creation theology, is conceived as neither original nor eternal, but rather as something good gone bad.

---

2. Fox, *Original Blessing*, 31.

Hope for humanity and the future of our planet must be based on a proper understanding of the doctrine of creation, one that is not antithetical to science but rather is the subject of the scientist's search, the source of the prophet's vision, and the subject of the mystic's commitment. According to Fox, the universe loves us every day, and the Creator loves us through creation. The following quotation captures his perspective beautifully:

> Creation is the source, the matrix, and the goal of all things—the beginning and the end, the alpha and the omega. Creation is our common parent, when "our" stands for all things. Creation is the mother of all beings and the father of all beings, the birther and the begetter. It is all-holy; it is awe-filled. . . . Creation is never finished, never satisfied, never bored, never passive. Creation is always newly born, always making new. . . . How can such a drama be jeopardized as it is today? Only because our species, with its religions, education, moralities, governments, and economics, has lost the sense of creation. When that happens, nothing is holy; nothing seems worth the struggle for justice that is necessary to preserve it. Community dies, and relations no longer exist.[3]

In *Original Blessing*, Fox describes spirituality as a way of life characterized by four paths: (1) The Via Positiva: Befriending Creation; (2) The Via Negative: Befriending Darkness; (3) The Via Creativa: Befriending Creativity; and (4) The Via Transformativa: Befriending New Creation. For each path he provides a signpost or commandment (italicized below):

- Via Positiva: *Thou shalt fall in love at least three times a day.* This applies to human beings, to nature in all its magnificence, and also to activities such as music, poetry, and dance. Creation has much to do with falling in love. This first commandment, one of praise, flows from the awe of being alive.

- Via Negativa: *Thou shalt dare the dark.* Every spiritual journey moves from the surface to the depths, and there is no moving from superficiality to depth without entering the dark. "Daring the dark" means entering nothingness and letting it be nothingness while it works its mystery on us. "Daring the dark" also means allowing pain to be pain and learning from it. Being at home in the dark involves relinquishing control—letting go and letting be.

3. Fox, *Creation Spirituality*, 10–11.

- Via Creativa: *Do not be reluctant to give birth*. Spiritual discipline in the creation tradition is focused on the development of the aesthetic. Beauty, and our role in co-creating it, lies at the heart of the spiritual journey. Such creativity wrestles with the demons and angels in the depths of our psyches, embracing our "shadow" side as well as our visions and dreams. "To give birth" is to enter the Creator's realm. The work of co-creation engages the image of God (*imago dei*) that is in every person, essential for assisting nature and history in carrying on the creativity of the universe.

- Via Transformativa: *Be compassionate, as your Creator is compassionate*. This commandment, the summation of Jesus' ethical teaching (Luke 6:36), corresponds in meaning to Matthew's passage from the Sermon on the Mount, translated "Be perfect, as your heavenly Father is perfect" (Matt 5:48). A better rendition of Matthew's Greek word *teleios* is: "Be mature" or "Be complete." As Luke's version makes clear, for humans to be perfect or complete is for them to be compassionate to all creatures (Luke 6:36). In this understanding, compassion is not about the actions that flow from a superior to an inferior, but as a result of our interdependence. True compassion, therefore, involves a deep respect for other cultures and traditions and the willingness to work together in our need for mutual wisdom.

It is important to note that Fox's four paths of spirituality are nonlinear and interdependent, not independent or consecutive. They can best be imagined as an open-ended spiral—and spirals are expansive as well as contractive, meaning they go forward as well as backward, and upward as well as downward. Thus, they are more cumulative than progressive. As Fox notes, "We weave through our paths like a spiral danced, not a ladder climbed."

In *Original Blessing*, Matthew Fox lays out a new direction for Christianity—a direction he believes is actually quite ancient and grounded in Jewish thinking. Fox believes that the teaching of original sin, which he finds foreign to the Bible, has led to disastrous consequences, whereas "original blessing"—the awareness of the original (and ongoing) goodness of creation—must take precedence. The implications are profound for spiritual (as well as psychological, sociological, and ecological) transformation. The sacredness of creation and of our role in it is a starting point—what the mystical tradition calls the Via Positiva, (the path of joy and delight, awe and gratitude); the Via Negativa (the past of darkness and silence and also of suffering and of letting go and letting be); the Via Creativa (the path of creativity); and the Via Transformativa (the path of justice and compassion).

All four paths constitute an adult spiritual journey, each feeding the others. In this book, Fox lays out twenty-seven themes that interweave among the Four Paths. In addition, each path ends with an examination of sin, salvation, and Christ from that path's theological perspective. For example, Path I ends with "a theology of creation and incarnation"; Path II, with "a theology of the cross"; Path III with ""a theology of resurrection"; and Path IV, with "a theology of the Holy Spirit." While the entire book is recommended reading, some may find the book's style initially disorienting. Hence, I suggest that you being with the introduction and the first three chapters.

The classic doctrine of original sin has two separable parts. One is the historical claim that the first human beings, Adam and Eve, sinned by eating fruit forbidden them by God. The second is the psychological claim that human nature was once virtuous, but was corrupted by the first sin. Both claims, however, can be disputed, for both can be shown to be false. As Patricia Williams demonstrates in her groundbreaking book *Doing without Adam and Eve*, the alleged corruption of human nature is found neither in Genesis 3 nor anywhere else in the Hebrew scriptures. Genesis 3 explicitly states that Adam and Eve became more like gods after they ate the fruit of the tree of knowledge (Gen 3:22). The idea of a fall—a corruption in human nature—is not prominent in the New Testament; the event of Genesis 3 is only mentioned in passages associated with the apostle Paul (Romans 5, 1 Corinthians 15, and 1 Timothy). Only later, in the writings of Augustine, does the doctrine of original sin become formulated in any significant way.[4]

In a chapter titled "The Demise of Adam and Eve," Williams asserts that it took the birth of modern science to challenge the predominant model of the universe and of human nature that had survived for over

---

4. Some Christians find a scriptural basis for original sin in Romans 5:12, but as Fox notes, the doctrine entered Christianity through Augustine's use of a faulty Latin translation. Translating correctly from the original Greek text, the NRSV text of Romans 5:12 reads, "Therefore, just as sin came into the world through one man, and death came through sin, and so death spread to all *because all have sinned*" (italics mine). By contrast, Augustine's Latin translation left out the word "death," leading him to read the sentence as "Through one man sin entered into the world and through sin death, and thus spread to all men, *in whom all have sinned*" (italics mine). Fox, *Original Blessing*, 48-49.

a thousand years. The scientific theory of biological evolution makes clear that successful species like humans do not pass through single-pair bottlenecks; there is certainly no evidence that this was true of *Homo sapiens*, a species that seems to have been well spread around the earth. Genetic evidence indicates that human populations never consisted of fewer than several thousand individuals.

Scientifically speaking, Adam and Eve can no longer be viewed as the progenitors of all humanity, for they were not historical figures. If not historical figures, they could not have disobeyed God. If they did not disobey God, then we have no basis for original sin and therefore no fall and no corruption of human nature.[5] Thus, the narrative about them cannot be used to explain the human inclination to sin or the origin of evil. That said, there is no need for despair. If one is prepared to accept a metaphorical interpretation of the Adam and Eve story, while insisting on the relevance of evolution, a ready understanding of original sin emerges.

As Darwinians have demonstrated, the struggle for existence and the consequent selection of variations leading to adaptations designed for success in this struggle often involve self-interest, if not outright selfishness, with the host of features, attitudes, and characteristics that most humans find offensive and that Christians judge as sinful. Of course, to be self-interested is not necessarily to be immoral. No one judges ill the person who eats a meal because he or she is hungry, or who falls in love with a pretty girl or a handsome young man and wants to have that person as a mate. However, all too quickly, self-interest degenerates into qualities like greed, lust, and boastfulness. There are good biological reasons for this. Those who feed themselves or their family are better off than those who have no food or just some leftover scraps. The man who impregnates a hundred women is ahead (in the Darwinian game of survival) of a man who impregnates just one. Those who lie and cheat their way to the top of the corporate ladder are more successful than those who lose.

Original sin as part of the biological package comes with being human. We inherit it from our parents and they from their parents. Moreover, overlapping our selfishness is a genuine altruism, a very necessary adaptation given the human path of sociality. We are loving, kind, and generous because that is just as much a part of our nature as is our selfishness. Acknowledging that sin remains central to the human condition,

---

5. Williams, *Doing without Adam and Eve*, xiv, 79–80.

Williams supplies insights from the field of sociobiology, such as the influence of genes, the environment, and the misuse of human freedom, to account for the origin of sin and to deal with the problem of evil. With respect to original sin, sociobiological *Homo sapiens* are practically identical to Christian *Homo sapiens*. Both camps see humans as deeply self-centered, selfish even, but with a genuine moral overlay, guiding (at least, instructing) our actions in social situations and interactions. The surface stories are very different, but the underlying concerns are the same: humans are truly sinful, with goodness fighting for control.[6]

As understood by Augustine, who coined the term, original sin is a biologically transmitted tendency to evil desires (*libido*) that arose with Adam and has contaminated all of humanity. However, most theologians today would consider such an interpretation extremely shallow. According to contemporary theological interpretation, original sin refers not to a specific act committed by a parental couple in the remote past, but to the general state of our present human estrangement from God, from each other, and from the natural world. Seeking new ways to account for the ambiguities of life and the presence of evil, Teilhard de Chardin spoke of original sin as "the reverse side of all creation."[7] We are all born into a world that is already deeply flawed, in great measure by human greed and violence. The notion of original sin, in this sense, also reminds us of our human incapacity to save ourselves from this state of affairs. In an evolving cosmos, life has not yet achieved a state of finality. This incompleteness of the cosmic project is nobody's fault, including the Creator's. The only universe a loving and caring God could create, after all, is an unfinished one. For God's love of creation to be actualized, the beloved world must be "other" than God. An instantly created ("finished") universe would in principle have been only an emanation or appendage of deity and not something truly other than God.

The assumption of an original perfection of creation, as envisioned by creationists, has in fact led religious speculation to imagine that the source of the enormous evil and suffering in the world must be either an original principle of evil—an idea unacceptable to biblical theism, which views the creation as inherently good—or else some intraworldly being or event. The latter supposition has led to the demonizing of various events, persons, animals, genders, and races. By contrast, it is enough

---

6. Ruse, *Can a Darwinian Be a Christian?*, 209–10.
7. Teilhard de Chardin, *Christianity and Evolution*, 40.

for us simply to wonder what a salutary thing it would be if religious thought were now to take the reality of evolution with complete seriousness. Understanding evil as the result of an initial transgression has made reparation and expiation a priority for all who follow biblical religion. The vital problem, both for Christ and for us, is to find a culprit and remove its influence. The assumption of original sin opened up the possibility of interpreting suffering essentially as punishment, necessitating an ethic of retribution.

Evolution means that the world is unfinished, and if it is unfinished, then we cannot justifiably expect perfection. There is inevitably a dark side. The notion that present evil can be attributed to a culprit that somehow spoiled the primordial creation has led to a misunderstanding of the "history of salvation" as a drama of "restoring" the original state of affairs. This emphasis has caused theologians to subordinate the expectation of the far more accurate and fulfilling understanding of the history of salvation as *transformation*—the novelty and surprise at the fulfillment of God's promises—to that of *restoration*—the recovery of a primal perfection of being. This is why evolution is potentially such good news for theology. Evolutionary cosmology invites us to complete the biblical vision of a life based on openness to the future and hope for surprise rather than allowing us to wax nostalgic for what we mistakenly imagine once was.

In an unfinished universe, we humans remain accomplices of evil, of course. However, our complicity in evil may now be interpreted less in terms of a hypothesized break from primordial innocence than as our systematic refusal to participate in the ongoing creation of the world. According to this new way of thinking, "original" sin is not simply the reverse side of an unfinished universe in process of being created. It is also the aggregation in human history and culture of all effects of our habitual refusal to take our appropriate place in the ongoing creation of the universe. It is this kind of corruption—and not the defilement of an allegedly original cosmic perfection—by which each of us is "stained."

For Fox, all religious seekers are mystics and prophets, and he shows the journey of both in this groundbreaking book that deliberately rejects the three paths of purgation, illumination and union, an approach based on original sin that fails to put justice or creativity at the heart of the spiritual journey. As Fox shows, Christianity once celebrated beauty, compassion, justice, and creativity and provided a path of ecstatic connection with all creation. If spirituality can be defined as "meeting with God in history," as Leonardo Boff defined it, and if a new spiritual era is emerging, then a new meeting with God is also upon us, providing a self-disclosure of God that is less warlike, less patriarchal, and more concerned with compassion, justice, celebration, beauty, and creativity.[8]

RICHARD ROHR'S *THE NAKED NOW*

Richard Rohr (born 1943), considered one of the West's preeminent spiritual teachers, is an internationally recognized author and speaker, known primarily for his focus on incarnational mysticism, nondual consciousness, and contemplation. A Franciscan priest, Rohr is also the founder and longtime director of the Center for Action and Contemplation in Albuquerque, New Mexico. He is the author of many devotional articles as well as of over thirty books, including *The Naked Now, Everything Belongs, Breathing Under Water, Falling Upward, Immortal Diamond, The Divine Dance,* and *The Universal Christ.*

Born in Kansas, Rohr received his Master of Theology degree in 1970 from the University of Dayton. He entered the Franciscans in 1961 and was ordained to the priesthood in 1970. Prior to establishing the Center for Action and Contemplation in 1986, Rohr founded the New Jerusalem Community in Cincinnati, Ohio in 1971. In his teaching on scripture, Rohr describes the biblical record as a human account of humanity's evolving experience with God. In *Immortal Diamond*, he suggests that Jesus' death and resurrection is an archetypal pattern for the individual's movement from the egocentric or False Self to the True Self, from the "self we think we are" to the "self we are in God."

An advocate of the Perennial Philosophy, Rohr teaches that a person does not have to follow Jesus or practices the tenets of any formal religion to experience salvation. Rather, such experience comes to those who "fall in love with the divine presence, under whatever name." Rohr's essential message focuses on the union of divine reality with all things, emphasizing the human potential and longing for this union. Rohr and other ecumenical spiritual leaders explore this Perennial Tradition in the Center for Action and Contemplation's issue of the publication *Oneing*. In addition to his soteriology and panentheistic theology, which lead to criticism that he is promoting universalism, Rohr has been faulted by members of the Religious Right for his Christology, which views creation as the first incarnation of "the universal Christ."

---

8. Fox, *Creation Spirituality*, 31.

In his 2009 volume *The Naked Now*, subtitled "Learning to See as the Mystics See,"[9] Rohr challenges spiritual seekers to give up the "either/or" dichotomies of dualistic thinking and to turn instead to the larger issues of love, infinity, suffering, God, ecology, war, and violence. Rohr honors religious mystics and describes them as having moved "from mere belief systems or belonging systems to actual inner experience."[10] These inner explorers are willing to surrender to the gift of grace that has opened their hearts "to the naked now of true prayer and full presence." They realize that although God is unspeakable, the divine is at the same time as close and as accessible as our breath. "Oneness is no longer merely a vague mystical notion, but a scientific fact." Thanks to their "third-eye" vision of understanding, mystics are able to grasp the big picture.[11]

Rohr claims that Jesus was the first nondualistic religious teacher of the West and as one who would surely understand and affirm the nonpolarity thinking of Hinduism, Buddhism, and Taoism. Along with Native religions, these three traditions emphasize the overcoming of conflicts and oppositional thinking by conversions of the heart, mind, and emotions. They are more concerned with this world than the world to come. In contrast, the traditional accent of the monotheistic religions (Christianity, Judaism and Islam) on individual salvation and "us versus them" thinking has led to elitism, ethnic hatred, war, violence, homophobia, poverty, and the savaging of animals and the earth. Much of this conflict stems from the judging mind, which ranks and excludes in its quest for

---

9. As noted previously, students in this study are encouraged to read recommended titles in their entirety. However, if that is not currently possible, for the purpose of this study I suggest that you read pages 9–38 of *The Naked Now*, which includes Rohr's preface and the book's first four chapters. While scholars do not always agree on definitions of the term "mystic," true mystics, such as Moses, Isaiah, the Buddha, Jesus, Origen of Alexandria, Gregory of Nyssa, Evagrius of Pontus, Denys the Areopagite, Muhammad, Francis of Assisi, Meister Eckhart, John of the Cross, Mohandas Gandhi, Martin Luther King, Jr., and Richard Rohr, have been to the mountain top, have received the divine vision, and have returned to share their encounter with God, a journey of ascending and descending, of height and depth, light and darkness, of contemplation and action. Mysticism, however, need not be esoteric or occasional. As Catholic theologian Karl Rahner noted, "The devout Christian of the future will either be a 'mystic' or he will cease to be anything at all." Cited in Rohr, *Naked Now*, 38.

10. Rohr, *Naked Now*, 29–39.

11. Citing the twelfth-century Hugh and Richard of the monastery of St. Victor in Paris, Rohr speaks of the first eye as the eye of the flesh (thought or sight), the second as the eye of reason (meditation or reflection), and the third as the eye of true understanding (contemplation), Rohr, *Naked Now*, 28.

certainty. Rohr laments the resistance to the radical change that Jesus proclaimed and embodied in his teachings on nonviolence, a simple lifestyle, love of the poor, forgiveness, love of enemies, inclusivity, and compassion.

Rohr celebrates what he calls "a renaissance of the contemplative mind, the one truly unique alternative that religion has to offer the world."[12] He discusses how the contemplative mind approaches faith, great love, suffering, paradox, mystery, being awake, and leadership. One of the hallmarks of this spiritual path is the "Principle of Likeness." Here is how Rohr explains it: "The enormous breakthrough is that when you honor and accept the divine image within yourself, you cannot help but see it in everybody else, too, and you know it is just as undeserved and unmerited as it is in you. That is why you stop judging, and that is how you start loving unconditionally and without asking whether someone is worthy or not. The breakthrough occurs at once, although the realization deepens and takes on greater conviction over time."[13] Imagine what would happen in America and around the world if Christians abandoned dualistic thinking and began to live out the radical teachings of Jesus that have been ignored. Imagine what would happen if governments would be prodded by the world's religions to practice the contemplative mind and move beyond the need for war, demonizing of the enemy, and "us" versus "them" thinking!

At the outset of life, God unites body and soul and sends us into the world. As a parting gift, the Creator presents us with an unassembled jigsaw puzzle representing the true and unique self God created us to be. Our mission is to search for and find all the scattered pieces, and assemble as much of the puzzle as we can. By the end of our lives, we hope to have discovered the greater picture of who we are in God's sight. Another way of saying this is that the primary goal of our lives is to discover our purpose for being and to shape our history accordingly. Most of us, I would guess, do not arrive at the hour of death completely assembled. It remains for God to "finish us" on the other side.

"True spirituality," Rohr says, "is not a search for perfection or control or the door to the next world; it is a search for divine union *now*. The great discovery is always that what we are searching for has already been given! I did not find it; it found me. It is Jacob's shout of Eureka! at

---

12. Rohr, *Naked Now*, 114.
13. Rohr, *Naked Now*, 159.

the foot of his ladder to heaven in Genesis 28:16-17."[14] At the heart of *The Naked Now* is Rohr's call for Christians to reject a narrow, dualistic (either/or) understanding of the mysteries of God and church in favor of a nondualistic (both/and) mindset that celebrates truth wherever it is found. Dualistic people view themselves as humans trying desperately to become human. However, as the Christian revelation makes clear, we are already spiritual ("in God"), and our difficult but necessary task is to learn how to become human.[15]

Citing Thomas Aquinas's observation that "Whatever is received is received according to the mode of the receiver," Rohr notes that whatever one teaches or receives is heard on at least nine different levels, according to the inner, psychological, and spiritual maturity of the listener.[16] Level 1 people misuse scripture, sacraments, and any other spiritual tool that is presented to them, whereas Level 7–9 people "make lemonade out of even sour or unripe lemons." While discerning these levels from his own pastoral and teaching experience, Rohr is quick to note that his levels serve a didactic purpose; real life is much more subtle.

Rohr's list includes:

1. *My body and self-image are who I am.* Such a view represents dualistic/polarity thinking and leads to dominance of security, safety, and defensive needs.

2. *My external behavior is who I am.* People at this level need to look good to others, and in so doing hide or disguise contrary evidence from themselves and from others. This stage is common among conservatives.

3. *My thoughts/feelings are who I am.* People at this level develop intellect and will in order to have better thoughts and feelings, and in so doing control them to the extent that neither they nor others see their self-serving character. This education as a substitute for transformation is common among liberals and the educated.

4. *My deeper intuitions and felt knowledge are who I am.* This level, while a breakthrough from previous levels, keeps people stymied, for it substitutes individualism, self-absorption, and inner work for true encounter with otherness.

---

14. Rohr, *Naked Now*, 16.
15. Rohr, *Naked Now*, 69.
16. Rohr's list of nine levels is adapted from *Naked Now*, 164–66.

5. *My shadow self is who I am.* People at this level are overwhelmed by their own weakness; without guidance, grace, and prayer, many go back to previous identities.

6. *I am empty and powerless.* At this level most attempts to save the self by superior behavior, techniques, morality, positive roles, or religious devotion lead to regression. All one can do is wait, ask, and trust. People at this level learn faith and discover the superior mentoring qualities of darkness. Such people are discovering for themselves the reality of God.

7. *I am much more than who I thought I was.* People at this level undergo the death of the false self and the birth of the True Self. Since such people are not yet fully yielded to the loss of ego, their experience feels like a void, even if a wonderful void. Such people, embarking on the second-half journey, are learning the meaning of "dark splendor."

8. *"I and the Father are one"* (John 10:30). At this level there is only God—or as Teresa of Ávila states, "One knows God in oneself, and knows oneself in God." All else is seen as passing ego possession, which need not be protected, promoted, or proved—to anyone.

9. *I am who I am.* At this level one accepts oneself fully, warts and all; no window dressing is necessary. This level represents the most radical critique of religion, viewed now as just a pointer to reality and not reality itself. People at this stage need not appear to be anything but who they are. Fully detached from self-image, such people live in the image of God for themselves, which includes and loves both the good and the bad. Here one experiences total nonduality, the serenity and freedom of the saints.

Rohr's goal, like that of every religious seeker, is to keep people moving deeper into faith, knowing they receive all necessary information and experience at each level to travel onward. Like Fox, Rohr's spirituality is comprehensive and progressive, yet engages fully with orthodox Christian doctrine and the contemplative tradition.

QUESTIONS FOR DISCUSSION AND REFLECTION

In addition to the questions listed at the end of the preface, answer the following questions, writing your answers in a journal. If you are in a group study, be prepared to share your answers with those in the group.

1. In your own words, explain the distinction between orthodoxy and orthopraxy, and their relevance to Christian spirituality.
2. Explain and assess the merit of Franciscan spirituality as an "alternative orthodoxy."
3. Evaluate the merit or deficiency of fundamentalism as an authentic form of religious spirituality.
4. Identify and assess John Haught's four components of wholesome religion.
5. Explain the adequacy or inadequacy of viewing nature/reality as sacramental.
6. Do you agree with Matthew Fox that the fall/redemption paradigm is essentially foreign to scripture? If so, how do you explain its predominance in Christian theology?
7. Explain the adequacy or inadequacy of creation spirituality. If possible, state its core principle in one sentence.
8. In your own experience, which of Fox's four paths of spirituality seems most attractive to you at this time? Explain your answer. Which path currently seems least attractive? Explain your answer.
9. Explain the adequacy or inadequacy of the doctrine of original sin. After reading this chapter, which aspect of Patricia Williams's discussion on original sin did you find most helpful or useful? Explain your answer.
10. Assess the strengths and weaknesses of Rohr's nondualist message.
11. Explain and assess Rohr's "Principle of Likeness."
12. Assess the merit of Rohr's statement, "True spirituality is not a search for perfection or control or the door to the next world; it is a search for divine union *now*."
13. *For reflection only*: In light of Rohr's spectrum of religious maturity, which level best summarizes your current self-understanding? Explain your choice.

Chapter 12

John Shelby Spong's *Why Christianity Must Change* and Marcus Borg's *Heart of Christianity*

IN ADDITION TO READING some of Christianity's greatest classics, this study has been designed to prompt you to examine your religious beliefs and practices, the goal being to move your focus and attention from orthodoxy (a form of spirituality concerned with correct belief) to orthopraxy (a form of spirituality concerned with useful practice). As you examine your attitudes and beliefs, what role do they play in your spiritual journey? Perhaps a better way to pose the question is, what is the role of religion or of spirituality in your human journey? Do religion or spirituality function as anchors to keep you securely in place, or as sails to propel you forward? In other words, should theology be steady, certain, and unchanging, or should it be fluid, dynamic, and adaptive to the changes in our life and in our environment?

In my experience, religion and spirituality function as pathways or "route-findings" through the ultimate limits of our lives. These limits include not only death and meaninglessness but also anything that threatens our wellbeing, anything that stands between us and lasting peace or happiness. To accomplish this task, every generation of believers benefits by reexamining its theology, thereby providing society with vision and hope. A stagnant theology reflects a religion that is limited in both usefulness and effectiveness.

Life on planet earth is fragile, and our lives are immensely complex. *Rebuilding the Temple* celebrates the many voices of Christian literature, spanning thousands of years and speaking to us from a variety of sociological, ecclesiastical, and theological perspectives.

In this closing chapter we examine the life and writings of Anglican Bishop John Shelby Spong and Lutheran New Testament scholar Marcus Borg, both advocates of progressive Christianity. Recently deceased, both individuals addressed the relationship of theology to changing social issues, and their views have been regularly criticized by conservative clergy for beliefs and practices deemed heretical, unchristian, or antichristian. Nevertheless, both thinkers considered themselves authentic followers of Jesus Christ and therefore faithfully Christian. While both were concerned with the dilemma of being Christian in a postmodern secular world, Spong challenged the very foundation of Christianity, viewing the theological and ecclesiastical task as requiring deconstruction (radical discovery and transformation), whereas Borg viewed the task as requiring reconstruction (radical rediscovery and reformation). To appreciate and understand the theological views of modern scholars such as Spong and Borg, readers may find helpful the following perspectives on God and the scriptures.

UNDERSTANDING GOD PANENTHEISTICALLY

Theology is "talk about God." And the majority of people who use the term "God," particularly in the Western world, have in mind a theistic concept of God, meaning an all-powerful and supreme ruler of the universe. Supernatural theism, by implication, includes the view that all finite things are dependent in some way on this ultimate reality, a reality generally described in personal terms. After all, imaging God as a personal being is very common in the Bible. It is also the natural language of worship and prayer, and there is nothing wrong with it in such contexts. A transcendent reality that does not possess at the very least those qualities that constitute the dignity of human beings, qualities such as intelligence, feeling, freedom, power, initiative, and creativity, could not adequately inspire trust or reverence in human beings. In this sense God would have to be "personal" to be God. It is doubtful whether believers could worship something that does not have at least the stature of personality.

While the idea of a "personal God" is beneficial in that it makes God relational and accessible to humanity, the extremes of this position, such as presented in the Hebrew scriptures, raise insuperable problems for people in the modern era. This God fights wars and defeats enemies, chooses people and works through them, sends storms, heals the sick, spares the dying, rewards goodness, and punishes evil. Many people have trouble intellectually with these anthropomorphic renderings of God and with the seeming irrationality of belief in a personal God. While only the most traditional believers and the most literal readers of scripture believe such things anymore, this deity remains the primary object and substance of the Christian church's faith. It is this understanding of God that is becoming meaningless to increasing numbers in the modern world.

While it is attractive to speak of intimacy with God and accessibility to God, religious philosophers have long warned against ascribing human qualities and attributing human feelings to God. Still, the joy of familiarity with God and the need to recognize and be recognized by God override the philosopher's critique. There is, however, a critical flaw in this perspective: Once we conceive of God as a person like ourselves, God becomes open to criticism.

To protect God, apologists and theologians maintain that this way of thinking must be discarded. God is not like us, says Karl Barth; God is "Totally Other." Following this understanding, God is viewed as different not only in degree but also in kind. In using the model of transcendence, whereby God is said to be all knowing, all powerful, and all good, we instinctively know that we are not referring to the same kind of qualities we understand when speaking of attributes in humans. Does this mean, then, that God cannot be said to be moral in the manner that we are said to be moral? If so, that raises deep resentments. We hear it in the outburst of the philosopher John Stuart Mill: "I will call no being good who is not what I mean when I apply the epithet to my fellow creatures, and if such a being can sentence me to hell, to hell I will go."[1] In his publication, *The Sins of Scripture*, Bishop Spong examines biblical moral principles attributed to the will of God and concludes that those who wish to base their morality literally on the Bible have either not read it or not understood it.

But what are the alternatives? Is atheism (a-theism) the only alternative to theism? Technically, of course, there are numerous options, including polytheism (the belief that there are numerous deities), pantheism (the belief that God is in everything for everything is divine), henotheism (the notion of worshipping a territorial god, conceived as one

---

1. Cited by Schulweis, *Those Who Can't Believe*, 132.

god among many), animism (the belief that nature is filled with spirits or souls, which must be worshipped or appeased), and panentheism.

One can find historical traces of panentheism in both Western and Eastern Orthodox theology, though the word itself was popularized by English philosopher Alfred North Whitehead (1861–1947). Panentheism is not the same as pantheism, the concept that "all things are God." Rather, pan*en*theism is the concept that "all things are *in* God." Panentheism views God not as a supernatural being separate from the universe, beyond nature and history, but as the encompassing Spirit around us and within us. According to this conception, God is more than the universe, yet the universe is in God. Viewed spatially, God is not "out there" but "right here." Whereas supernatural theism emphasizes God's transcendence—God's otherness, God as more than the universe—panentheism affirms both the transcendence and immanence of God. It does not deny or subordinate one in order to affirm the other. For panentheism, God is both more than the universe and yet everywhere present in the universe.[2]

In this regard, panentheism is located between traditional theism and pantheism. As David Ray Griffin describes it, panentheism "combines features of both pantheism, which regards God as 'essentially immanent and in no way transcendent,' and traditional theism, which regards God 'as essentially transcendent and only accidentally immanent.'"[3] Griffin's work helps to explain why panentheism isn't just pantheism with a new name: "Panentheism is crucially different from pantheism because God transcends the universe in the sense that God has God's own creative power, distinct from that of the universe of finite actualities. Hence, each finite actual entity has its own creativity with which to exercise some degree of self-determination, so that it transcends the divine influence upon it."[4]

Theologians in various traditions have offered different ways of defining and modeling this God-world relationship. According to the influential German evangelical theologian Jürgen Moltmann, in the panentheistic view God, having created the world, also dwells in it, and

---

2. Critics of process theology dismiss this way of viewing God as unbiblical and claim that it represents a return to Greek and Roman paganism. This faulty understanding of panentheism leads Diogenes Allen to posit that the inspiration for Whitehead's God was Plato's *Timaeus*, in which Plato postulates a craftsman who took preexistent time, space, and matter and organized them, Allen, *Troubled Believer*, 48.

3. Griffin, *Reenchantment*, 141.

4. Griffin, *Reenchantment*, 142.

conversely the world which he has created exists in him. He writes of God "making space," a *nothing* (*nihil*) to which God gives being (*creatio ex nihilo*). "God does not create merely by calling something into existence . . . In a more profound sense he 'creates' by letting-be, by making room, by withdrawing himself."[5] Moltmann's language expresses the idea of the world, including humanity, as "enveloped by God without losing its true distinctiveness."[6] Consonant with Moltmann's theology, Anglican theologian Arthur Peacocke writes that "God is best conceived of as the circumambient [i.e., surrounding] reality enclosing all existing entities, structures and processes, and as operating in and through all, while being 'more' than all. Hence, all that is not God has its existence within God's operation and Being." Other panentheistic models have been suggested, but all reveal a common theme: the world is given existence, energy, life, nourishment, and continuous creation by the God in whom "we live and move and have our being" (Acts 17:28).

UNDERSTANDING THE SACREDNESS OF SCRIPTURE

Christians have always affirmed a close relationship between the Bible and God, just as other religions affirm a close connection between the sacred and their holy scriptures. Foundational to reading the Bible is a decision about how to view its origin. Does it come from God, or is it a human product?

Acknowledging the obvious human element in the Bible, modern Christians generally take a both/and stance regarding biblical authorship: the Bible is both divine and human. This approach, upon further review, is problematic and only compounds the confusion. When the Bible is seen as both divine and human, we have two options. One is to say that it is all divine and all human. That may sound good, but no one maintains such an unworkable tension. The other, more typical option is to attempt to separate the divine parts from the human parts—as if some of it comes from God and some is a human product. The parts that come from God are then given greater authority than the others. However, who's to say which parts are divine, and which human? The Bible does not come with footnotes that say, "This passage reflects the will of God; the next passage

---

5. Moltmann, *God in Creation*, 88–89.
6. Clayton and Peacocke, *In Whom We Live*, 145.

does not." So those who take the entire Bible as divine are consistent, but they might be consistently wrong.

Biblical scholars suggest three broad possibilities regarding the inspiration of the Bible:

- *verbal inspiration* – the view that every word of the Bible is divinely inspired and therefore inerrant;
- *human response to inspiration* – the view that biblical writers were witnesses to divine revelation; their words and experiences may be human but they serve as vehicles to a higher voice and a deeper reality;
- *inspired imagination* – the view that the Bible is great literature, designed to capture the imagination; though the books of the Bible contain heightened insight, their message is conditioned by historical, sociological, and cultural factors. When the Bible is studied academically, it is this view that scholars espouse.

JOHN SHELBY SPONG'S *WHY CHRISTIANITY MUST CHANGE OR DIE*

A prominent theme in Spong's writing is that popular and literal interpretations of Christian scripture are not sustainable and do not speak honestly to the situation of modern Christian communities. He favored an approach to scripture informed by scholarship and compassion, which would be compatible with contemporary (scientific) understandings of the universe. He believed that theism is no longer a valid conception of God's nature. Despite rejecting theism, he considered himself a Christian because he believed that Jesus Christ fully expressed the presence of a God of compassion and selfless love and that this was the meaning of the early Christian proclamation, "Jesus is Lord." Rejecting the historical truth claims of Christian doctrines such as the Virgin Birth and the Bodily Resurrection of Jesus, he was also a strong critic of the doctrine that saw one church, such as the Roman Catholic Church, as the one true Church and Jesus Christ as the one and only Savior for humanity.

Spong was a strong proponent of the church reflecting the changes in society at large. Toward that end, he called for a new Reformation, though in fact he was really arguing for anthropological, theological, and ecclesiastical transformation, affirming that Christianity's basic doctrines should be reformulated. His views on the future of Christianity were that we have to start with the present, not the past, and that the scriptures and creeds of Christianity are works in progress that must not be understood literally to perceive their meaning. Like most modernists, he believed that institutions and ideas are always evolving, forcing a dialogue between yesterday's words and today's knowledge. In his estimation, the past, even the Christian past, should never claim to offer eternal truth, for religious truths, like political, economic, philosophic, and scientific theories, are always subject to modification and correction.

John Shelby Spong (1931–2021), was born in Charlotte, North Carolina. A lifelong Episcopalian, he attended the University of North Carolina at Chapel Hill, graduating in 1952. He then attended the Virginia Theological Seminary, receiving his degree in 1955. Serving as rector of various churches in North Carolina and Virginia, in 1979 he was elected Bishop of Newark, New Jersey, serving in that capacity until 2000.

As pastor and later as bishop, he became an outstanding proponent of gender, sexual, and racial equality. A liberal Christian theologian, religion commentator, and author, he called for a fundamental rethinking of Christian belief away from theism and traditional doctrines. In 1977, Spong was one of the first American bishops to ordain a woman into the clergy, and he was the first to ordain an openly gay man in 1989. Throughout his ministry, he held visiting positions and gave lectures around the world, including at major American theological institutions such as Harvard Divinity School. Receiving many awards, including 1999 Humanist of the Year, Spong was a guest on numerous national television broadcasts.

As author of about thirty books, including controversial titles such as *Living in Sin?*, *Rescuing the Bible from Fundamentalism*, *Born of a Woman*, *Resurrection: Myth or Reality?*, *Liberating the Gospels*, *Why Christianity Must Change or Die*, *A New Christianity for a New World*, *The Sins of Scripture*, *Jesus for the Non-Religious*, *Eternal Life: A New Vision*, and commentaries on the Bible as well as on the gospels of John and Matthew, his writings evoked both great support and great condemnation from differing segments of the Christian church. Most of the response was positive, the vast majority of these coming from laypeople, whereas the negative response came mostly from clergy, who characterized his role with labels such as heretic, Antichrist, hypocrite, the Devil incarnate, and ecclesiastical whore. Some calls and letters carried threats of punitive action, including his murder, supposedly under instruction from God.

By way of response, Spong claimed that he was attempting to make religion relevant for a new generation that no longer could believe in the supernatural.

In 1998, after publishing his controversial *Why Christianity Must Change or Die*, Spong posted on the Internet, in Luther-like fashion, twelve theses that he believed needed to be debated as part of Christianity's inevitable transformation. The response to the theses and to the book was immense. In the first fifteen months of his book's publication, he received over six thousand letters from his readers, a total that continued to rise into the tens of thousands. Clearly his message had struck a chord. Spong's "Twelve Points for Reform," available on the Internet and elaborated in his 2001 book, *A New Christianity for a New World*, can be summarized as follows:

1. Theism, as a way of defining God, is dead. So most theological God-talk is today meaningless. A new way to speak of God must be found.

2. Since God can no longer be conceived in theistic terms, it becomes nonsensical to seek to understand Jesus as the incarnation of the theistic deity. Hence, the Christology of the ages is bankrupt.

3. The biblical story of the perfect and finished creation from which human beings fell into sin is pre-Darwinian mythology and post-Darwinian nonsense.

4. The Virgin Birth, understood as literal biology, makes Christ's divinity, as traditionally understood, impossible.

5. The miracle stories of the New Testament can no longer be interpreted in a post-Newtonian world as supernatural events performed by an incarnate deity.

6. The view of the cross as the sacrifice for the sins of the world is a barbarian idea based on primitive concepts of God and must be dismissed.

7. Resurrection is an action of God. Jesus was raised into the meaning of God. It therefore cannot have been a physical resuscitation occurring inside human history.

8. The story of the Ascension assumes a three-tiered universe and is therefore not capable of being translated into the concepts of a post-Copernican space age.

9. There is no external, objective, revealed standard written in scripture or on tablets of stone that can govern our ethical behavior for all time.

10. Prayer cannot be a request made to a theistic deity to act in human history in a particular way.

11. The hope for life after death must be separated forever from the behavior control mentality of reward and punishment. Therefore, the church must abandon its reliance on guilt as a motivator of behavior.

12. All human beings bear God's image and each must be respected uniquely. Therefore, no external description of one's being, whether based on race, ethnicity, gender, or sexual orientation, can properly be used as the basis for rejection or discrimination.

Spong referred to himself as a believer in exile. He believed the world into which Christianity was born was limited and provincial, particularly when viewed from the perspective of the progress in knowledge and technology made over the past two millennia. This makes any ideas or beliefs formulated in first-century Judea inadequate to modern minds and lives. Spong begins his book *Why Christianity Must Change or Die* by commenting on the Apostles' Creed line by line, then methodically moving on through the heart of Christian belief, exploring aspects such as theism, Christology, prayer, morality, and ecclesiology, demonstrating in each case the inadequacies of Christianity as detailed in the Bible and in church traditions. The epilogue includes Spong's own creed, recast to reflect the beliefs he considered relevant to Christianity at the end of the twentieth century.

Critics of Spong should know that he advocated nothing that had not already been proposed and debated within biblical scholarship. He merely popularized deeply debated discussions among clergy and academics. In his estimation, doctrines and beliefs such as the inerrancy of scripture, the miracles of Jesus, and doctrines such as the Resurrection and the Virgin Birth, needed to be explained in ways that modern, ordinary believers could understand. As a result, he made clear to clergy and laypeople alike what it means to have an informed faith that "makes sense" in the contemporary world, and helped deepen and broaden the Christian exploration of scripture, faith, and discipleship.

MARCUS BORG'S *THE HEART OF CHRISTIANITY*

American New Testament scholar Marcus Borg (1942–2015) is among the most widely known and influential voices in recent Liberal or Progressive Christianity. As a fellow of the Jesus Seminary, a group of 159 critical scholars tasked with reexamining the traditions surrounding the historicity of Jesus, particularly his deeds and sayings, Borg was a major figure in historical Jesus scholarship.

Born in Minnesota and raised in a Lutheran family in North Dakota, after high school he attended Concordia College in Moorhead, Minnesota, determined to become an astrophysicist. He soon changed his major to math and physics, and then again to political science and philosophy. As a young man, he experienced deep doubts about his Christian faith and decided to pursue postgraduate studies at Union Theological Seminary in New York City, where he became familiarized with Liberal theology. After graduating from Union, Borg went overseas to Oxford University, where he earned his Master of Theology and Doctor of Philosophy degrees. He then embarked in a teaching career, first at Concordia College, then at South Dakota University and Carleton College in Northfield, Minnesota. He finished his career at Oregon State University, where he held positions in culture, religious studies, and philosophy from 1979 until his retirement in 2007. During his time at Oregon State, he also served as Visiting Professor of New Testament at the Pacific School of Religion in Berkeley, distinguishing himself in professional organizations such as the Society of Biblical Literature and the Anglican Association of Biblical Scholars. In 2009 he was installed as canon theologian at Trinity Episcopal Cathedral in Portland, Oregon, where he was a longtime member.

The author of more than twenty-five books, including the bestselling *Meeting Jesus Again for the First Time*, *Reading the Bible Again for the First Time*, and *The God We Never Knew*, Borg wrote clearly and concisely about life as a journey of transformation. His books are always surprising and delightful, for they take us boldly into fresh fields of wonder, mystery, and passion regarding Jesus, God, the Bible, and the Christian life. In his posthumously published collection of essays, lectures, and sermons entitled *Days of Awe and Wonder: How to Be a Christian in the 21st Century*, Borg speaks explicitly about his personal mystical experiences, which underscore his move from the supernatural theism of his childhood toward panentheism (the view that "all things are in God").

Perhaps the central and strongest theme in this book and throughout Borg's career was his desire to present an alternative vision of the historical Jesus. A leading figure in the so-called "third quest" for the historical Jesus, Borg constructed a picture of Jesus as a non-eschatological "spirit person," rather than as an apocalyptic Jew proclaiming the imminent coming of God's kingdom and the end of time. Though only human, Jesus was, in Borg's view, still a striking person, "One of the most remarkable human beings who ever lived." In reading Borg's works, one gets the feeling that the de-emphasis of certain features in Jesus' Jewish background was not so much a neglect of Jesus' Jewishness as a yearning to see him as more like the modern "us" than like the ancient "them." Indeed, the Jesus we "meet again for the first time" in Borg's work could easily step out of the pages of the New Testament and slide into the pews of many liberal mainline churches.

Borg frequently collaborated on New Testament topics with his friend John Dominic Crossan, the popular Roman Catholic author, as well as co-authoring an important and insightful text on Jesus with conservative British theologian N. T. Wright entitled *The Meaning of Jesus: Two Visions*. In *Meeting Jesus Again for the First Time*, Borg drew on his own spiritual journey from the rigid and authoritarian Christianity of his childhood to the development of what he considered a deeper, richer, and more plausible set of beliefs based on a historical Jesus rather than on the theological Christ. At the moving eulogy delivered at Borg's memorial service by Barbara Brown Taylor, Taylor said with appreciation, "Marcus poured himself into many books and talks, all seeking to move us from secondhand to firsthand religion."

Despite his success and winsomeness, Borg has been criticized for thinking in terms of binaries. For example, his writings portray two views of Jesus (pre-Easter and post-Easter); two views of God (transcendence and immanence); two kinds of Christianity ("The Early Paradigm," a traditional form of Christianity with an inerrant Bible, a purity paradigm, and an emphasis on dogma, and "The Emerging Paradigm," with a mercy paradigm and an emphasis on relationships and personal transformation); and two kinds of salvation (one that focuses on forgiveness of sins and getting into heaven and another that focuses on living compassionately and justly in the present).

In *The Heart of Christianity*, Borg argues that the essential ingredients of a Christian life—faith, being born again, the kingdom of God, the gospel of love—are as vitally important today as they have always been. He clearly wants to show today's questioning Christians how to discover a life of faith by reconceptualizing familiar beliefs. Being born again, for example, has nothing to do with fundamentalist Christianity's assurance of salvation, but is a call to radical personal transformation. Talking about the kingdom of God does not mean that you are fighting against materialism or secularism, but that you have committed your life to the divine values of justice and love. And living the true Christian way is essentially about opening one's heart—to God, and to others. Above all else, Borg believed with passion and conviction that living the Christian life still makes sense.

Borg divides *The Heart of Christianity* into two sections. The first part is the theological section. In this segment, Borg addresses four areas viewed to be central to Christianity: faith, the Bible, God, and Jesus. In his chapter on faith, he contrasts faith as a matter of the head (as a way of belief) with faith as a matter of the heart (as way of life). In his chapter on the Bible, he contrasts the Bible as a divine product (that is, as divine revelation) with the Bible as a historical product (that is, as a human response to God). In his chapter on God, he contrasts supernatural theism with panentheism. In the chapter on Jesus, he contrasts the "pre-Easter" Jesus (the historical Jesus; what Jesus was before his death) with the "post-Easter" Jesus (the Jesus of faith; what Jesus became after his death).

The second part of *The Heart of Christianity* is the ethical section of Borg's work. In this segment he describes four areas viewed to be the most central to the Christian life: born again, the kingdom of God, relational and transformational visions of the Christian life, and ways of thinking about sin and salvation. In his chapter on born again, he combines one-time experiences of conversion with the necessity of a lifelong process of commitment to spirituality. In his chapter on the kingdom of God, he argues that the biblical vision of life has both personal (our life with God) and political (our commitment to social justice) components. In the chapter on "thin places," he contrasts the "closed heart" with the "open heart," noting that there are many ways to experience God, not all of them explicitly religious. In the chapter on sin and salvation, he underscores the biblical understanding of these as both individual and social. In his chapter on loving God, he emphasizes the importance of practice, which for him means paying attention to God personally as well as being committed to things that God is passionate about, such as compassion and justice. In his closing chapter, he contrasts three ways of being religious (absolutist, reductionist, and sacramental).

THE FOUR MEANINGS OF FAITH

As noted previously, students in this study are encouraged to read recommended titles in their entirety. However, if that is not possible, I suggest that you read chapter 1 in *The Heart of Christianity* as well as the discussion on the four meanings of faith in chapter 2, a topic that appears frequently in my writings. For those who are not familiar with this material, the following summary may be useful.[7]

In the history of Christianity, faith has four primary meanings. The first of these sees faith primarily as a "matter of the head," whereas the remaining three understand faith as a "matter of the heart." Each meaning is described with a Latin term to show its antiquity, as well as how it is understood in English. For each term the opposite is given, for antonyms are often as illuminating as synonyms.

1. Faith as Assent (*assensus*). In this first sense faith means simply "belief," which we take to mean holding a certain set of "beliefs," that is, "believing" certain doctrines or dogmas to be true. Understanding faith as belief is dominant today, both within the church and outside it. Its dominance in modern Western Christianity is due to the Protestant Reformation, which not only emphasized faith, but also produced numerous denominations, each defining itself by what it "believed," that is, by its distinctive doctrines or confessions. According to this understanding of faith, the opposite of faith as *assensus* is doubt or disbelief. In its fundamentalist permutation, those who doubt are said to lack faith, whereas those who disbelieve are said to have no faith. While this view is widespread, it puts the emphasis in the wrong place, for it suggests that what God really cares about is the beliefs in our heads, as if having "correct beliefs" is what saves us.

2. Faith as Trust (*fiducia*). In its second and higher sense, faith means "trust" in something or someone. In the Bible, it means radical trust in God. Significantly, it does not mean trusting in the truth of a set of statements about God, for that would simply be *assensus* under a different name. While our behavior is important, God seems to be less concerned with our actions than with our character, for our actions flow from our will. According to this meaning, the opposite of *fiducia* is not doubt or disbelief, but mistrust, which results in worry and anxiety. Four times in the extended passage from Matthew's Sermon on the Mount, Jesus says to his hearers, "Do not worry," and then adds, "You of little

---

7. The material in this segment is adapted from Borg, *Heart of Christianity*, 28–37.

faith" (Matt. 6:25–34). Lack of trust and anxiety go together; if you are anxious, you have little faith.

3. Faith as Faithfulness (*fidelitas*). In the Bible, faith is the trustful acceptance of God's promises, particularly of God's desire to bless all peoples and nations of the world. However, faith is also trust in God's faithfulness to the promise, that is, in God's ability to deliver Good News to everyone, something that God accomplishes through Jesus Christ and his followers. Because God is steadfast and faithful, we too are called to faithfulness. *Fidelitas* does not mean faithfulness to beliefs about God, whether biblical, creedal, or doctrinal. Rather it refers to radical centering in the God to whom the Bible and creeds and doctrines point. The English equivalent to *fidelitas* is "fidelity." Faith as fidelity means loyalty, allegiance, the commitment of the self at its deepest level. Its opposite is not doubt or disbelief. Rather, as in human relationships, its opposite is infidelity, being unfaithful to our relationship with God. To use a striking biblical metaphor, the opposite of this meaning of faith is adultery. Another vivid biblical term for infidelity to God is idolatry, meaning not so much the worship of idols as false gods, but centering in something finite rather than the sacred, which is infinite and beyond all images. As the opposite of idolatry, faith means being loyal to God "and not to the seductive would-be lords of our lives," whether one's nation, affluence, achievement, family, or desire.[8]

4. Faith as Vision (*visio*). As the English word "vision" suggests, faith is a way of seeing reality, and how we view the whole affects how we respond to life. There are basically three ways we can see the whole: (a) We can see reality as *hostile and threatening*, and therefore respond to life defensively, doing whatever we can to survive, for that is all that matters. (b) We can see reality as *indifferent* to human purposes and ends. Although this response to life will be less anxious than that of the first way, we are still likely to be defensive and precautionary. (c) We can see reality as *life-giving, nourishing, and full of promise*. To use a traditional theological term, to see reality as filled with wonder and beauty, and to nourish and spread this goodness, leads to radical trust. It frees us from the anxiety, self-preoccupation, and concern to protect the self with systems of security that mark the first two viewpoints. It leads to the ability to love and to be present to the moment.

---

8. Borg, *Heart of Christianity*, 33.

To understanding faith as *visio* is to see reality as gracious; its opposite, un-faith, views reality as hostile and indifferent. This meaning of faith is closely related to *fiducia*, to faith as trust. Trust and vision go together; trust in God—the God of promise and faithfulness—and how we view God go together. In this way of life, radical centering in God leads to a deepening trust that transforms the way we view reality and live our lives. Seeing, living, trusting, and centering are all related in complex and salutary ways.

As we have noted, faith is relational, but this does not mean that beliefs don't matter. There are affirmations that are central to the Christian faith, affirmations such as the reality of God, the centrality of Jesus, and the significance of the Bible. These beliefs are essential, not only for Christians, but for people of all faiths, when properly understood. Faith as a way of seeing at the deepest level requires avoiding the human tendency toward excessive precision and certitude. Christian theology has often been plagued by both—the desire to know too much and to know it too precisely. Our minds tell us that such knowledge is not possible—perhaps not even desirable—and people cannot easily give their heart to something that their mind rejects. Properly understood, a deep but humble understanding of Christian faith as *assensus* is close to faith as *visio*. As we have seen, biblical and theological faith need not be viewed as assent to narrow propositions or as fulfilling specific requirements, but as a persuasive and compelling way of seeing reality.

While faith involves the mind, faith is primarily the way of the heart. Given the premodern meaning of "believe," to believe in God is to love God and to love that which God loves. The Christian life is as simple and challenging as that.

In his writings, there is no question that Borg is responding to a conservative brand of North American Christianity, namely fundamentalist evangelicalism. However, his conclusions have far wider implications for the church as a whole. As a modern believer, Borg emphasizes building a faith on three foundational premises: *rationality* ("rational" for Borg means adhering to modern norms of rationality); *relevance* (related closely to Borg's notion that everything modern Christians embrace in the Christian tradition be relevant to modern thought and understanding); and *relational*. Borg places great emphasis on the Christian life being a relationship with God. While maintaining that all humans are in a relationship with God from birth, he believes that modern humans have a sense of living "East of Eden," desiring to return to spiritual wellbeing and wholeness.

Throughout his teaching career, Borg was renowned as a gifted writer adept at popularizing difficult concept in a lively and meditative style. A personable and outgoing individual, Borg modeled for the world and the church what it is like to build collegial relationships with people who hold deep yet differing conviction, and to discover greater truth and friendship in the midst of that kind of dialogue. Almost single-handedly among progressive Christians, Borg opened up new avenues of experience and thought for lapsed Christians or nonbelievers interested in rethinking the Christianity of their youth. He was most convincing to people caught between resentment over issues in Christianity such as human guilt, evil, and damnation, and the equally unacceptable alternative of outright atheism. In the face of opposition between orthodoxy and unbelief, Borg always looked for a third way.

QUESTIONS FOR DISCUSSION AND REFLECTION

In addition to the questions listed at the end of the preface, answer the following questions, writing your answers in a journal. If you are in a group study, be prepared to share your answers with those in the group.

1. In your estimation, do your religious attitudes and beliefs function more as anchors to keep you securely in place, or as sails to propel you forward? Explain your answer.
2. Explain the advantages and disadvantages of the idea of a "personal" God.
3. Explain and assess the merit of panentheism for spirituality.
4. In the segment on the sacredness of scripture, which view of scripture do you find most useful, that scripture is primarily divine or primarily human? Assess the viability of the author's statement regarding the unworkability of the view we all wish were true, that scripture is both fully divine and fully human.
5. Do you agree with Spong that a literal interpretation of the Bible is neither adequate nor sustainable? Explain your answer.
6. In your estimation, what is Spong's greatest contribution to Christian spirituality? Explain your answer.

7. Of Spong's "Twelve Points for Reform," which do you find most persuasive, and which least persuasive? Explain your answer.

8. Of Borg's four meanings of faith, which best characterize your current stance? Explain your answer.

9. In your estimation, what is Borg's greatest contribution to Christian spirituality?

Chapter 13

Conclusion

HAVING FINISHED THIS BOOK, you may still be wondering, "What is this experience we call the spiritual journey"? Is it a way of thinking, a way of living, or both? Is spirituality similar or identical with religion, and if so, is being "religious" the same as being spiritual? Unfortunately, the answer to these latter questions is ambiguous and unclear, for the answer is subjective rather than objective. As no two people are alike, physically, intellectually, psychologically, and emotionally, no two people are alike spiritually. What characterizes one person's faith, beliefs, values, interests, and lifestyle cannot define or suit other people. While it is possible to live religiously in a truncated or inauthentic manner, such as when one's religion is reduced to religiosity—that is, when it is expressed mostly in cultural, intellectual, or legalistic ways—this is not the case for spirituality, which can be expressed occasionally or immaturely, but not inauthentically.

Unlike religiosity, which is limiting and confining, spirituality is an adventure, characterized by openness, risk-taking, and ongoing growth. In most cases, the spiritual journey consists of identifiable stages. While Christians might disagree on nomenclature—that is, on the names or numbers of stages of the spiritual journey—there is widespread agreement on the impetus and goal of the journey. As noted in chapter 1 above, spirituality is the journey of life "from God, to God, and with God," a journey defined by Christians as "life in the Spirit." As you may have discovered in your reading and study of great Christian literature, the process of coming to know or to experience God is also the process of knowing oneself.

According to the apostle Paul, believers should view their bodies as temples of the Holy Spirit (1 Cor 6:19). However, in an earlier passage, Paul uses the temple metaphor to speak of a person's entire being, "Do you not know that you are God's temple, and that God's Spirit dwells in you? . . . For God's temple is holy, and you are that temple" (1 Cor 3:16–17). While our bodies may be described as a temple of God, our souls and spirits are also a wondrous residence. This hidden part of us, in union with divinity, is where God-ness (our image of God or original goodness) exists.

As we saw in chapter 6, the sixteenth-century Spanish mystic Teresa of Ávila agreed with Paul, expanding his imagery by describing the inner sphere of a believer's spirituality as an interior castle. She divides this castle into seven distinct mansions or dwelling places, the seventh or innermost mansion being a dwelling place of God, where the human soul achieves transformation and spiritual marriage with God. Like Teresa, the thirteenth-century Sufi (Muslim) poet Jalaluddin Rumi described a person's inner soul-space as a magnificent cathedral, sweet and beautiful beyond description. Likewise, twentieth-century Jesuit paleontologist Teilhard de Chardin understood the necessity of opening our spiritual door inward to find and claim our inner goodness. Reflecting on his own spiritual journey, Teilhard observed this truth: "The deeper I descend into myself, the more I find God at the heart of my being."[1]

However we describe our inner terrain, one thing seems certain: we tend to live in only a few rooms of our inner landscape. The full person God created us to be contains more than we can imagine, but most of us dwell within only a small portion of the superb temple, castle, or cathedral within. Opening the door of our heart allows us entrance to the vast treasure of who we are and to the divine presence within us. To say this, however, is not to dismiss the reality of this same loving presence being fully alive in our external world. The Eternal One is with us in *all* of life. Our purpose in opening the door inward is to help us know and claim who we are so that we can more completely join with God in expressing God's love in every part of our external world.

---

1. Teilhard de Chardin, *Writings in the Time of War*, 61.

FIRST AND SECOND HALF OF LIFE LIVING AND THINKING

While many models—biological, social, psychological, cognitive, moral, ecological, religious, existential, mystical—exist to help conceptualize life's journey, one I find compelling is known as the "second half of life." This "further journey" is not chronological, nor does one magically stumble upon it at midlife or in times of crisis, though these often serve as catalysts. While the second journey represents the culmination of one's faith journey, it is largely unknown today, even by people we consider deeply religious, since most individuals and institutions remain stymied in the preoccupations of the first half of life, establishing identity, creating boundary markers, and seeking security. The first-half-of-life task, while essential, is not the full journey. Furthermore, one cannot walk the second journey with first-journey tools. One needs a new toolkit.

The first task is to build a strong "container" or identity; the second is to find the contents that the container is meant to hold.[2] The first task—surviving successfully—is obvious, one we take for granted as the purpose of life. We all want to complete successfully the task that life first hands us: establishing an identity, a home, a career, relationships, friends, community, and security, all foundational for getting started in life. Many cultures throughout history, most empires in antiquity, and the majority of individuals in the modern period have focused on first-half-of-life tasks, primarily because it is all they have time for, but also for lack of vision.

Most of us are never told that we can set out from the known and the familiar to take on a further journey. Our institutions, including our churches, are almost entirely configured to encourage, support, reward, and validate the tasks of the first half of life. Shocking and disappointing as it may be, we struggle more to survive than to thrive, focusing on "getting through" or on getting ahead rather than on finding out what is at the top or was already at the bottom. As wilderness guide Bill Plotkin puts it, many of us learn to do our "survival dance," but we never get to our actual "sacred dance."

According to Plotkin, the stage of adolescence—beyond which most adults never move—holds the key to both individual development and human evolution. In this stage individuals develop their distinctive ego-based consciousness, which represents both their greatest liability as well

---

2. Rohr, *Falling Upward*, xiii.

as their greatest potential. If they are to become fully human and move to the stages of genuine adulthood, people in the adolescent stage must let go of the familiar and comfortable while submitting to a journey of descent into "the mysteries of nature and the human soul." Individuals who remain within the constraints of a largely adolescent world regress into "pathological adolescence," characterized by materialism, sexism, competitive violence, racism, egoism, and self-destructive patterns. Patho-adolescent societies are perpetuated by leaders and celebrities described as self-serving politicians, moralizing religious leaders, drug-induced entertainment icons, and greedy captains of industry. If society is going to develop soulcentrically, it must be overseen by wise elders, not by adolescent politicians and corporate officers.

How can you know you are entering the second half of life? The following road markers are quite reliable: when you

- experience new urges
- sense a new vision
- are ready to let go of old securities
- are ready to risk giving up the patterns of the past for the promise of the future
- are ready to embrace your shadow self[3]
- are as focused on the "inner" life as on the outer dimension of life.

FIRST AND SECOND HALF OF LIFE SPIRITUALITY

While we are now familiar with the expression "the first half of life," we should not, indeed we cannot equate it with first half of life spirituality. While there are similarities and overlap between the two formulations, the first expression refers essentially to chronology, distinguishing immaturity from maturity, youth and adulthood from midage and old age, starting life from concluding life.

---

3. The shadow self, something everyone possesses, represents the least developed part of one's personality. The shadow uses relatively childish and primitive forms of judgment and perception, often as an escape from the conscious personality and in defiance of conscious standards. One's shadow includes "good" qualities as well as "bad" or "shameful" qualities that one denies. As one makes room for one's polarities, one becomes healthier and more open to transforming grace.

First half of life spirituality, while often working in tandem with first half of life living and thinking, is a way of life and thought that though religious in nature, is centered on encounter with deity/divine Spirit, with opening to grace as the foundational event. However, for many if not for most individuals, piety, religion, morality, and even culture take the place of spirituality. In such cases, nominal religion becomes religiosity, a substitute for authentic spirituality, and in speaking of religiosity, we find we are no longer describing spirituality but rather an acculturated form of first half of life living and thinking.

In my experience and from my vantage point as a scholar of spirituality and religious studies, the entry point to authentic spirituality, unlike religion, is not ritual or indoctrination, although these can be catalysts for first half of life spirituality, but rather a personal or individual encounter with the divine. This experience, called a "second birth" by evangelicals, is frequently described as a conversion. As the foundational experience for first half of life spirituality, such an experience is generally followed by adherence to a religious mindset and a moral lifestyle.

While such a conversion can be foundational for second half of life spirituality as well, the difference is that for this second "half" of life, such an experience is not based on a decision one makes or a commitment one controls. Rather, this experience is an absolute gift of grace, for it comes more as a realization or revelation than as an act of the will. Unlike entrance into first half of life spirituality, this second experience is best described as a realization or awakening, for such transformation simply happens over time, more like a process than an event, and it may take time before individuals become conscious of the changes within themselves. More commonly, awareness occurs retrospectively, brought to our attention by those around us who notice the difference in our attitude, nature, and demeanor.

While individuals can describe their own experience of the second spiritual journey and even serve as mentors, they cannot define or outline the journey for others. This is due both to the uniqueness of the journey and to a subtle factor, known by generations of mystics and spiritual masters but elusive to many of our contemporaries: One does not choose this second spiritual journey; rather it chooses you. It finds you by means of your soul, your personal center and true home, the source of your true belonging. The soul comes to our aid through dreams, deep emotion, love, the quiet voice of guidance, synchronicities, revelations, hunches, and visions, and at times through illness, nightmares, and terrors. This is the identity that defines us, aligning us with our powers of nurturing, transforming, and creating, with our powers of presence and wonder. It is the soul that guides us, preparing the way and declaring us ready for this further journey.

As you may have noticed in your reading of classic Christian literature, most of the works written during the church's first eighteen hundred years had first half of life religious or spiritual tasks in mind: establishing, maintaining, cultivating, and deepening one's faith identity. This lifestyle and mindset was often based on the three supernatural virtues of faith, hope, and love, a paradigm found in scripture, developed by the church, and lived out in faithful witness with fellow believers. Only during the modern period, primarily in the twentieth and twenty-first centuries (with notable exceptions such as George Fox and William Blake), do we find Christian writers clearly pointing us to the possibility of second half of life spirituality. Viewing A. W. Tozer, Henry Drummond, Andrew Murray, Henri Nouwen, and Russell Conwell as transitional figures, it isn't until our final five authors—Brian McLaren, Matthew Fox, Richard Rohr, John Shelby Spong, and Marcus Borg—that we find clear exemplars of second half of life spirituality.

THE JOURNEY OF FAITH: A CONTEMPORARY MODEL

In light of the questions and concerns these five authors raise in their writings, it is obvious that society has changed dramatically since Christianity emerged in the first century. During that period, as society changed, Christians changed accordingly, both in lifestyle and belief. Perhaps an appropriate way to conclude our discussion of spirituality and classic Christian literature is with the following well-known paradigm for the journey of faith, one I introduced into my writings in 2012 in *Beyond Belief*.

Having taught religious studies at the college and graduate levels for four decades, I noticed that the mindset of college students changed dramatically during that period. In almost every discipline, the level of engagement with the subject matter transformed students from passive to active learners. In addition, the theological preunderstanding of students in my classes changed as well. While a majority continue to be reared in Christian homes, an increasing number enroll in religion courses not simply to build upon an existing foundation but to wrestle with matters of faith. Large numbers of college students today self-designate as agnostics and atheists, and those who arrive at these positions thoughtfully rather than out of boredom or apathy add profoundly to class dynamics. Skeptical students often become exemplary students, for they approach life passionately rather than perfunctorily. Overall, people today find themselves attracted to a religious paradigm that describes one's faith story as a journey through three stages. This journey is instructive for many because it articulates their own faith story.

Precritical understanding (also called *first naiveté*) is an early state in which children accept whatever significant authority figures in their lives tell them to be true as indeed true. For some this state is short-lived; for others, it can last a lifetime. In this stage, children generally accept conflicting teachings that God is everywhere present and that God is in heaven. Theologians speak of this tension as the relationship between the immanence and transcendence of God. While most children live with the ambiguity, others feel the need to resolve the tension one way or another.

In their early teens, some begin to doubt the existence of God, an experience that can be traumatic for those who believe in hell or who fear eternal punishment. From a psychological perspective, such an experience represents a collision between one's childhood beliefs and those of modernity. Those who undergo this transition are entering the stage of *critical understanding*, and there seems to be no way back.

In late adolescence, college students often become exposed to the scholarly study of religion. The answers provided by the great intellectual figures of Western theology may not restore their former beliefs, but they do provide a framework that allows then to take their perplexity seriously. Those who wrestle with the nature of scripture and learn about early Christianity discover that the Bible, including the gospels and the rest of the New Testament, is neither a divine document nor a straightforward historical record. Some are exposed to the well-known scholarly distinction between "the Jesus of history" and "the Christ of faith," a distinction Borg notes in his writings.

The first concept refers to Jesus as he truly was—a Galilean Jew who was executed by the Romans—and the second concept refers to what Jesus became in the faith of the early Christian communities: the Christ of the developing Christian tradition. The gospels, it seems, contain mostly later traditions about Jesus, so it is the "Christ of faith" rather than the "Jesus of history" that one encounters in the gospels and in the later creeds. From this perspective, the image of Jesus as divine Savior, central to the church's theology, is not something Jesus had taught concerning himself but rather came from the church's later understanding. The longer one studies the Christian tradition, the more transparent its human origins become. The same applies to all of the world's religions; all seem products of culture. Those who accept this become perplexed about God and conclude that there probably is no such reality.

Eventually those who persevere in their faith journey discover that agnosticism and atheism are not final destinations but temporary stops. Their religious perception is transformed by what might be called "an experience of sacred mystery." Something happens to them—a mystical experience, something traumatic, a relationship, a sudden realization, a wilderness experience, an experience of "something more"—and the word "God" becomes meaningful once again, only this time not as a reference to a supernatural being "out there" but to the sacred at the center of existence, the holy mystery that is all around us and within us. God is no longer a mere idea or an article of belief external to oneself but rather an element of experience. Such persons have reached the state of *postcritical understanding* (also called *second naiveté*), a state where one participates in religious rituals because they are meaningful and not because they are required, where one hears ancient biblical stories as "true" while knowing them as not literally true.

Though the expression "postcritical understanding" or "postcritical naiveté" seems to represent accurately this sophisticated state of innocence, I prefer "mature faith." By faith, I refer to an existential state that is unique to each individual, and by "mature" I refer to a conscious, heartfelt examination of conviction based upon one's cumulative life experience. Mature faith challenges one's conceptual framework and provides a new understanding of the religious task. In this regard, *Rebuilding the Temple* is written that you may remain open to truth wherever it appears, growing ever more deeply in your spirituality and enjoying more fully its benefits.

A POSTMODERN MODEL OF FAITH DEVELOPMENT

In his book, *Faith After Doubt*, theologian Brian McLaren proposes a postmodern model of faith development, in which questions and doubt are not the enemy of faith but rather a portal to a more mature and fruitful kind of faith. Based on his own journey of faith, his model correlates with my own experience. McLaren's four-stage approach best describes the faith journey for people reared in traditional forms of religion.

Like love, which progresses in stages through one's life, from the "securing" phase in childhood to the "exploring" phase in adolescence and early adulthood, to the "giving" stage in marriage and career, and to the "enjoying" stage in late adulthood and retirement, faith is intended to grow and develop throughout life. Doubt, it turns out, is the passageway from one stage of faith to the next. Without doubt, there can be growth within a stage, but growth from one stage to another usually requires us to doubt the assumptions that give shape to our current stage. We will call the first period of growth Stage One, and the next period Stage Two, and so on. Each new stage, like a ring on a tree, embraces and builds upon the previous stage, while growing beyond its limits. Alternatively, each stage includes and transcends its predecessors. McLaren labels the four stages: Simplicity, Complexity, Perplexity, and Harmony.

McLaren compares these stages to the four sequential seasons of spring, summer, fall, and winter, likening Simplicity to the springlike season of spiritual awakening, Complexity to the summerlike season of spiritual strengthening, Perplexity to the autumnlike season of spiritual surviving, and Harmony to the winterlike season of spiritual discovery. Like living with nature, the point is not to stay in spring or summer forever, nor is it the point to get to (or through) winter as soon as possible, any more than the point of life is advancing from infancy to old age as soon as possible. Rather, the point is to live each stage fully, to learn well what each day and season has to teach, and to live and enjoy life in companionship with God and others through all of life's seasons. As with nature, the journey of faith is not a neat progression, and the lines between stages are certainly arbitrary. The fact is, there is no more of a clear line between stages than there is a clear line between seasons. You can have warm days in winter and snowfall in spring, and just as calendars don't tell the whole story, neither can any schema. There is no shame, pride, or regret in being at the stage of development in which we find ourselves. If there is anything to regret, I suppose it is refusing to grow when life invites us to do so, or rushing through our current stage without learning all it has to teach us.

In *Stage One* (Simplicity), which begins around the age of two, infants become increasingly independent, and it is the parents' task to teach them how to provide for their own needs and desires in appropriate ways. This stage revolves around the simple mental function of sorting nearly everything into one of two categories (things are either permitted or prohibited, others are either friend or foe, and one is either happy or sad). For that reason, in Stage One, you set out to master the mental skills of dualism, of seeing the world in twos (this or that, in or out, right or wrong).

Authorities—your parents, grandparents, teachers, political and religious leaders—are central to this stage; hence, Stage One is the stage of authority as well as the stage of dualism. As far as you are concerned, the authorities know everything, and you don't, so you feel highly dependent on them. You trust them and want to please them, and you aspire someday to be as certain and all-knowing as they are. Before long, you find out that the authorities in your life dislike or distrust other authorities, and your dualism adds a new category: us versus them. This social dualism creates a strong sense of loyalty and identity among "us." It also creates a strong sense of anxiety and even hostility about "them," the "others," the "outsiders," and the "outcasts." Stage One is built on trust, because for the child, trust is an absolute necessity, a matter of survival. Simple trust, unquestioning loyalty, that's what matters in Stage One.

Stage One is the baseline of what being raised means in our culture. Here one is taught the difference between right and wrong and other basic dualisms of Stage One. While this stage works well from the age of two to twelve, many people spend their entire lives in Stage One, submitting to authorities and following all the rules. Then, when it is time for them to become authorities themselves, they demand the same submission from the next generation that they themselves gave to the previous generation. For that reason, it shouldn't be a surprise that faith and religion are a strictly Stage One phenomenon for millions, even billions, of people.

Thus far, Stage One may have felt like a school to help us learn the basic morals necessary for independence. However, at some point, it begins to feel like detention, even a prison. The only way out is doubt. We may doubt that the authorities are always right. We may doubt that all the rules are always absolute and appropriate. Add hormones, puberty, sexual curiosity, and changing brains to the mix, and Simplicity stops feeling appropriate anymore. This may happen at twelve or twenty-two or forty-five, but eventually, many of us doubt our way out of Simplicity and enter Stage Two.

If Stage One is about dualism and dependence, *Stage Two* (Complexity) is about pragmatism and independence. We have our own lives to live, and we have to find a way to become who we are on our own.

In Stage One we were drawn to authority figures who told us what to think and do, but in Stage Two we seek out coaches who teach us how to think for ourselves and help us develop our own goals, along with our own skills to attain those goals. In Stage One, we saw life as a matter of survival, but in Stage Two we see life as a game, as a contest of competing and winning. In Stage One everything was either known or knowable, but in Stage Two, everything is learnable and doable, if only we can find the right models, mentors, and coaches, and master the right techniques, skills, and know-how.

In terms of our faith, we are no longer content merely to listen to a sermon by an authority figure; we want to learn methods of studying the Bible for ourselves. Learning and studying, thinking for ourselves and reaching our own conclusions, are part of what it means to be a good Stage Two Christian. People in Simplicity and Complexity become active consumers in the religious market. Every year, they need more sermons, books, radio and TV shows, podcasts, conferences, courses, retreats, camps, churches, and mission trips. For some people, the only faith they will ever know is either the authoritarian, dualistic faith of Stage One, or the pragmatic independent faith of Stage Two. However, what happens if you start to question your religious goals?

When people run into problems with Stage One or Two faith, some make a lateral transfer to another faith community. Other disillusioned Stage Two believers may temporarily or permanently revert to Stage One forms of faith. When Stage Two people find religious teaching or programming doesn't produce the results they expected, many sincere believers simply amp up their effort, assuming the fault is their own. But eventually their confidence cracks, doubts pour in, and their Stage Two project starts to sink. For most Stage Two believers, however, there is no going back, at least not in the long term. Having felt increasingly alienated from Stage One dualism and Stage Two pragmatism, they lose faith in both the authoritarian leaders of Simplicity and the success coaches of Complexity, whether inside or outside the church. Both types of leaders make promises they can't deliver on, and neither type is honestly facing life's deeper questions and challenges.

After trying lateral transfers among two or more Stage Two faith communities, some start doubting the whole faith project. They begin to feel so stuck, trapped, and stagnant they decide to burn down the whole structure. Other people aren't so easily satisfied. Their quest for honesty and depth burns like a fire in the belly and they move into *Stage Three*

(Perplexity). Life for people in Stage Three feels more than simple and more than complex; it is simultaneously perplexing and mysterious. Because this stage embraces relativism, Stage Three people feel more comfortable lurking on the fringes of a group rather than belonging squarely in its center. Even better, they might be fringe members of a number of groups, to gain a variety of viewpoints. Unable to find a community that fits their stage, many become unaffiliated "nones," working out their questions alone. If they find community at all, it tends to be among alienated individuals like themselves.

Stage Three, even though it brings new gains, with multiple highs and thrills, often feels conflicted and heavy, like a feeling of descent and loss. Stage Two built so naturally on Stage One, and even the portal of doubt between the two was a relatively easy passage compared to Stage Three. Now, however, everything we once constructed we now deconstruct. The summits we climbed in Stage Two we now leave behind. Will anything remain, or will we end up in a state of spiritual bankruptcy?

Over time, we come to see that our grim "all is lost" assessment isn't the whole story. For example, in Stage Three, we still retain powerful and valuable treasures that we gained in Stage One. We learned, through dualism, to care about whether we are doing right or wrong. We learned to tell the truth. We learned to stand for something. Now, in Stage Three, our courageous commitment to honesty in the face of great cost and loss shows how well we learned the moral lessons of Simplicity. Similarly, in Stage Three we retain powerful treasures that we gained in Stage Two. We learn to be curious and flexible. We learn that different spheres of life are like games that operate by different sets of rules, and we become fluent in the complex rules of multiple games. We learn independence, and become self-motivated learners and self-managers, adults who begin to take responsibility for our own successes and failures.

Thus, despite the feelings of loss, the lasting gains of Stages One and Two sustain us in Perplexity. In addition, Stage Three will do the same for Stage Four. The fact is, Perplexity brings some of the greatest spiritual gifts life has to offer, gifts such as humility, honesty, courage, and sensitivity, for it is the doorstep to Stage Four. Whereas Perplexity is a path of descent, it is also a path of dissent. It gives us the courage to speak our truth, even when we are threatened for doing so. That courage is not simply an intellectual matter; it is also ethical, a matter of integrity and character.

If Stage Three dissenters keep descending through Perplexity, they will encounter a moment of crisis. Will their power of critical thinking become a gift that undoes them, or will the seeing through of skeptical doubt lead them into mystical or contemplative insight? Will they see through and beyond Simplicity, Complexity, and Perplexity to a deeper narrative, a more mysterious coherence, a revolutionary Harmony that embraces and integrates all it includes, producing a way to see things whole again?

People deep in Perplexity, feeling disillusioned with naïve dualism and pragmatism, face a stark choice. Will they become cynical nihilists, seeing everything so critically that meaning, purpose, value, reverence, and wonder become increasingly distant and elusive? For some people, this cynicism is the only intellectually honest option, so they surrender to perpetual Perplexity, all dressed up in critical thinking with nowhere to go. Nevertheless, some people can't be satisfied with that choice. They become cynical of their own cynicism, skeptical of their own skepticism, critical of their own critical thinking, even doubting their doubtfulness. They begin to wonder, hope, and imagine, and they dare to believe that there is another option beyond Stage Three. To maintain momentum, to keep growing and developing, however, requires a kind of dying, a death to ego or pride, a relinquishment of our right to judge, to know, and to control. You might call this a death to privilege, superiority, or supremacy, as seekers realize that all people share in the human condition.

Stage Four (Harmony) builds on "the still more excellent way of love" described by Paul in his letter to the Corinthians (1 Cor 12:31–14:1). In this passage, Paul makes clear that nearly everything religious people strive for will eventually be embraced by something deeper. Even faith and hope don't have the last word. Only love, he says, is the more excellent way. In his masterpiece *The Brothers Karamazov*, Dostoevsky captured this shift to Harmony when he admonished his readers to "Love all God's creation, the whole and every grain of sand in it. Love every leaf, every ray of God's light. Love the animals, love the plants, love everything. If you love everything, you will perceive the divine mystery in things. Once you perceive it, you will begin to comprehend it better every day. And you will come at last to love the whole world with an all-embracing love."

At some point, this discovery of unifying Harmony beyond disintegrating Perplexity seems very simple, almost childish, like a return home. Perhaps this is what T. S. Eliot had in mind when he wrote, "We shall not cease from exploring, and the end of our exploring will be to arrive where we started and know the place for the first time." For this reason, Harmony has been described as a second naiveté, a second simplicity or innocence best described as transcendence, a transcendence, however, that combines the best of the conservative and the best of the progressive positions, because it brings along or includes the previous stages rather than leaving them behind.

If in Stage One we know that everything is knowable, in Stage Two we know that everything is doable, and in Stage Three we know that everything is relative, in Stage Four we come to know that everything is suitable for its time (Eccl 3:11). In this stage we can finally accept that all our knowing, past and present, is partial (1 Cor 13:12). Now we finally see authority figures neither as omniscient and trustworthy (as in Stages One and Two) nor as fake or deluded (as in Stage Three), but rather as human beings like us, mortal and fallible. This awareness also allows us to find our identity in new ways in relation to others; not in Stage One dependence, nor in Stage Two independence, and not in Stage Three counterdependence, but in the more mature interdependence of nonduality. This humility before others morphs into what some call paradoxy—the realization that no statement about God—or even about what is true—can be final or complete.

This new realization—likened to a second Simplicity—eventually matures into a higher Complexity, and so on, in an ascending spiral of growth and discovery that continues as long as life itself. Far from feeling we have finally arrived, in Stage Four we finally begin to understand that arrival has never been the goal.

In Stage Four we discover amazing truths. For example, we discover that spirituality is about love; that knowing is loving; that we know ourselves by loving ourselves; that we know others by loving them; that we know God by loving ourselves and others. Those who reach Stage Four do not experience Certainty, however, for that is the concern of those in Stages One and Two. Stage Four people never feel they have arrived. They are not obsessed with misguided notions of certainty or supremacy—more the opposite. Committed to the faith journey, they know there is no such thing as certainty in faith. Faith, like all creativity, flourishes not in certainty but in questioning, not in security but in venturing. In Stage Four, it is trust that matters, and qualities such as peace, harmony, joy, relationships, intimacy, and unity.

Those who reach Stage Four can also look back and see love's gravitational pull all along. When they loved correctness in Stage One, the love with which they pursued correctness mattered more. When they loved effectiveness in Stage Two, the love that moved them to pursue effectiveness mattered still more. When they loved honesty and justice in Stage Three, honesty and love mattered, but the love that burned in their heart for them mattered still more. Faith was about love all along. They just didn't realize it, and it took doubt to help them see it.

QUESTIONS FOR DISCUSSION AND REFLECTION

In addition to the questions listed at the end of the preface, answer the following questions, writing your answers in a journal. If you are in a group study, be prepared to share your answers with those in the group.

1. Describe the difference between religion and spirituality. What positive—or negative—thoughts come to mind when you think about being religious versus being spiritual? Which term ("religion" or "spirituality") best describes your approach to God or to your deeper Self? Explain your answer.

2. Do you consider yourself to be in the first or second half of the spiritual journey? Explain your answer.

3. Assess the strengths and weaknesses of the author's spiritual paradigm as a journey through the precritical, critical, or postcritical stages of faith. Which of these stages best describes the current location of your spiritual journey? In your estimation, is it possible to revert from a postcritical stage to a precritical or critical stage? Why or why not?

4. Evaluate the viability of the postcritical stage, beginning with the idea that Christians can read the biblical accounts as true while knowing them as not literally true.

5. Assess the usefulness of the four-stage model of faith development presented in this chapter.

6. In which phase or stage of faith do you currently find yourself? Explain your answer.

7. Do you believe it is possible to be in more than one stage of faith simultaneously, or to be able to move backward as well as forward along the faith spectrum? Explain your answer.

8. If you ever found yourself in the spiritual stage of Perplexity, were you able to move forward to Stage Four? If so, how did this change occur? If not, why not?

9. Do you believe, with the apostle Paul, that "love is the answer" to life's perplexities, or does the word "love" sound too naïve, simplistic, or sentimental? Explain your answer.

10. What holds true for individuals also applies to institutions. If you are a member of a church or other religious organization, does this organization appear to be focused on only one stage of faith, or does it adequately provide for the needs of members in more than one stage? Explain your answer.

11. After completing this book (or course or seminar), has your reflection changed the way you relate to God, to yourself, and to others? If so, how?

Bibliography

Allen, Diogenes. *Christian Belief in a Postmodern World: The Full Wealth of Conviction.* Louisville, KY: Westminster John Knox, 1989.

———. *Theology for a Troubled Believer: An Introduction to the Christian Faith.* Louisville, KY: Westminster John Knox, 2010.

Augustine of Hippo. *Confessions and Enchiridion.* Translated and edited by Albert C. Outler. The Library of Christian Classics 7. Philadelphia: Westminster, 1955.

Augustine of Hippo. *Selected Writing.* Translated by Mary T. Clark. The Classics of Western Spirituality 47. New York: Paulist, 1984.

Blake, William. "The Marriage of Heaven and Hell." In *The Complete Poetry and Prose of William Blake*, 33–45. Rev. ed, edited by David V. Erdman. Berkeley. University of California Press, 1982.

Borg, Marcus J. *The God We Never Knew.* San Francisco: HarperSanFrancisco, 1998.

———. *The Heart of Christianity: Rediscovering a Life of Faith.* San Francisco: HarperSanFrancisco, 2003.

———. *Meeting Jesus Again for the First Time.* San Francisco: HarperSanFrancisco, 1995.

———. *Reading the Bible Again for the First Time.* San Francisco: HarperSanFrancisco, 2002.

Bradford, Richard. *The Complete Critical Guide to John Milton.* New York: Routledge, 2001.

Brown, Peter. *Augustine of Hippo: A Biography.* Berkeley: University of California Press, 1967.

Brueggemann, Walter. *Theology of the Old Testament.* Minneapolis, Fortress, 1997.

Calvin, John. *Institutes of the Christian Religion.* 2 vols. Translated by Ford Lewis Battles and edited by John T. McNeill. The Library of Christian Classics 20–21. Philadelphia: Westminster, 1960.

Cary, Phillip. *Augustine: Invention of the Inner Self: The Legacy of a Christian Platonist.* New York: Oxford University Press, 2000.

———. *The History of Christian Theology.* The Great Courses Guidebook. Chantilly, VA: Teaching Company, 2008.

———. *Luther: Gospel, Law, and Reformation.* The Great Courses Guidebook. Chantilly, VA: Teaching Company, 2004.

Clayton, Philip. "God Beyond Orthodoxy: Process Theology for the 21st Century," 1–16. Online: http://www.philipclayton.net/files/papers/GodBeyondOrthodoxy-r3.pdf.

———, and Arthur Peacocke. *In Whom We Live and Move and Have our Being: Panentheistic Reflections on God's Presence in a Scientific World*. Grand Rapids, MI: Eerdmans, 2004.

Conwell, Russell. *Acres of Diamonds*. Includes a biography of Conwell by Robert Shackleton. New York: Harper & Row, 1943.

Cook, William R., and Ronald B. Herzman. *Dante's Divine Comedy: Course Guidebook*. Chantilly, VA: The Teaching Company, 2007.

Danielson, Dennis. *The Cambridge Companion to Milton*. New York: Cambridge University Press, 1989.

Dante Alighieri. *The Divine Comedy*. 3 vols. Translated by Charles S. Singleton. Bollingen Series. Princeton, NJ: Princeton University Press, 1970.

Davidson, Hugh M. *Blaise Pascal*. Boston: Twayne, 1983.

Drummond, Henry. *The Greatest Thing in the World*. New York: Grosset & Dunlap, n. d.

Eaves, Morris. *The Cambridge Companion to William Blake*. Cambridge: Cambridge University Press, 2003.

Fitzgerald, Allan D. *Augustine through the Ages: An Encyclopedia*. Grand Rapids, MI: Eerdmans, 1999.

Fox, Matthew. *Creation Spirituality*. San Francisco: HarperSanFrancisco, 1991.

———. *Original Blessing*. Santa Fe, NM: Bear & Co., 1983.

Frye, Northrop. *The Return of Eden: Five Essays on Milton's Epics*. Toronto: University of Toronto Press, 1965.

Griffin, David Ray. *Reenchantment without Supernaturalism: A Process Philosophy of Religion*. Ithaca, NY: Cornell University Press, 2001.

Harkness, Georgia. *Mysticism: Its Meaning & Message*. Nashville: Abingdon, 1973.

Haught, John F. *The Promise of Nature: Ecology and Cosmic Purpose*. Mahwah, NJ: Paulist, 1993.

Hazelton, Roger. *Blaise Pascal: The Genius of His Thought*. Philadelphia: Westminster, 1974.

Holmes, Urban T. *The History of Christian Spirituality*. New York: Seabury, 1980.

Jones, Cheslyn, et al. *The Study of Spirituality*. New York: Oxford University Press, 1986.

Kavanaugh, Kieran. *John of the Cross: Selected Writings*. The Classics of Western Spirituality 53. New York: Paulist, 1987.

——— and Otilio Rodriguez. *Teresa of Avila: The Interior Castle*. The Classics of Western Spirituality 14. Mahway, NJ: Paulist, 1979.

Kirpatrick, Robin. *Dante: The Divine Comedy*. Landmarks of World Literature. New York: Cambridge University Press, 1987.

Lansing, Richard. *The Dante Encyclopedia*. New York: Garland, 2000.

Leith, John H. *An Introduction to the Reformed Tradition*. Rev. ed. Louisville: Westminster John Knox, 1981.

Lull, Timothy. *Martin Luther's Basic Theological Writings*. Minneapolis: Fortress, 1989.

MacCulloch, Diarmaid. *Christianity: The First Three Thousand Years*. New York: Viking, 2009.

———. *The Reformation: A History*. New York: Viking, 2003.

May, Gerald G. *Addiction and Grace*. New York:HarperOne, 1991.

McLaren, Brian D. *A Generous Orthodoxy*. Grand Rapids, MI: Zondervan, 2004.

McNeill, John T. *The History and Character of Calvinism*. New York: Oxford University Press, 1954.

Milton, John. "Paradise Lost." In *John Milton*, edited by Stephen Orgel and Jonathan Goldberg, 355–618. The Oxford Authors. New York: Oxford University Press, 1991.

Moltmann, Jürgen. *God in Creation: A New Theology of Creation and the Spirit of God*. Minneapolis, MN: Fortress, 1993.

Murray, Andrew. *Humility: The Beauty of Holiness*. Fort Washington, PA: Christian Literature Crusade, 1980.

Noll, Mark A. *Turning Points: Decisive Moments in the History of Christianity*. 3rd ed. Grand Rapids, MI: Baker Academic, 2012.

Nouwen, Henri J. M. *Reaching Out: The Three Movements of the Spiritual Life*. New York: Image Doubleday, 1986.

Pascal, Blaise. *Pascal's Pensées*. New York: Dutton, 1958.

Pelikan, Jaroslav. *Luther's Works*. St. Louis: Concordia, and Philadelphia: Fortress, 1955–1976.

Rist, J. M. *Augustine: Ancient Thought Baptized*. New York: Cambridge University Press, 2003.

Rohr, Richard. *Falling Upward: A Spirituality for the Two Halves of Life*. San Francisco: Jossey-Bass, 2011.

———. *Immortal Diamond: The Search for Our True Self*. San Francisco: Jossey-Bass, 2013.

———. *The Naked Now: Learning to See as the Mystics See*. New York: Crossroad, 2009.

———. *The Universal Christ*. New York: Convergent, 2019.

———. *What the Mystics Know*. New York: Crossroad, 2015.

Ruse, Michael. *Can a Darwinian be a Christian?* Cambridge: Cambridge University Press, 2001.

Schulweis, Harold M. *For Those Who Can't Believe*. New York: HarperPerennial, 1995.

Snyder, James L. *In Pursuit of God: The Life of A. W. Tozer*. Camp Hill, PA: Christian Publications, 1991.

Spong, John Shelby. *A New Christianity for a New World*. New York: HarperOne, 2001.

———. *Eternal Life: A New Vision*. New York: HarperOne, 2009.

———. *Liberating the Gospels: Reading the Bible with Jewish Eyes*. San Francisco: HarperSanFrancisco, 1996.

———. *Rescuing the Bible from Fundamentalism*. San Francisco: HarperSanFrancisco, 1991.

———. *The Sins of Scripture*. New York: HarperOne, 2006.

———. *Why Christianity Must Change or Die*. New York: HarperOne, 1999.

Steere, Douglas V. *Quaker Spirituality: Selected Writings*. The Classics of Western Spirituality 41. Mahwah, NJ: Paulist, 1984.

Stewart, H. F. *Pascal's Pensées*. New York: Pantheon, 1950.

Teilhard de Chardin, Pierre. *Christianity and Evolution*. Translated by René Hague. New York: Harcourt Brace and Co., 1969.

———. *Writings in the Time of War*. Translated by René Hague. New York: Harper and Row, 1968.

Tozer, A. W. *The Pursuit of God*. Harrisburg, PA: Christian Publications, 1948.

Urban, Linwood. *A Short History of Christian Thought*. Rev. ed. New York: Oxford University Press, 1995.

Vande Kappelle, Robert P. *The Arc of Spirituality: The Western Love Affair with God*. Eugene, OR: Wipf & Stock, 2021.

———. *Dark Splendor: Spiritual Fitness for the Second Half of Life*. Eugene, OR: Resource, 2015.

———. *Deep Splendor: A Study of Spirituality in Modern Literature*. Eugene, OR: Wipf & Stock, 2021.

———. *Deeper Splendor: Spirituality and Personality in Modern Literature*. Eugene, OR: Wipf & Stock, 2022.

———. *The New Creation: Church History Made Accessible, Relevant, and Personal*. Eugene, OR: Wipf & Stock, 2018.

———. *Refined by Fire: Rethinking Essential Teachings in Scripture*. Eugene, OR: Wipf & Stock, 2018.

———. *The Second Journey: Visions and Voices on First- and Second-Half-of-Life Spirituality*. Eugene, OR: Wipf & Stock, 2020.

———. *Wading in Water: Spirituality and the Arts*. Eugene, OR: Wipf & Stock, 2021.

Whaling, Frank. *John and Charles Wesley: Selected Prayers, Hymns, Journal Notes, Sermons, Letters and Treatises*. The Classics of Western Spirituality 27. New York: Paulist, 1981.

Williams, Patricia A. *Doing without Adam and Eve: Sociobiology and Original Sin*. Minneapolis: Fortress, 2001.

Index

Abraham (patriarch), 12, 13, 17
  call of, 15–16
  testing of, 147
Allport, Gordon, 164
Apostles' Creed, 42, 43, 72, 80, 81, 208
Aquinas, Thomas, 31, 54, 92, 186
Aristotle, 31, 50, 55, 74
Arminianism, 120, 121
Augustine of Hippo, 2, 27–44, 108, 190n4
  City of God, 29, 35, 38, 39, 42
  Confessions, 29, 30, 35–42, 118
  conversion of, 33, 38, 39, 41
  Enchiridion, 29, 30, 42–44
  and free will, 40
  life of, 27, 31–35
  On the Trinity, 38
  and psychology, 30, 39–40

Baptist(s), 113, 114, 119, 121, 169
Barth, Karl, 202
Bernard of Clairvaux, 55, 56, 67, 92, 98
Beza, Theodore, 78, 79
Bible. *See* scripture
Blake, William, 123, 124, 131, 222
  life of, 136–40
  The Marriage of Heaven and Hell, 136, 137, 139, 140, 141–43
  role of Christ in, 138, 139, 140, 143
  role of religion in, 139–40, 141
Boccaccio, Giovanni, 45
Boff, Leonardo, 193
Bonaventure, 54
Bonhoeffer, Dietrich, viiin1, 104, 168

Borg, Marcus, 200, 201, 222
  Heart of Christianity, 210–15
  life of, 209–10
Brainerd, David, 104
Britten, Benjamin, 138
Brother Lawrence, viiin1, 104, 120
Brueggemann, Walter, 23
Bucer, Martin, 83
Buddha, the, 7, 195n9
Bunyan, John, viiin1, 87, 118

Calvin, John, 31
  Institutes, 78, 80–83
  life of, 77–80
Calvinism, 120, 130
Cary, Phillip, 154
Chambers, Oswald, 105
Cicero, 32, 38, 45, 51
Cloud of Unknowing, 89, 104
Commonwealth period in England, 116, 120, 121, 125, 132, 136
Conwell, Russell, 222
  Acres of Diamonds, 169, 172–74
  life of, 169–72
Cowan, L. B., 104
creation, doctrine of, 13–15, 88, 188
creationism, creationists, 192
Cromwell, Oliver, 116, 125, 135
Crossan, John Dominic, 210

Dante Alighieri, 87, 133, 139, 141
  De Monarchia, 47, 48
  Divine Comedy, 45, 46, 47, 48, 49–63
  La Vita Nuova, 45, 48, 58

(Dante Alighieri continued)
   life of, 45–49
Davidson, Hugh, 112
Dawkins, Richard, 112
death, 130, 167, 198, 200
Denys the Areopagite, 88–90, 195n9
Descartes, René, 105
Dillard, Annie, 104
Donatism, 35–36
Dostoevsky, Fyodor, 90, 229
doubt, role of, 224, 231
Drummond, Henry, 104, 222
   The Greatest Thing in the World, 152–55
   life of, 151–52
dualism, nondualism, 32, 123, 141, 151, 176, 181, 187, 195, 196, 197, 198, 226, 227, 228
Durant, Will, 107
Dylan, Bob, 138

Eckhart, Meister, 104, 195n9
Einstein, Albert, 3
election, doctrine of, 13, 15–16, 108
Elijah, 12, 19
Eliot, T. S., 45, 106, 229
Erasmus, Desiderius, 76
Evagrius of Pontus, 195n9
evil. *See* good and evil
Exodus, the, 12, 17–19, 63

faith, 4, 11, 16, 25, 29, 42–43, 54, 67, 71, 74, 75, 76, 82, 90, 107, 109, 112, 149, 150, 198, 210, 211, 212–14, 217, 224
   journey of, 222–24
   mature, 224
   model of faith development, 224–31
faith-reason problem, 107–13
fall, doctrine of the, 14, 15
Farel, William, 78
first half of life, 2, 85, 219, 220–21
Fox, George, 104, 120, 121, 222
   Journal of, 115, 116, 117, 118
   life of, 114–17
Fox, Matthew, 181, 183, 222
   life of, 185–87

Original Blessing, 181, 185, 187–94
Francis of Assisi, 120, 195n9
Frei, Hans, 176n2
Freud, Sigmund, 138
Frye, Northrop, 129
fundamentalism, 182, 211, 214

Gandhi, Mohandas, 195n9
Glorious Revolution, 117, 119n4
Ginsberg, Allen, 138
God, 1, 2, 3, 23–24, 82, 177, 201–2, 214, 218, 223, 224
   belief in, 2
   as Creator, 13, 43, 80, 81, 182, 192, 196
   existence of, 109, 223, 224
   experiencing, vii, 29, 85
   as faithful, 213
   intimacy with, 91, 147, 148, 202, 225
   knowledge of, 80–81, 87, 89, 90, 147, 148, 149, 198, 230
   as love, 2, 43, 67, 89
   love for, 67, 91, 96, 153, 160, 214
   love of, 13–14, 19, 28, 56, 154
   models of, 3
   name of, 18, 150
   as personal, 4, 13, 147, 201–2
   presence of, 16–19, 88, 120, 149
   pursuit of, 146–51
   as relational, 2, 3, 10
   seeing, 29, 50, 55, 56, 89
   union with, 85, 88, 89, 90, 92, 96, 99, 100
   worship of, 9–10
Goethe, Johann von, 154
good and evil, 32, 33, 123, 124, 131, 132, 141, 142, 143, 187, 192, 193, 198
good works, doctrine of, 67, 71
grace, doctrine of, 43, 70, 71
Gregory of Nyssa, 195n9
Griffin, David Ray, 203

Hale, Edward Everett, 120
Hammarskjöld, Dag, 104
Haught, John F., 184, 185
Homer, 46, 51, 52

Hugh of St. Victor, 195n11
humility, 150–51, 153, 157–61, 177
Huxley, Aldous, 138

imagination, 138
indulgences, 65, 69

Jansenism, Jansenist, 105, 106, 108, 111, 112
Jesus Christ, 6, 9, 11, 12, 14, 20, 21–24, 25, 81–82, 86, 147, 149, 150, 176, 177, 178, 179, 188, 195, 196, 210, 214, 223–24
   and humility, 157, 158, 160
   and incarnation, 43, 49, 194, 207
   and nondualism, 195
   role in heaven, 128
   as Savior, 177, 178
   trusting in, 177
John of the Cross, 85, 90, 91, 92, 104, 120
   The Ascent of Mount Carmel, 96, 99
   The Dark Night, 92, 96, 99
   dark night of the soul, 99–102
   life of, 95–96
Julian of Norwich, viiin1, 104
Julius Caesar, 51
Jung, Carl, 138
Justinian, 54, 55

Kempis, Thomas à, 104, 120
Kierkegaard, Søren, 104
King, Martin Luther, Jr., 195n9

Laplace, Pierre Simon de, 110
Laubach, Frank, 104, 168
lectio divina, vii
Lewis, C. S., 45
Limbo, 51
literature
   Christian, viii, 7, 200
   devotional, 104, 145
   and spirituality, vii, 1, 9
Lord's Prayer, 42, 68, 72, 80
love, 2, 14, 22, 23, 25, 26, 28, 29, 35, 37, 42–44, 56, 61, 67, 74, 90, 91, 97, 102, 113, 151, 225, 229, 230, 231
   as *Amore*, 49
   courtly, 49
Loyola, Ignatius, 95, 101
Luther, Martin, 31, 66, 76, 77, 83, 121
   and faith, 67, 71, 74, 75
   and law and grace, 67
   life of, 66–73
   On the Freedom of a Christian, 71, 73–76

Manicheism, 32–33, 37, 41, 123, 138
May, Gerald, 14
McLaren, Brian, 222
   A Generous Orthodoxy, 176–79
   life of, 175
   model of faith development, 224–31
Melanchthon, Philip, 72
Merton, Thomas, 104
Milton, John, 45, 117, 123, 124, 135, 136, 139, 141, 143
   Aeropagitica, 125, 135
   The Christian Doctrine, 126, 131
   life of, 124–26
   Of Education, 124, 130
   Paradise Lost, 123, 126–35, 136, 140, 143
   role of Christ in, 127, 129–30, 132, 134
   role of God in, 127, 128, 129, 130, 131, 132
   role of Satan in, 127, 128–29, 131–33, 134
   Paradise Regained, 126, 133, 134, 136
   Samson Agonistes, 126, 133, 134
Moltmann, Jürgen, 203, 204
Moses, 11, 17–18, 19
Muhammad, 195n9
Murray, Andrew
   Humility, 157–61
   life of, 155–56
mystic, mysticism, 85–102, 120, 142, 153, 178, 183, 185, 188, 189, 193, 195n9, 209, 221
   definition of, 86
myth, mythology, 15, 32, 35, 51, 58, 63, 124, 127, 137, 140

Napoleon Bonaparte, 21
Nasr, Seyyed, 183
Neoplatonism, 33, 36, 37, 38, 39, 41
Newman, John Henry, 104, 118, 120
Norris, Kathleen, 104
Nouwen, Henri, 222
　life of, 163–64
　Reaching Out, 164–68
　The Wounded Healer, 164

Odysseus (Ulysses), 52, 127n1
Origen of Alexandria, 195n9
original sin, doctrine of, 34, 56, 108, 186, 187, 189, 190n4, 191–93, 207
orthodoxy, 177, 178, 181, 200, 215
　alternative, 182
orthopraxy, 177, 181, 200
Ovid, 45, 51

panentheism, 3, 149, 194, 201–4, 209, 211
pantheism, 3, 145, 149, 202, 203
Pascal, Blaise, 14, 104
　conversion of, 106
　life of, 105–7
　Pensées, 105, 107–9, 112, 113
　wager, 108–13
Paul (apostle), 6, 9, 11, 12, 22, 24–26, 31, 33, 41, 43, 86, 87, 121, 147, 153, 156, 218, 229
Peacocke, Arthur, 204
Pelagian, Pelagius, 41
Pence, Mike, 176
Penington, Isaac, 120
Penn, William, 117, 119
Pentecostal(ism), 156, 177
Perennial Philosophy, 194
personality
　corporate, 12, 13
Plato, 31, 203n2
Plotkin, Bill, 219
poetry, 63, 142
postcritical, 224
prayer, 39, 58, 60, 70, 86–92, 97, 101, 156, 165, 167–68, 208
precritical, 223
purgatory, 52, 59, 60, 68, 69

Quakers, 113, 114, 115–21

Rahner, Karl, 195n9
Reformation, the, 65, 66, 69, 70, 73, 77, 79, 98, 113, 121, 212
religion, religious, 1, 6–7, 57, 81, 118, 139–40, 142, 184–85, 200, 217
religiosity, 138, 217
religious conversion, 221
Renan, Ernst, 21
Revelation, book of, 10–11
revelation, general and special, 81
Reynolds, Joshua, 137
Richard of St. Victor, 195n11
Rohr, Richard, 3, 104, 181, 195n9, 222
　life of, 194
　The Naked Now, 181, 195–98
Rumi, Jalaluddin, 218

sacrament, sacramental, 184–85, 211
　definition of, 184
salvation, 18, 30, 67, 73, 150, 159, 193, 195, 210, 211
　definition of, 158-59, 177
　symbol of, 48
scripture, 9, 25, 32, 85, 115, 118–19, 178, 201, 211, 214, 224
　literal interpretation of, 205
　as sacred, vii, 204–5
　and spirituality, 9–26
second half of life, 3, 86, 198, 219–22
self, 6–7, 82, 196, 198, 213
　shadow, 220n3
Shakespeare, William, 46
Simpson, A. B., 146
Singer, June, 138
sociobiology, 192
soul, 2, 221
Spirit, Holy, 2, 3, 6, 25, 43, 82, 114, 115, 118, 121, 148–49, 156, 190, 217, 218
spiritual director, 101
spiritual journey, vii, 1, 29, 165, 190, 200, 219, 221, 224
spirituality, 1, 3, 67–68, 145, 147, 149, 165, 196, 211, 217, 221, 230
　apophatic, 88, 89
　biblical, 9–26

creation, 185, 186, 187–90
and dark night, 99–101
definition of, 1, 2, 181, 182, 193, 217
as energy field, 3
Franciscan, 182
and God, 3, 146
kataphatic, 88, 89
and literature, vii, 1, 9
mature, 4, 6
medieval, 27-29, 67
New Testament, 20–26
Old Testament, 12–20
paths of, 188–90
primary principle of, 154
and religion, 1, 6, 200, 217
role of, 6
sacramental, 182–85
secular, 1
task of, 1–2, 154
test of, 155
Spong, John Shelby, 90, 201, 208, 222
life of, 206–7
A New Christianity for a New World, 206, 207–8
Sins of Scripture, 202, 206
Why Christianity Must Change or Die, 206, 207, 208
Swedenborg, Emmanuel, 138, 141

Taylor, Barbara Brown, 210
Taylor, Hudson, 104
Teilhard de Chardin, Pierre, 192, 218
temple, 5, 6
liturgy, 9

as metaphor, 6, 7
Teresa of Ávila, 85, 90, 91, 92, 101, 104, 120, 198, 218
life of, 93–95
Mansions of the Interior Castle, 96–98
Theologia Germanica, 104
theology
definition of, 201
nature and role of, 200
Tozer, A. W. 104
life of, 145-46
The Pursuit of God, 145, 146–51
Trinity, Holy, 2, 3, 38, 55, 56, 89, 111
Troelsch, Ernst, 65

Virgil, 31, 46, 48, 49, 50, 51, 52, 53, 54, 58, 61, 62–63
Aeneid, 52, 58–59
Virgin Mary, 27, 54, 55, 59, 93
Voltaire, 111

Wells, H. G., 21
Wesley, John, 31, 104, 120, 175
Whitehead, Alfred North, 203
Williams, Patricia, 190, 192
Wollstonecraft, Mary, 137
Woolman, John, 104, 119
Wordsworth, William, 139
Wright, N. T., 210

Yeats, William Butler, 138

Zwingli, Ulrich, 72, 76, 77

www.ingramcontent.com/pod-product-compliance
Lightning Source LLC
Chambersburg PA
CBHW051635230426
43669CB00013B/2315